Honoré de Balzac

The Wild Ass' skin and Other Stories

Honoré de Balzac

The Wild Ass' skin and Other Stories

ISBN/EAN: 9783744751407

Printed in Europe, USA, Canada, Australia, Japan

Cover: Foto ©Thomas Meinert / pixelio.de

More available books at **www.hansebooks.com**

H. DE BALZAC

THE COMÉDIE HUMAINE

Portrait of Balzac.

H. DE BALZAC

———

THE

WILD ASS' SKIN

(LA PEAU DE CHAGRIN)

AND OTHER STORIES

TRANSLATED BY

ELLEN MARRIAGE

WITH A PREFACE BY

GEORGE SAINTSBURY

PHILADELPHIA

THE GEBBIE PUBLISHING CO., Ltd.

1897

CONTENTS

LIST OF ILLUSTRATIONS

PREFACE.

THE "Wild Ass' Skin" is the one book of Balzac's which it is difficult for those who know it to approach without a somewhat uncritical enthusiasm. It is not faultless; no book of his is, and this cannot challenge the epithet even to the extent to which not a few others can challenge it. It is earlier than almost any of the mature novels, except "The Chouans;" and it bears in some respects the marks of its earliness as well as, in others, those of that rather artificial scheme of representing life, which was so strongly characteristic of the author, and which, while it helped him in conceiving the "Comédie Humaine," imposed a certain restraint and hamper on the "Comédie" itself. We could spare a good deal of the journalist and other talk at the orgie; and more persons than Emile have gone to sleep over, or have escaped sleep only by skipping, the unconscionable length of Raphael's story.

But these are the merest and most miserable of details. In the first place, the conception is of the very finest. You may call it a philosophic study, or you may not; you may class it as an "allegory" on the banks of the Nile or the Seine, or any other river, if you like. Neither title will do it any harm, and neither can explain it or exalt it higher. The law of Nemesis—the law that every extraordinary expansion or satisfaction of heart or brain or will is paid for—paid for inevitably, incommutably, without the possibility of putting off or transferring the payment—is one of the truths about which no human being with a soul a little above the brute has the slightest doubt. It may be put religiously as, "Know that for all these things God will bring thee into judgment;" or philosophically, as in the same book, "All things are double, one against the other;" or in any other fashion or language.

But it is an eternal and immutable verity, and the soul of man bears witness to it.

It is Balzac's way to provide abundant, and not always economically arranged backgrounds and contrasts for his central pictures; and the gaming-house (the model of how many gaming-houses since!), the gorgeous disorder of the curiosity shop, and the "orgie" provide these in the present case lavishly enough. The orgie is undoubtedly the weakest. It is only touched with others by the pleasant and good-humor skit of Gautier in "Les Jeune-France;" but the note there struck is, as usual with "Théo," the right one. You cannot "organize" an orgie; the thing comes naturally or not at all; and in the splendors of Taillefer, as in those of Trimalchio, there is a certain coldness.

But this is soon forgotten in the absorbing interest of the skin and its master. The only adverse comment which has ever occurred to me is, that one might perhaps have expected a longer period of indifference, of more or less reckless enjoyment of the privileges, to elapse before a vivid consciousness of the curse and of the penalty. I know no answer, unless it be that Balzac took the orgie itself to be, as it were, the wild oats of Raphael's period—in which case he had not much to show for it. But when the actual consciousness wakes, when the Skin has been measured on the napkin, and its shrinking noted, nothing is questionable any longer. The frenzied anxiety of the victim is not overdone; the way in which his very frenzy leads him to make greater and ever greater drafts on his capital of power without any corresponding satisfaction is masterly. And the close is more masterly still. To some tastes the actual conclusion may be a thought too allegorical, but in eighteen–hundred–and–thirty your allegory was your only wear; and Gautier, in the pleasant book above cited, was thoroughly in the fashion when he audaciously put a hidden literary meaning on the merry tale of "Celle-ci et celle-là." Here, too, if anywhere, the opposition of Pauline and Fœdora in this way is justified. It softens off the too high-strung tragedy of the catastrophe at the same time that it points the moral, and it rounds as much as it adorns the tale.

It has been observed, in no carping or hypercritical spirit, that passages of the book are somewhat high-flown in style. The fact is that Balzac had rather a tendency to this style, and only outgrew it, if he ever did outgrow it, by dint of its greater and greater unfitness for his chosen subjects. Here, if anywhere, it was excusable, just as here, if anywhere, the gigantic element in his genius found scope and play. There had been some "inventories" in literature before, and there have been many more since the description of the curiosity shop; but none, if we except the brief Shakespearian perfection of that in Clarence's dream, and none at all in a heaped and minute style, can approach this. The thing is night-marish—you *see* the *magots* and the armor, the pictures and the statues, and amongst them all the sinister "piece of shag-reen,"* with the ineffaceable letters stamped on it.

And so over all the book there is the note of the seer, of the seer who sees and who makes others see. This note is seldom an idyllic or merely pleasant one; the writer who has it must have, even in such a book as the "Country Doctor," a black thread in his twist, a sombre background to his happy valley. Here the subject not only excuses, but demands a constant sombreness, a tone of thunder in the air, of eclipse and earthquake. And the tone is given. A very miserable person would he be who endeavored to pick out burlesque points in the "Wild Ass' Skin," the most apoc-alyptic of the novels of the nineteenth century, and yet one of the most soberly true in general theme and theory. When one thinks of the tireless efforts which have been made, especially of late years, to "pejorate" pessimism and blacken

---

*I hesitated between "The Piece of Shagreen" and "The Wild Ass' Skin" for the title, but Balzac's own remarks decided me. "The Magic Skin" is very weak, and "The Skin of Shagreen" hideous.

gloom, and of the too general conclusion of yawn or laugh to which they bring us, it is doubly curious to come back to this sermon by a very unpriestly preacher on the simple text, "Whom the gods curse, to him they grant the desires of his heart."

"The Wild Ass' Skin" appeared first in August, 1831, published in two volumes, by Gosselin and Canel, with a Preface and a "Moral," which the author afterwards cut out. Of its four chapters or divisions the first originally bore the title of the whole book, and the last that of "Conclusion," not "Epilogue," which was afterwards affixed to it. One or two fragments, not incorporated in the finished book, exist, having been previously published. Balzac reviewed it himself, more than once, in the *Caricature* and elsewhere, both at its first appearance and afterwards, when it reappeared in the same year with other stories and a new preface by Philarète Chasles as "Philosophical Tales and Romances." This was republished more than once till, in 1835, it took rank anew in the "Philosophical Studies," while ten years later, under the same sub-title, it was finally classed in the first complete arrangement of the "Comédie Humaine."

"L'Elixir de longue Vie" (The Elixir of Life), in which Balzac acknowledges (I do not know whether by trick or not) indebtedness to Hoffmann or somebody else, is also "style of 1830," and to speak with perfect frankness, would have been done much better by Mérimée or Gautier than by Balzac. But it is done well.

The first "Étude de Femme" (A Study of Woman) came out in *La Mode* in March, 1830, next year at the end of the "Peau de Chagrin," in 1835 (with a new title, *Profil de Marquise*) in "Scènes de la vie Parisienne." When the "Comédie" was collected its actual title was taken and it was given a position among the shorter stories.

G. S.

BRIEF SKETCH

OF

HONORÉ DE BALZAC.

Honoré de Balzac was born at Tours on the 20th of May, 1799. The family was a respectable one, though its right to the particle which Balzac always carefully assumed, subscribing himself (with dubious correctness, though the point is an argued one) "*de* Balzac" was contested. And there appears to be no proof of their connection with Jean Guez de Balzac, the founder, as some will have him, of modern French prose, and the contemporary and fellow-reformer of Malherbe. Indeed, as the novelist pointed out with sufficient pertinence, his earlier namesake had no hereditary right to the name at all, and merely took it from some property. Balzac's father, who, as the *zac* pretty surely indicates, was a southerner and a native of Languedoc, was fifty-three years old at the birth of his son, whose Christian name was selected on the ordinary principle of accepting that of the saint on whose day he was born. Balzac the elder had been a barrister before the Revolution, but under it he obtained a post in the commissariat, and rose to be head of that department for a military division. His wife, who was much younger than himself, and who survived her son, is said to have possessed both beauty and fortune, and was evidently endowed with the business faculties so common among Frenchwomen. When Honoré was born, the family had not long been established at Tours, where Balzac the elder (besides his duties) had a house and some land ; and this town continued to be their headquarters till

the novelist, who was the eldest of the family, was about six-
teen.   He had two sisters (of whom the elder, Laure, after-
wards Madame Surville, was his confidante and his only
authoritative biographer) and a younger brother, who seems
to have been, if not a scapegrace, rather a burden to his
friends, and who later went abroad.

The eldest boy was, in spite of Rousseau, put out to nurse,
and at seven years old was sent to the Oratorian grammar-
school at Vendôme, where he stayed another seven years,
going through, according to his own account, the future ex-
periences and performances of Louis Lambert, but making no
reputation for himself in the ordinary school course.   If, how-
ever, he would not work in his teacher's way, he overworked
himself in his own by devouring books; and was sent home
at fourteen in such a state of health that his grandmother
(who, after the French fashion, was living with her daughter
and son-in-law), ejaculated, "And this is the way the college
returns the fine children we send her!"   It would seem,
indeed, that after making all due allowance for grand-
motherly and sisterly partiality, Balzac was actually a very
good-looking boy and young man, though the portraits of
him in later life may not satisfy the more romantic expecta-
tions of his admirers.   He must have had at all times eyes
full of character, perhaps the only feature that never fails in
men of intellectual eminence; but he certainly does not seem
to have been in his manhood either exactly handsome or ex-
actly (to use a foolish-sounding term which yet has no exact
equivalent of better sound) "distinguished-looking."   But
the portraits of the middle of the century are, as a rule,
rather wanting in this characteristic when compared with
those of its first and last periods.

For a short time he was left pretty much to himself, and
recovered rapidly.   But late in 1814 a change of official
duties removed the Balzacs to Paris, and when they had estab-
lished themselves in the famous old *bourgeois* quarter of the

Marais, Honoré was sent to divers private tutors or private schools till he had "finished his classes" in 1816 at the age of seventeen and a half. Then he attended lectures at the Sorbonne, where Villemain, Guizot aud Cousin were lecturing, and heard them, as his sister tells us, enthusiastically, though there are probably no three writers of any considerable repute in the history of French literature who stand further apart from Balzac. For all three made and kept their fame by spirited and agreeable generalizations and expatiations, as different as possible from the savage labor of observation on the one hand and the gigantic developments of imagination on the other, which were to compose Balzac's appeal. His father destined him for the law; and for three years more he dutifully attended the offices of an attorney and a notary, besides going through the necessary lectures and examinations. All these trials he seems to have passed, if not brilliantly, yet sufficiently.

And then came the inevitable crisis, which was of an unusually severe nature. A notary, who was a friend of the elder Balzac and owed him some gratitude, offered not merely to take Honoré into his office, but to allow him to succeed to his business, which was a very good one, in a few years on very favorable terms. Most fathers, and nearly all French fathers, would have jumped at this; and it so happened that about the same time M. de Balzac was undergoing that unpleasant process of compulsory retirement which his son has described in one of the best passages of the "Works of His Youth,"* the opening scene of "Argow le Pirate." It does not appear that Honoré had revolted during his probation—indeed he is said, and we can easily believe it from his books, to have acquired a very solid knowledge of law, especially in bankruptcy matters, of which he was himself to have a very close shave in future. A solicitor, indeed, told Laure de Balzac that he found "César Birotteau," a kind of "Balzac on

* *Œuvres de Jeunnesse.*

Bankruptcy;" but this may have been only the solicitor's fun.

It was no part of Honoré's intentions to use this knowledge—however content he had been to acquire it—in the least interesting, if nearly the most profitable, of the branches of the legal profession ; and he protested eloquently, and not unsuccessfully, that he would be a man of letters and nothing else.   Not unsuccessfully ; but at the same time with distinctly qualified success.   He was not turned out of doors ; nor were the supplies, as in Quinet's case only a few month's later, absolutely withheld even for a short time.   But his mother (who seems to have been less placable than her husband) thought that cutting them down to the lowest point might have some effect.   So, as the family at this time (April, 1819) left Paris for a house some twenty miles out of it, she established her eldest son in a garret furnished in the most Spartan fashion, with a starvation allowance and an old woman to look after him.   He did not literally stay in this garret for the ten years of his astonishing and unparalleled probation ; but without too much metaphor it may be said to have been his Wilderness, and his Wanderings in it to have lasted for that very considerable time.

We know, in detail, very little of him during this period. For the first years, between 1819 and 1822, we have a good number of letters to Laure ; between 1822 and 1829, when he first made his mark, very few.   He began, of course, with verse, for which he never had the slightest vocation, and almost equally of course with a tragedy.   But by degrees, and apparently pretty soon, he slipped into what was his vocation, and like some, though not very many, great writers, at first did little better in it than if it had not been his vocation at all.   The singular tentatives which, after being allowed for a time a sort of outhouse in the structure of the "Comédie Humaine," were excluded from the octavo "Édition Défini-tive" five-and-twenty years ago, have never been the object of that exhaustive bibliographical and critical attention which has been bestowed on those which follow them. They were not absolutely unproductive—we hear of sixty, eighty, a hundred pounds being paid for them, though whether this was the amount of Balzac's always sanguine expectations, or hard cash actually handed over, we cannot say. They were very numerous, though the reprints never extended to more than ten.

It is generally agreed that these singular "Works of His Youth" were of service to Balzac as exercises, and no doubt they were so; but something may be said on the other side. They must have done a little, if not much, to lead him into and confirm him in those defects of style and form which distinguish him so remarkably from most writers of his rank. It very seldom happens when a very young man writes very much, be it book-writing or journalism, without censure and without "editing," that he does not at the same time get into loose and slipshod habits. And we may set down to this peculiar form of apprenticeship of Balzac's not merely his failure ever to attain, except in passages and patches, a thoroughly great style, but also that extraordinary method of composition which in after days cost him and his publishers so much money.

However, if these ten years of probation taught him his trade, they taught him also a most unfortunate avocation or by-trade, which he never ceased to practise, or to try to practise, which never did him the very least good, and which not unfrequently lost him much of the not too abundant gains which he earned with such enormous labor. This was the "game of speculation." His sister puts the tempter's part on an unknown "neighbor," who advised him to try to procure independence by a good speculation. Those who have read Balzac's books and his letters will hardly think that he required much tempting. He began by trying to publish—an attempt which has never yet succeeded with a single man of letters, so far as we can remember. His scheme was not a bad one; indeed, it was one which has brought much money to other pockets since, being neither more nor less than the issuing of cheap one-volume editions of French classics. But he had hardly any capital; he was naturally quite ignorant of his trade, and as naturally the established publishers and booksellers boycotted him as an intruder. So his "Molière" and his "La Fontaine" are said to have been sold as waste paper, though if any copies escaped they would probably bring a very comfortable price now. Then, such capital as he had having been borrowed, the lender, either out of good nature or avarice, determined to throw the helve after the hatchet. He partly advanced himself, and partly induced Balzac's parents to advance more, in order to start the young man as a printer, to which business Honoré himself added that of typefounder. The story was just the same: knowledge and capital were again wanting, and though actual bankruptcy was avoided, Balzac got out of the matter at the cost not merely of giving the two businesses to a friend (in whose hands they proved profitable), but of a margin of debt from which he may be said never to have fully cleared himself.

He had more than twenty years to live, but he never cured himself of this hankering after a good speculation. Sometimes it was ordinary stock-exchange gambling; but his special weakness was, to do him justice, for schemes that had something more grandiose in them. Thus, to finish here with the subject, though the chapter of it never actually finished till his death, he made years afterwards, when he was a successful and a desperately busy author, a long, troublesome, and costly journey to Sardinia to carry out a plan of resmelting the slag from Roman and other mines there. Thus in his very latest days, when he was living at Vierzschovnia with the Hanska and Mniszech household, he conceived the magnificently absurd notion of cutting down twenty thousand acres of oak wood in the Ukraine, and sending it *by railway* right across Europe to be sold in France. And he was rather reluctantly convinced that by the time a single log reached its market the freight would have eaten up the value of a whole plantation.

It was perhaps not entirely chance that the collapse of the printing scheme, which took place in 1827, the ninth year of the Wanderings in the Wilderness, coincided with or immediately preceded the conception of the book which was to give Balzac passage into the Promised Land. This was "The Chouans," called at its first issue, which differed considerably from the present form, "The Last Chouan or Brittany in 1800" (later 1799). It was published in 1829 without any of the previous anagrammatic pseudonyms, and whatever were the reasons which had induced him to make his bow in person to the public, they were well justified, for the book was a distinct success, if not a great one. It occupies a kind of middle position between the melodramatic romance of his nonage and the strictly analytic romance-novel of his later time ; and, though dealing with war and love chiefly, inclines in conception distinctly to the latter. Corentin, Hulot, and other personages of the actual Comedy (then by no means planned or at least avowed) appear ; and though the influence of Scott is in a way paramount on the surface, the under-work is quite different, and the whole scheme of the loves of Montauran and Mademoiselle de Verneuil is pure Balzac.

It would seem as if nothing but this sun of popular approval had been wanted to make Balzac's genius burst out in full bloom. Although we have a fair number of letters for the ensuing years, it is not very easy to make out the exact sequence of production of the marvelous harvest which his genius gave. It is sufficient to say that in the three years following 1829 there were actually published the charming story of "The Sign of the Cat and the Racket," the "Wild Ass' Skin," the most original and splendid, if not the most finished and refined of all Balzac's novels, most of the short "Philosophical Stories," of which some are among their author's greatest triumphs, many other stories (chiefly included in the "Scenes of Private Life,") and the beginning of the "Droll Stories."

It is well known that from the time almost of his success as a novelist he was given, like too many successful novelists (*not* like Scott), to rather undignified and foolish attacks on critics. The explanation may or may not be found in the fact that we have abundant critical work of his, and that it is nearly all bad. Now and then we have an acute remark in his own special sphere; but as a rule he cannot be complimented on these performances, and when he was half-way through his career this critical tendency of his culminated in the unlucky *Revue Parisienne*, which he wrote almost entirely himself, with slight assistance from his friends, MM. de Belloy and de Grammont. It covers a wide range, but the literary part of it is considerable, and this part contains that memorable and disastrous attack on Sainte-Beuve, for which the critic afterwards took a magnanimous revenge in his obituary chat. Although the thing is not quite unexampled, it is not easily to be surpassed in the blind fury of its abuse. Sainte-Beuve was by no means invulnerable, and an anti-critic who kept his head might have found, as M. de Pontmartin and others did find, the joints in his armor. But when, apropos of the "Port Royal" more especially, and of the other works in general, Balzac informs us that Sainte-Beuve's great characteristic as a writer is tediousness, tediousness knee-deep—that his style is intolerable, that his historical handling is like that of Gibbon, Hume and other dull people, when he jeers at him for exhuming "The Holy Mother," and scolds him for presuming to obscure the glory of the "Sun King," the thing is partly ludicrous, partly melancholy. One remembers that agreeable Bohemian, who at a symposium once interrupted his host by crying,

"Man o' the hoose, gie us less o' yer clack and mair o' yer Jairman wine!" Only in human respect and other, we phrase it: "Oh, dear M. de Balzac! give us more 'Eugénie Grandets,' more 'Père Goriots,' more 'Peaux de Chagrin,' and don't talk about what you do not understand!"

Balzac was a great politician also, and here, though he may not have been very much more successful, he talked with more knowledge and competence. He must have given himself immense trouble in reading the papers, foreign as well as French; he had really mastered a good deal of the political religion of a French publicist. It is curious to read, sixty years after date, his grave assertion that "France should make a conquest of Madagascar," and with certain very pardonable defects (such as his Anglophobia), his politics may be pronounced not unintelligent and not ungenerous, though somewhat inconsistent and not very distinctly traceable to any coherent theory. As for the Anglophobia, the Englishman who thinks the less of him for that must have very poor and unhappy brains. A Frenchman who does not more or less hate and fear England, an Englishman who does not regard France with a more or less good-humored impatience, is usually "either a god or a beast," as Aristotle saith. Balzac began with an odd but not unintelligible compound, something like Hugo's, of Napoleonism and Royalism. In 1824, when he was still in the shades of anonymity, he wrote and published two by no means despicable pamphlets in favor of primogeniture and the Jesuits, the latter of which was reprinted in 1880 at the last Jesuitical Congress in France. His "Letters on Paris," in 1830–31, and his "France and the Foreigner," in 1836, are two considerable series of letters from "Our Own Correspondent," handling the affairs of the world with boldness and industry if not invariably with wisdom. They rather suggest (as does the later *Revue Parisienne* still more) the political writing of the age of Anne in England, and perhaps a little later, when "the wits" handled politics and society, literature and things in general with unquestioned competence and an easy universality.

Besides this work in books, pamphlets, etc., Balzac, as has been said, did a certain amount of journalism, especially in the *Caricature*, his performances including, we regret to say, more than one puff of his own work ; and in this, as well as by the success of "The Chouans," he became known about 1830 to a much wider circle, both of literary and of private acquaintance. It cannot indeed be said that he ever mixed much in society ; it was impossible that he should do so, considering the vast amount of work he did and the manner in which he did it. This subject, like that of his speculations, may be better finished off in a single passage than dealt with by scattered indications here and there. He was not one of those men who can do work by fits and starts in the intervals of business or of amusement ; nor was he one who, like Scott, could work very rapidly. It is true that he often achieved immense quantities of work (subject to a caution to be given presently) in a very few days, but then his working day was of the most peculiar character. He could not bear disturbance ; he wrote (as probably most people do) best at night, and he could not work at all after heavy meals. His favorite plan (varied sometimes in detail) was therefore to dine lightly about five or six, then to go to bed and sleep till eleven, twelve, or one, and then to get up, and with the help only of coffee (which he drank very strong and in enormous quantities) to work for indefinite stretches of time into the morning or afternoon of the next day. He speaks of a sixteen hours' day as a not uncommon shift or spell of work, and almost a regular one with him ; and on one occasion he avers that in the course of forty-eight hours he took but three of rest, working for twenty-two hours and a half continuously on each side thereof. In such spells, supposing reasonable facility of composition, and mechanical power in the hand to keep going all the time, an enormous amount can of course be accomplished. A thousand words an hour is anything but an extraordinary rate of writing, and fifteen hundred by no means unheard of with persons who do not write rubbish.

The references to this subject in Balzac's letters are very numerous; but it is not easy to extract very definite information from them. It would be not only impolite but incorrect to charge him with unveracity. But the very heat of imagination which enabled him to produce his work created a sort of mirage, through which he seems always to have regarded it; and in writing to publishers, editors, creditors, and even his own family, it was too obviously his interest to make the most of his labor, his projects, and his performance. Even his contemporary, though elder, Southey, the hardest-working and the most scrupulously honest man of letters in England who could pretend to genius, seems constantly to have exaggerated the idea of what he could perform, if not of what he had performed in a given time. The most definite statement of Balzac's is one which claims the second number of "Sur Catherine de Medicis" (" La Confidence des Ruggieri ") as the production of a single night, and not one of the most extravagant of his nights. Now, " La Confidence des Ruggieri " fills, in the small edition, eighty pages of nearer four hundred than three hundred words each, or some thirty thousand words in all. Nobody in the longest of nights could manage that, except by dictating it to shorthand clerks. But in the very context of this assertion Balzac assigns a much longer period to the correction than to the composition, and this brings us to one of the most curious and one of the most famous points of his literary history.

Some doubts have been thrown on the most minute account of his ways of composition which we have, that of the publisher Werdet. But there is too great a consensus of evidence as to his general system to make the received description of it doubtful. According to this, the first draft of Balzac's work never presented it in anything like fulness, and sometimes did not amount to a quarter of the bulk finally published. This being returned to him from the printer "in slip" on sheets with very large margins, he would set to work on the correction; that is to say, on the practical rewriting of the thing, with excisions, alterations, and above all, additions. A "revise" being executed, he would attack this revise in the same manner, and not unfrequently more than once, so that the expenses of mere composition and correction of the press were enormously heavy (so heavy as to eat into not merely his publisher's but his own profits), and that the last state of the book, when published, was something utterly different from its first state in manuscript. And it will be obvious that if anything like this was usual with him, it is quite impossible to judge his actual rapidity of composition by the extent of the published result.

However this may be (and it is at least certain that in the years above referred to he must have worked his very hardest, even if some of the work then published had been more or less excogitated and begun during the wilderness period), he certainly so far left his eremitical habits as to become acquainted with most of the great men of letters of the early thirties, and also with certain ladies of more or less high rank, who were to supply, if not exactly the full models, the texts and starting-points for some of the most interesting figures of the "Comédie." He knew Victor Hugo, but certainly not at this time intimately; for as late as 1839 the letter in which he writes to Hugo to come and breakfast with him at Les Jardies (with interesting and minute directions how to find that frail abode of genius) is couched in anything but the tone of a familiar friendship. The letters to Beyle of about the same date are also incompatible with intimate knowledge. Nodier (after some contrary expressions) he seems to have regarded as most good people did regard that true man of letters and charming tale-teller; while among the younger generation Théophile Gautier and Charles de Bernard, as well as Gozlan and others, were his real and constant friends. But he does not figure frequently or eminently in any of the genuine gossip of the time as a haunter of literary circles, and it is very nearly certain that the assiduity with which some of his heroes attend *salons* and clubs had no counterpart in his own life. In the first place he was too busy; in the second he would not have been at home there. Like the young gentleman in *Punch*, who "did not read books but wrote them," though in no satiric sense, he felt it his business not to frequent society but to create it.

He was, however, aided in the task of creation by the ladies already spoken of, who were fairly numerous and of divers degrees. The most constant after his sister Laure was that sister's schoolfellow, Madame Zulma Carraud, the wife of a military official at Angoulême and the possessor of a small country estate at Frapesle, near Tours. At both of these places Balzac, till he was a very great man, was a constant visitor, and with Madame Carraud he kept up for years a correspondence which has been held to be merely friendly, and which was certainly in the vulgar sense innocent, but which seems to us to be tinged with something of that feeling, midway between love and friendship, which appears in Scott's letters to Lady Abercorn, and which is probably not so rare as some think. Madame de Berny, another family friend of higher rank, was the prototype of most of his "angelic" characters, but she died in 1836. He knew the Duchess d'Abrantès, otherwise Madame Junot, and Madame de Girardin, otherwise Delphine Gay; but neither seems to have exercised much influence over him. It was different with another and more authentic duchess, Madame de Castries, after whom he dangled for a considerable time, who certainly first encouraged him and probably then snubbed him, and who is thought to have been the model of his wickeder great ladies. And it was comparatively early in the thirties that he met the woman whom, after nearly twenty years, he was at last to marry, getting his death in so doing, the Polish Madame Hanska. These, with some relations of the last named, especially her daughter, and with a certain "Louise"—an unknown who never ceased to be so—were Balzac's chief correspondents of the other sex, and as far as is known, his chief friends in it.

About his life, without extravagant "padding" of guess-work or of mere quotation and abstract of his letters, it would be not so much difficult as impossible to say much; and accordingly it is a matter of fact that most lives of Balzac, including all good ones, are rather critical than narrative. From his real *début* with "The Last Chouan" to his departure for Poland on the long visit, or brace of visits, from which he returned finally to die, this life con-sisted solely of work. One of his earliest utterances, "I must keep digging away," was his motto to the very last, varied only by a certain amount of traveling. Balzac was always a considerable traveler; indeed if he had not been so his constitution would probably have broken down long before it actually did; and the expense of these voyagings (though by his own account he generally conducted his affairs with the most rigid economy), together with the interruption to his work which they occasioned, entered no doubt for some-thing into his money difficulties. He would go to Baden or Vienna for a day's sight of Madame Hanska; his Sar-dinian visit has been already noted; and as a specimen of others it may be mentioned that he once journeyed from Paris to Besançon, then from Besançon right across France to Angoulême, and then back to Paris on some business of selecting paper for one of the editions of his books, which his publishers would probably have done much better and at much less expense.

Still his actual receipts were surprisingly small, partly, it may be, owing to his expensive habits of composition, but far more, according to his own account, because of the

Belgian piracies, from which all popular French authors suffered till the government of Napoleon the Third managed to put a stop to them. He also lived in such a thick atmosphere of bills and advances and cross-claims on and by his publishers, that even if there were more documents than there are it would be exceedingly difficult to get at facts which are, after all, not very important. He never seems to have been paid much more than $2500 for the newspaper publication (the most valuable by far because the pirates could not interfere with its profits) of any one of his novels. And to expensive fashions of composition and complicated accounts, a steady back-drag of debt and the rest, must be added the very delightful, and to a novelist not useless, but very expensive mania of the collector. Balzac had a genuine taste for, and thought himself a genuine connoisseur in, pictures, sculpture, and objects of art of all kinds, old and new; and though prices in his day were not what they are in these, a great deal of money must have run through his hands in this way. He calculated the value of the contents of the house, which in his last days he furnished with such loving care for his wife, and which turned out to be a chamber rather of death than of marriage, at some $80,000. But part of this was of Madame Hanska's own purchasing, and there were offsets of indebtedness against it almost to the last. In short, though during the last twenty years of his life such actual "want of pence" as vexed him was not due, as it had been earlier, to the fact that the pence refused to come in, but only to imprudent management of them, it certainly cannot be said that Honoré de Balzac, the most desperately hard worker in all literature for such time as was allotted him, and perhaps the man of greatest genius who was ever a desperately hard worker, falsified that most uncomfortable but truest of proverbs, "Hard work never made money."

If, however, he was but scantily rewarded with the money for which he had a craving (not absolutely devoid of a touch

of genuine avarice, but consisting chiefly of the artist's desire
for pleasant and beautiful things, and partly presenting a
variety or phase of the grandiose imagination, which was his
ruling characteristic), Balzac had plenty of the fame, for
which he cared quite as much as he cared for money. Per-
haps no writer except Voltaire and Goethe earlier made such
a really European reputation ; and his books were of a kind
to be more widely read by the general public than either
Goethe's or Voltaire's. In England, this popularity was, for
obvious reasons, rather less than elsewhere. The respectful
vogue which French literature had had in England in the
eighteenth century had ceased, owing partly to the national
enmity revived and fostered by the great war, and partly to
the growth of a fresh and magnificent literature at home dur-
ing the first thirty years of the nineteenth. But Balzac could
not fail to be read almost at once by the lettered ; and he
was translated pretty early, though not perhaps to any great
extent.

It was in England, it may be said, that by far his greatest
follower appeared, and appeared very shortly. For it would
be absurd in the most bigoted admirer of Thackeray to deny
that the author of " Vanity Fair," who was in Paris and
narrowly watching French literature and French life at the
very time of Balzac's most exuberant flourishing and educa-
tion, owed something to the author of " Father Goriot."
There was no copying or imitation ; the lessons taught by
Balzac were too much blended with those of native masters,
such as Fielding, too much informed and transformed by indi-
vidual genius. Some may think—it is a point at issue not
merely between Frenchmen and Englishmen, but between
good judges of both nations on each side—that in absolute
veracity and likeness to life, in limiting the operation of the
inner consciousness on the outward observation to strictly
artistic scale, Thackeray excelled Balzac as far as he fell short
of him in the powers of the seer and in the gigantic imagina-

tion of the prophet.   But the relations of pupil and master in at least some degree are not deniable.

So things went on in light and in shade, in home-keeping and in travel, in debts and in earnings, but always in work of some kind or another, for eighteen years from the turning point of 1829.   By degrees he gained fame and ceased to be in the most pressing want of money, Balzac left off to some extent, though never entirely, those miscellaneous writings— reviews (including puffs), comic or general sketches, political diatribes, " physiologies " and the like—which with his discarded prefaces and much other interesting matter, were at last, not many years ago, included in four stout volumes of the " Édition Définitive." With the exception of the " Physiologies " (a sort of short satiric analysis of this or that class, character or personage), which were very popular in the reign of Louis Philippe in France, and which Albert Smith and others introduced into England, Balzac did not do any of this miscellaneous work extremely well.   Very shrewd observations are to be found in his reviews, for instance, his indication, in reviewing La Touche's " Fragoletta," of that common fault of ambitious novels, a sort of woolly and " ungraspable " looseness of construction and story, which constantly bewilders the reader as to what is going on.   But, as a rule, he was thinking too much of his own work and his own principles of working to enter very thoroughly into the work of others.   His politics, those of a moderate but decided Royalist and Conservative, were, as has been said, intelligent in theory, but in practice a little distinguished by that neglect of actual business detail which has been noticed in his speculations.

At last, in the summer of 1847, it seemed as if the Rachel for whom he had served nearly if not quite the full fourteen years already, and whose husband had long been out of the way, would at last grant herself to him.   He was invited to Vierzschovnia in the Ukraine, the seat of Madame Hanska, or in strictness of her son-in-law, Count Georges Mniszech ; and

as the visit was apparently for no restricted period, and Bal-
zac's pretensions to the lady's hand were notorious, it might
have seemed that he was as good as accepted.   But to assume
this would have been to mistake what perhaps the greatest
creation of Balzac's great English contemporary and coun-
terpart on the one side, as Thackeray was his contemporary
and counterpart on the other, considered to be the malignity
of widows.   What the reasons were which made Madame
Hanska delay so long in doing what she did at last, and might
just as well, it would seem, have done years before, is not
certainly known, and it would be quite unprofitable to discuss
them.   But it was on the 8th of October, 1847, that Balzac
first wrote to his sister from Vierzschovnia, and it was not till
the 14th of March, 1850, that, "in the parish church of Saint
Barbara at Berditchef, by the Count Abbé Czarski, represent-
ing the Bishop of Jitomir [this as characteristic of Balzac in
one way as what follows is in another], a Madame Eve de
Balzac, born Countess Rzevuska, or a Madame Honoré de
Balzac or a Madame de Balzac the elder " came into existence.

It does not appear that Balzac was exactly unhappy during
this huge probation, which was broken by one short visit to
Paris.   The interest of uncertainty was probably much for his
ardent and unquiet spirit, and though he did very little literary
work for him, one may suspect that he would not have done
very much if he had stayed at Paris, for signs of exhaustion,
not of genius but of physical power, had shown themselves
before he left home.   But it is not unjust or cruel to say that
by the delay " Madame Eve de Balzac " (her actual baptismal
name was Evelina) practically killed her husband.   These
winters in the severe climate of Russian Poland were abso-
lutely fatal to a constitution, and especially to lungs already
deeply affected.   At Vierzschovnia itself he had illnesses, from
which he narrowly escaped with life, before the marriage ; his
heart broke down after it ; and he and his wife did not reach
Paris till the end of May.   Less than three months afterwards,

on the 18th of August, he died, having been visited on the very day of his death in the Paradise of bric-à-brac which he had created for his Eve in the Rue Fortunée—a name too provocative of Nemesis—by Victor Hugo, the chief maker in verse as he himself was the chief maker in prose of France. He was buried at Père la Chaise. The after fortunes of his house and its occupants were not happy; but they do not concern us.

In person Balzac was a typical Frenchman, as indeed he was in most ways. From his portraits there would seem to have been more force and address than distinction or refinement in his appearance, but, as has been already observed, his period was one ungrateful to the iconographer. His character, not as a writer, but as a man, must occupy us a little longer. For some considerable time—indeed it may be said until the publication of his letters—it was not very favorably judged on the whole. We may, of course, dismiss the childish scandals (arising, as usual, from clumsy or malevolent misinterpretation), which gave rise to caricatures of him such as that of which we read, representing him in a monk's dress at a table covered with bottles and supporting a young person on his knee, the whole garnished with the epigraph: "Scenes of Hidden Life." They seem to have given him, personally, a very unnecessary annoyance, and indeed he was always rather sensitive to critcism. This kind of stupid libel will never cease to be devised by the envious, swallowed by the vulgar, and simply neglected by the wise. But Balzac's peculiarities, both of life and of work, lent themselves rather fatally to a subtler misconstruction which he also anticipated and tried to remove, but which took a far stronger hold. He was represented—and in the absence of any intimate male friends to contradict the representation, it was certain to obtain some currency—as in his artistic person a sardonic libeler of mankind, who cared only to take foibles and vices for his subjects, and who either left goodness and virtue out

of sight altogether, or represented them as the qualities of
fools.   In private life he was held up as at the best a self-
centred egotist who cared for nothing but himself and his own
work, capable of interrupting one friend who told him of the
death of a sister by a suggestion that they should change the
subject and talk of "something real, of 'Eugénie Grandet,'"
and of levying a fifty per cent. commission on another who
had written a critical notice of his, Balzac's life and works.
With the first of these charges he himself, on different occa-
sions, rather vainly endeavored to grapple, once drawing up
an elaborate list of his virtuous and vicious women, and show-
ing that the former outnumbered the latter ; and, again, labor-
ing (with that curious lack of sense of humor which distin-
guishes of all Frenchmen but a very few, and distinguished him
eminently) to show that though no doubt it is very difficult
to make virtuous persons interesting, he, Honoré de Balzac,
had attempted it, and succeeded in it, on a quite surprising
number of occasions.

The fact is that if he had handled this last matter rather
more lightly his answer would have been a sufficient one, and
that in any case the charge is not worth answering.   It does
not lie against the whole of his work ; and if it lay as con-
clusively as it does against Swift's, it would not necessarily
matter.   To the artist in analysis as opposed to the romance-
writer, folly always, and villainy sometimes, does supply a
much better subject than virtuous success, and if he makes his
fools and his villains lifelike and supplies them with a fair
contrast of better things, there is nothing more to be said.
He will not, indeed, be a Shakespeare, or a Dante, or even a
Scott ; but we may be very well satisfied with him as a Field-
ing, a Thackeray, or a Balzac.   His education in a lawyer's
office, the accursed advice about the *bonne spéculation*, and
his constant straitenings for money, will account for his some-
times looking after the main chance rather too narrowly ; and
as for the "Eugénie Grandet" story it requires no great

stretch of charity or comprehension to see in it nothing more than the awkward, very easily misconstrued, but not necessarily in the least heartless or brutal attempt of a rather absent and very much self-centred recluse absorbed in one subject, to get his interlocutor as well as himself out of painful and useless dwelling on sorrowful matters. Self-centred and self-absorbed Balzac no doubt was; he could not have lived his life or produced his work if he had been anything else. And it must be remembered that he owed extremely little to others; that he had the independence as well as the isolation of the self-centred; that he never spunged or fawned on a great man, or wronged others of what was due to them. The only really unpleasant thing about him, perhaps due to ignorance of all sides of the matter, is a slight touch of snobbishness now and then, especially in those late letters from Vierzschovnia to Madame de Balzac and Madame Surville, in which, while inundating his mother and sister with commissions and requests for service, he points out to them what great people the Hanskas and Mniszechs are, what infinite honor and profit it will be to be connected with them, and how desirable it is to keep struggling engineer brothers-in-law and ne'er-do-well brothers in the colonies out of sight lest they should disgust the magnates.

But these are "sma' sums, sma' sums," as Bailie Jarvie says; and smallness of any kind has, whatever it may have to do with Balzac the man, nothing to do with Balzac the writer. With him as with some others, but not as with the larger number, the sense of greatness increases the longer and the more fully he is studied. He resembles Goethe more than any other man of letters—certainly more than any other of the present century—in having done work which is very frequently, if not even commonly, faulty, and in yet requiring that his work shall be known as a whole. His appeal is cumulative; it repeats itself on each occasion with a slight difference, and though there may now and then be the same faults to be noticed, they are almost invariably accompanied, not merely by the same, but by fresh merits.

There are two things which it is more especially desirable to keep constantly before one in reading Balzac—two things, which, taken together, constitute his almost unique value, and two things which not a few critics have failed to take together in him, being under the impression that the one excludes the other, and that to admit the other is tantamount to a denial of the one.   These two things are, first, an immense attention to detail, sometimes observed, sometimes invented or imagined; and, secondly, a faculty of regarding these details through a mental lens or arrangement of lenses almost peculiar to himself, which at once combines, enlarges, and invests them with a peculiar magical halo or mirage.   The two thousand personages of the "Comédie Humaine" are, for the most part, "signaled," as the French official word has it, marked and denoted by the minutest traits of character, gesture, gait, clothing, abode, what not; the transactions recorded are very often (more often indeed than not) given with a scrupulous and microscopic accuracy of reporting which no detective could outdo.   Defoe is not more circumstantial in detail of fact than Balzac; Richardson is hardly more prodigal of character-stroke.   Yet a very large proportion of these characters, of these circumstances, are evidently things invented or imagined, not observed.   And in addition to this the artist's magic glass, his Balzacian speculum, if we may so say (for none else has ever had it) transform even the most rigid observation into something flickering and fanciful, the outline as of shadows on the wall, not the precise contour of etching or of the camera.

It is curious, but not unexampled, that both Balzac himself when he struggled in argument with his critics and those of his partisans who have been most jealously devoted to him, have usually tried to exalt the first and less remarkable of these gifts over the second and infinitely more remarkable. Balzac protested strenuously against the use of the word "gigantesque" in reference to his work; and of course it is susceptible of an unhandsome innuendo. But if we leave that innuendo aside, if we adopt the same reflection that "gigantesque" does not exclude "gigantic," or assert a constant failure of greatness, but only indicates that the magnifying process is carried on with a certain indiscriminateness, we shall find none, I think, which so thoroughly well describes him.

The effect of this singular combination of qualities, apparently the most opposite, may be partly anticipated, but not quite. It results occasionally in a certain shortcoming as regards the very truth, absolute artistic truth to nature. Those who would range Balzac in point of such artistic veracity on a level with poetical and universal realists like Shakespeare and Dante, or prosaic and particular realists like Thackeray and Fielding, seem not only to be utterly wrong but to pay their idol the worst of all compliments, that of ignoring his own special qualifications. The province of Balzac may not be—I do not think it is—identical, much less coextensive, with that of nature. But it is his own—a partly real, partly fantastic region, where the lights, the shades, the dimensions, and physical laws are slightly different from those of this world of ours, but with which, owing to things it has in common with that world, we are able to sympathize, which we can traverse and comprehend. Every now and then the artist uses his observing faculty more, and his magnifying and (since there is no better word) distorting lens less; every now and then he reverses the proportion. Some tastes will like him best in the one stage; some in the other; the happier constituted will like him best in both. These latter declined to put "Eugénie Grandet" above the "Wild Ass' Skin," or "Father Goriot" above the wonderful handful of tales which includes "The Quest of the Absolute" and "The Unknown Masterpiece," though they will no doubt recognize that even

in the two first named members of these pairs of the Bal-
zacian quality, that of magnifying and rendering grandiose,
is present, and that the martyrdom of Eugénie, the avarice
of her father, the blind self-devotion of Goriot to his thank-
less and worthless children, would not be what they are if they
were seen through a perfectly achromatic and normal medium.

This specially Balzacian quality is unique. It is like—it
may almost be said to *be*—the poetic imagination, present in
magnificent volume and degree, but in some miraculous way
deprived and sterilized of the specially poetical quality. By
this we do not of course mean that Balzac did not write in
verse; we have a few verses of his, and they are pretty poor,
but that is neither here nor there. The difference between
Balzac and a great poet lies not in the fact that the one fills
the whole page with printed words, and the other only a part
of it—but in something else. If we could put that something
else into distinct words we should therein attain the philoso-
pher's stone, the elixir of life, the first cause, the great
secret, not merely of criticism but of all things. It might
be possible to coast about it, to hint at it, by adumbrations
and in consequences. But it is better and really more helpful
to face the difficulty boldly, and to say that Balzac, approach-
ing a great poet nearer perhaps than any other prose writer in
any language, is distinguished from one by the absence of the
very last touch, the finally constituting quiddity, which makes
a great poet different from Balzac.

Now, when we make this comparison, it is of the first in-
terest to remember—and it is one of the uses of the compari-
son, that it suggests the remembrance of the fact—that the
great poets have usually been themselves extremely exact ob-
servers of detail. It has not made them great poets; but
they would not be great poets without it. And when Eugénie
Grandet starts from the little wooden bench at the reference to
it in her scoundrelly cousin's letter (to take only one instance
out of a thousand), we see in Balzac the same observation.

subject to the limitations just mentioned, that we see in Dante and Shakespeare, in Chaucer and Tennyson. But the great poets do not as a rule *accumulate* detail. Balzac does, and from his very accumulation he manages to derive that singular gigantesque vagueness—differing from poetic vague, but ranking next to it—which we have here ventured to note as his distinguishing quality. He bewilders us a very little by it, and he gives us the impression that he has slightly bewildered himself. But the compensations of the bewilderment are large.

For in this labyrinth and whirl of things, in this heat and hurry of observation and imagination, the special intoxication of Balzac consists. Every great artist has his own means of producing this intoxication, and it differs in result like the stimulus of beauty or of wine. Those persons who are unfortunate enough to see in Balzac little or nothing but an ingenious piler-up of careful strokes—a man of science taking his human documents and classing them after an orderly fashion in portfolio and deed-box—must miss this intoxication altogether. It is much more agreeable as well as much more accurate to see in the manufacture of the "Comédie" the process of a Cyclopean workshop—the bustle, the hurry, the glare and shadow, the steam and sparks of Vulcanian forging. The results, it is true, are by no means confused or disorderly —neither were those of the forges that worked under Lipari— but there certainly went much more to them than the dainty fingering of a literary fretwork-maker or the dull rummagings of a realist *à la* Zola.

In part no doubt, and in great part, the work of Balzac is dream-stuff rather than life-stuff, and it is all the better for that. What is better than dreams? But the coherence of his visions, their bulk, their solidity, the way in which they return to us and we return to them, make them such dream-stuff as there is all too little of in this world. If it is true that evil on the whole predominates over good in the vision of this "Voyant," as Philarete Chasles so justly called him (and we think it does, though not to the same extent as we once thought), two very respectable, and in one case very large, though somewhat opposed divisions of mankind, the philosophic pessimist and the convinced and consistent Christian believer, will tell us that this is at least not one of the points in which it is unfaithful to life. If the author is closer and more faithful in his study of meanness and vice than in his studies of nobility and virtue, the blame is due at least as much to his models as to himself. If, as we fear must be confessed, he has seldom succeeded in combining a really passionate with a really noble conception of love, very few of his countrymen have been more fortunate in that respect. If in some of his types—his journalists, his married women, and others—he seems to have sacrificed to conventions, let us remember that those who know attribute to his conventions such a powerful if not altogether such a holy influence that two generations of the people he painted have actually lived more and more up to his painting of them.

And last of all, but also greatest, has to be considered the immensity of his imaginative achievement, the huge space that he has filled for us with vivid creation, the range of amusement, of instruction, of (after a fashion) edification which he has thrown open for us to walk in. It is possible that he himself and others more or less well-meaningly, though more or less maladroitly, following his lead, may have exaggerated the coherence and the architectural design of the "Comédie." But it has coherence and it has design; nor shall we find anything exactly to parallel it. In mere bulk the "Comédie" probably, if not certainly, exceeds the production of any novelist of the first class in any kind of fiction except Dumas, and with Dumas, for various and well-known reasons, there is no possibility of comparing it. All others yield in bulk; all in a certain concentration and intensity; none even aims at anything like the same system and completeness. It must be remembered that owing to shortness of life, lateness of beginning, and the diversion of the author to other work, the " Comédie " is the production, and not the sole production, of some seventeen or eighteen years at most. Not a volume of it, for all that failure to reach the completest perfection in form and style which has been acknowledged, can be accused of thinness, of scamped work, of mere repetition, of mere cobbling up. Every one bears the marks of steady and ferocious labor, as well as of the genius which had at last come where it had been so earnestly called and had never gone away again. It is possible to overpraise Balzac in parts or to mispraise him as a whole. But so long as inappropriate and superfluous comparisons are avoided and as his own excellence is recognized and appreciated, it is scarcely possible to overestimate that excellence in itself and for itself. He stands alone ; even with Dickens, who is his nearest analogue, he shows far more points of difference than of likeness. His vastness of bulk is not more remarkable than his peculiarity of quality ; and when these two things coincide in literature or elsewhere, then that in which they coincide may be called, and must be called, Great, without hesitation and without reserve.

INTRODUCTION.

In giving the general title of "The Comédie Humaine" to a work begun nearly thirteen years since, it is necessary to explain its motive, to relate its origin, and briefly sketch its plan, while endeavoring to speak of these matters as though I had no personal interest in them. This is not so difficult as the public might imagine. Few works conduce to much vanity; much labor conduces to great diffidence. This observation accounts for the study of their own works made by Corneille, Molière, and other great writers; if it is impossible to equal them in their fine conceptions, we may try to imitate them in this feeling.

The idea of "The Comédie Humaine" was at first as a dream to me, one of those impossible projects which we caress and then let fly; a chimera that gives us a glimpse of its smiling woman's face, and forthwith spreads its wings and returns to a heavenly realm of phantasy. But this chimera, like many another, has become a reality; has its behests, its tyranny, which must be obeyed.

The idea originated in a comparison between humanity and animality.

It is a mistake to suppose that the great dispute which has lately made a stir, between Cuvier and Geoffroi Saint-Hilaire, arose from a scientific innovation. Unity of structure, under other names, had occupied the greatest minds during the two previous centuries. As we read the extraordinary writings of the mystics who studied the sciences in their relation to infinity, such as Swedenborg, Saint-Martin, and others, and the works of the greatest authors on Natural History—Leibnitz, Buffon, Charles Bonnet, etc., we detect in the *monads* of Leibnitz, in the *organic molecules* of Buffon, in the *vegetative force* of Needham, in the correlation of similar organs of Charles Bonnet—who in 1760 was so bold as to write, " Animals vegetate as plants do "—we detect, I say, the rudiments of the great law of self for self, which lies at the root of *unity of plan*. There is but one animal. The Creator works on a single model for every organized being. " The animal " is elementary, and takes its external form, or, to be accurate, the differences in its form, from the environment in which it is obliged to develop. Zoölogical species are the result of these differences. The announcement and defence of this system, which is indeed in harmony with our preconceived ideas of divine power, will be the eternal glory of Geoffroi Saint-Hilaire, Cuvier's victorious opponent on this point of higher science, whose triumph was hailed by Goethe in the last article he wrote.

I, for my part, convinced of this scheme of nature long before the discussion to which it has given rise, perceived that in this respect society resembled nature. For does not society modify man, according to the conditions in which he lives and acts, into men as manifold as the species in zoölogy ? The differences between a soldier, an artisan, a man of business, a lawyer, an idler, a student, a statesman, a merchant, a sailor, a poet, a beggar, a priest, are as great, though not so easy to define, as those between the wolf, the lion, the ass, the crow, the shark, the seal, the sheep, etc. Thus social species have always existed, and will always exist, just as there are zoölogical species. If Buffon could produce a magnificent work by attempting to represent in a book the whole realm of zoölogy, was there not room for a work of the same kind on society ? But the limits set by nature to the variations of animals have no existence in society. When Buffon describes the lion, he dismisses the lioness with a few phrases ; but in society a wife is not always the female of the male. There may be two perfectly dissimilar beings in one household. The wife of a shopkeeper is sometimes worthy of a prince, and the wife of a prince is often worthless compared with the wife of an artisan. The social state has freaks which nature does not allow herself; it is nature *plus* society. The description of social species would thus be at least double that of animal species, merely in view of the two sexes. Then, among animals the drama is limited; there is scarcely any confusion; they turn and rend each other—that is all. Men, too, rend each other; but their greater or less intelligence makes the struggle far more complicated. Though some savants do not yet admit that the animal nature flows into human nature through an immense tide of life, the grocer certainly becomes a peer, and the noble sometimes sinks to the lowest social grade. Again, Buffon found that life was extremely simple among animals. Animals have little property, and neither arts nor sciences; while man, by a law that has yet to be sought, has a tendency to express his culture, his thoughts, and his life in everything he appropriates to his use. Though Leuwenhoek, Swammerdam, Spallanzani, Réaumur, Charles Bonnet, Müller, Haller, and other patient investigators have shown us how interesting are the habits of animals, those of each kind are, at least to our eyes, always and in every age alike; whereas the dress, the manners, the speech, the dwelling of a prince, a banker, an artist, a citizen, a priest, and a pauper are absolutely unlike, and change with every phase of civilization.

Hence the work to be written needed a threefold form—men, women, and things; that is to say, persons and the material expression of their minds; man, in short, and life.

As we read the dry and discouraging list of events called history, who can have failed to note that the writers of all periods, in Egypt, Persia, Greece, and Rome, have forgotten to give us the history of manners? The fragment of Petronius on the private life of the Romans excites rather than satisfies our curiosity. It was from observing this great void in the field of history that the Abbé Barthélemy devoted his life to a reconstruction of Greek manners in "Le Jeune Anacharsis."

But how could such a drama, with the four or five thousand persons which a society offers, be made interesting? How, at the same time, please the poet, the philosopher, and the masses who want both poetry and philosophy under striking imagery? Though I could conceive of the importance and of the poetry of such a history of the human heart, I saw no way of writing it; for hitherto the most famous story-tellers had spent their talent in creating two or three typical actors, in depicting one aspect of life. It was with this idea that I read the works of Walter Scott. Walter Scott, the modern troubadour, or finder (*trouvère—trouveur*), had just then given an aspect of grandeur to a class of composition unjustly regarded as of the second rank. Is it not really more difficult to compete with personal and parochial interests by writing of Daphnis and Chloe, Roland, Amadis, Panurge, Don Quixote, Manon Lescaut, Clarissa, Lovelace, Robinson Crusoe, Gil Blas, Ossian, Julie d'Etanges, My Uncle Toby, Werther, Corinne, Adolphe, Paul and Virginia, Jeanie Deans, Claverhouse, Ivanhoe, Manfred, Mignon, than to set forth in order facts more or less similar in every country, to investigate the spirit of laws that have fallen into desuetude, to review the theories which mislead nations, or, like some metaphysicians, to explain what *Is?* In the first place, these actors, whose existence becomes more prolonged and more authentic than that of the generations which saw their birth, almost always live solely on condition of there being a vast reflection of the present. Conceived in the womb of their own period, the whole heart of humanity stirs within their frame, which often covers a complete system of philosophy. Thus Walter Scott raised to the dignity of the philosophy of history the literature which, from age to age, sets perennial gems in the poetic crown of every nation where letters are cultivated. He vivified it with the spirit of the past; he combined drama, dialogue, portrait, scenery, and description; he fused the marvelous with truth—the two elements of the times; and he brought poetry into close contact with the familiarity of the humblest speech. But as he had not so much devised a system as hit upon a manner in the ardor of his work, or as its logical outcome, he never thought of connecting his compositions in such a way as to form a complete history of which each chapter was a novel, and each novel the picture of a period.

It was by discerning this lack of unity, which in no way detracts from the Scottish writer's greatness, that I perceived at once the scheme which would favor the execution of my purpose, and the possibility of executing it. Though dazzled, so to speak, by Walter Scott's amazing fertility, always himself and always original, I did not despair, for I found the source of his genius in the infinite variety of human nature. Chance is the greatest romancer in the world; we have only to study it. French society would be the real author; I should only be the secretary. By drawing up an inventory of vices and virtues, by collecting the chief facts of the passions, by depicting characters, by choosing the principal incidents of social life, by composing types out of a combination of homogeneous characteristics, I might perhaps succeed in writing the history which so many historians have neglected: that of manners. By patience and perseverance I might produce for France in the nineteenth century the book which we must all regret that Rome, Athens, Tyre, Memphis, Persia, and India have not bequeathed to us; that history of their social life which, prompted by the Abbé Barthélemy, Monteil patiently and steadily tried to write for the middle ages, but in an unattractive form.

The work, so far, was nothing. By adhering to the strict lines of a reproduction a writer might be a more or less faithful, and more or less successful painter of types of humanity, a narrator of the dramas of private life, an archæologist of social furniture, a cataloguer of professions, a registrar of good and evil; but to deserve the praise of which every artist must be ambitious, must I not also investigate the reasons or the cause of these social effects, detect the hidden sense of this vast assembly of figures, passions, and incidents? And finally, having sought—I will not say having found—this reason, this motive power, must I not reflect on first principles, and discover in what particulars societies approach or deviate from the eternal law of truth and beauty? In spite of the wide scope of the preliminaries, which might of themselves constitute a book, the work, to be complete, would need a conclusion. Thus depicted, society ought to bear in itself the reason of its working.

The law of the writer, in virtue of which he is a writer, and which I do not hesitate to say makes him the equal, or perhaps the superior, of the statesman, is his judgment, whatever it may be, on human affairs, and his absolute devotion to certain principles. Machiavelli, Hobbes, Bossuet, Leibnitz, Kant, Montesquieu *are* the science which statesmen apply. "A writer ought to have some settled opinions on morals and politics; he should regard himself as a tutor of men; for men need no masters to teach them to doubt," says Bonald. I took these noble words as my guide long ago; they are the written law of the monarchical writer. And those who would confute me by my own words will find that they have misinterpreted some ironical phrase, or that they have turned against me a speech given to one of my actors—a trick peculiar to calumniators.

As to the intimate purpose, the soul of this work, these are the principles on which it is based.

Man is neither good nor bad; he is born with instincts and capabilities; society, far from depraving him, as Rousseau asserts, improves him, makes him better; but self-interest also develops his evil tendencies. Christianity, above all, Catholicism, being—as I have pointed out in the " Country

Doctor " (*Le Médecin de Campagne*)—a complete system for the repression of the depraved tendencies of man, is the most powerful element of social order.

In reading attentively the presentment of society cast, as it were, from the life, with all that is good and all that is bad in it, we learn this lesson—if thought, or if passion, which combines thought and feeling, is the vital social element, it is also its destructive element. In this respect social life is like the life of man. Nations live long only by moderating their vital energy. Teaching, or rather education, by religious bodies is the grand principle of life for nations, the only means for diminishing the sum of evil and increasing the sum of good in all society. Thought, the living principle of good and ill, can only be trained, quelled, and guided by religion. The only possible religion is Christianity (see the letter from Paris in " Louis Lambert,'' in which the young mystic explains, á propos to Swedenborg's doctrines, how there has ever been but one religion since the world began). Christianity created modern nationalities, and it will preserve them. Hence, no doubt, the necessity for the monarchical principle. Catholicism and royalty are twin principles.

As to the limits within which these two principles should be confined by various institutions, so that they may not become absolute, every one will feel that a brief preface ought not to be a political treatise. I cannot, therefore, enter on religious discussion, nor on the political discussions of the day. I write under the light of two eternal truths—religion and monarchy; two necessities, as they are shown to be by contemporary events, towards which every writer of sound sense ought to try to guide the country back. Without being an enemy to election, which is an excellent principle as a basis of legislation, I reject election regarded as *the only social instrument,* especially so badly organized as it now is; for it fails to represent imposing minorities, whose ideas and interests would occupy the attention of a monarchical government.

Elective power extended to all gives us government by the masses, the only irresponsible form of government, under which tyranny is unlimited, for it calls itself law. Besides, I regard the family and not the individual as the true social unit. In this respect, at the risk of being thought retrograding, I side with Bossuet and Bonald instead of going with modern innovators. Since election has become the only social instrument, if I myself were to exercise it no contradiction between my acts and my words should be inferred. An engineer points out that a bridge is about to fall, that it is dangerous for any one to cross it ; but he crosses it himself when it is the only road to the town. Napoleon adapted election to the spirit of the French nation with wonderful skill. The least important members of his legislative body became the most famous orators of the chamber after the Restoration. No chamber has ever been the equal of the " *Corps Législatif*," (Legislative Body), comparing them man for man. The elective system of the empire was, then, indisputably the best.

Some persons may, perhaps, think that this declaration is somewhat autocratic and self-assertive. They will quarrel with the novelist for wanting to be an historian, and will call him to account for writing politics. I am simply fulfilling an obligation—that is my reply. The work I have undertaken will be as long as a history ; I was compelled to explain the logic of it, hitherto unrevealed, and its principles and moral purpose.

Having been obliged to withdraw the prefaces formerly published, in response to essentially ephemeral criticisms, I will retain only one remark.

Writers who have a purpose in view, were it only a reversion to principles familiar in the past because they are eternal, should always clear the ground. Now every one who, in the domain of ideas, brings his stone by pointing out an abuse, or setting a mark on some evil that it may be removed—every such man is stigmatized as immoral. The accusation of immorality, which has never failed to be cast at the courageous writer, is, after all, the last that can be brought when nothing else remains to be said to a romancer. If you are truthful in your pictures; if by dint of daily and nightly toil you succeed in writing the most difficult language in the world, the word "immoral" is flung in your teeth. Socrates was immoral; Jesus Christ was immoral; they both were persecuted in the name of the society they overset or reformed. When a man is to be killed he is taxed with immorality. These tactics, familiar in party warfare, are a disgrace to those who use them. Luther and Calvin knew well what they were about when they shielded themselves behind damaged worldly interests! And they lived all the days of their life.

When depicting all society, sketching it in the immensity of its turmoil, it happened—it could not but happen—that the picture displayed more of evil than of good ; that some part of the fresco represented a guilty couple ; and the critics at once raised the cry of immorality, without pointing out the morality of another portion intended to be a perfect contrast. As the critic knew nothing of the general plan I could forgive him, all the more because one can no more hinder criticism than the use of eyes, tongues and judgment. Also the time for an impartial verdict has not yet come for me. And, after all, the author who cannot make up his mind to face the fire of criticism should no more think of writing than a traveler should start on his journey counting on a perpetually clear sky. On this point it remains to be said that the most conscientious moralists doubt greatly whether society can show as many good actions as bad ones; and in the picture I have painted of it there are more virtuous figures than reprehensible ones. Blameworthy actions, faults and crimes, from the lightest to the most atrocious, always meet with punishment, human or divine, signal or secret. I have done better than the historian, for I am free. Cromwell here on earth escaped all punishment but that inflicted by thoughtful men.

And on this point there have been divided schools. Bossuet even showed some consideration for the great regicide. William of Orange, the usurper, Hugues Capet, another usurper, lived to old age with no more qualms or fears than Henri IV. or Charles I. The lives of Catherine II. and of Frederic of Prussia would be conclusive against any kind of moral law, if they were judged by the twofold aspect of the morality which guides ordinary mortals, and that which is in use by crowned heads; for, as Napoleon said, for kings and statesmen there are the lesser and the higher morality. My scenes of political life are founded on this profound observation. It is not a law to history, as it is to romance, to make for a beautiful ideal. History is, or ought to be, what it was; while romance ought to be "the better world," as was said by Mme. Necker, one of the most distinguished thinkers of the last century.

Still, with this noble falsity, romance would be nothing if it were not true in detail. Walter Scott, obliged as he was to conform to the ideas of an essentially hypocritical nation, was false to humanity in his picture of woman, because his models were schismatics. The Protestant woman has no ideal. She may be chaste, pure, virtuous; but her unexpansive love will always be as calm and methodical as the fulfilment of a duty. It might seem as though the Virgin Mary had chilled the hearts of those sophists who have banished her from heaven with her treasures of lovingkindness. In Protestantism there is no possible future for the woman who has sinned; while, in the Catholic Church, the hope of forgiveness makes her sublime. Hence, for the Protestant writer there is but one woman, while the Catholic writer finds a new woman in each new situation. If Walter Scott had been a Catholic, if he had set himself the task of describing truly the various phases of society which have successively existed in Scotland, perhaps the painter of Effie and Alice—the two figures for which he blamed himself in his later years—might have admitted passion with its sins and punishments, and the virtues revealed by repentance. Passion is the sum-total of humanity. Without passion, religion, history, romance, art, would all be useless.

Some persons, seeing me collect such a mass of facts and paint them as they are, with passion for their motive power, have supposed, but wrongly, that I must belong to the school of sensualism and materialism—two aspects of the same thing —Pantheism. But their misapprehension was perhaps justified—or inevitable. I do not share the belief in indefinite progress for society as a whole; I believe in man's improvement in himself. Those who insist on reading in me the intention to consider man as a finished creation are strangely mistaken. *Séraphita*, the doctrine in action of the Christian Buddha, seems to me an ample answer to this rather heedless accusation.

In certain fragments of this long work I have tried to popularize the amazing facts, I may say the marvels of electricity, which in man is metamorphosed into an incalculable force; but in what way do the phenomena of brain and nerves, which prove the existence of an undiscovered world of psychology, modify the necessary and undoubted relations of the worlds to God? In what way can they shake the Catholic dogma? Though irrefutable facts should some day place thought in the class of fluids which are discerned only by their effects while their substance evades our senses, even when aided by so many mechanical means, the result will be the same as when Christopher Columbus detected that the earth is a sphere, and Galileo demonstrated its rotation. Our future will be unchanged. The wonders of animal magnetism, with which I have been familiar since 1820; the beautiful experiments of Gall, Lavater's successor; all the men who have studied mind as opticians have studied light—two not dissimilar things—point to a conclusion in favor of the mystics, the disciples of St. John, and of those great thinkers who have established the spiritual world—the sphere in which are revealed the relations of God and man.

A sure grasp of the purport of this work will make it clear that I attach to common, daily facts, hidden or patent to the eye, to the acts of individual lives, and to their causes and principles, the importance which historians have hitherto ascribed to the events of public national life. The unknown struggle which goes on in a valley of the Indre between Mme. de Mortsauf and her passion is perhaps as great as the most famous of battles (*Le Lys dans la Vallée*). In one the glory of the victor is at stake; in the other it is heaven. The misfortunes of the two Birotteaus, the priest and the perfumer, to me are those of mankind. La Fosseuse (in " The Country Doctor ")and Mme. Graslin(in " The Village Pastor ") are almost the sum-total of woman. We all suffer thus every day. I have had to do a hundred times what Richardson did but once. Lovelace has a thousand forms, for social corruption takes the hues of the medium in which it lives. Clarissa, on the contrary, the lovely image of impassioned virtue, is drawn in lines of distracting purity. To create a variety of virgins it needs a Raphael. In this respect, perhaps literature must yield to painting.

Still, I may be allowed to point out how many irreproachable figures—as regards their virtue—are to be found in the portions of this work already published: Pierrette, Lorrain, Ursule Mirouët, Constance Birotteau, La Fosseuse, Eugénie Grandet, Marguerite Claës, Pauline de Villenoix, Madame Jules, Madame de la Chanterie, Eve Chardon, Mademoiselle d'Esgrignon, Madame Firmiani, Agathe Rouget, Renée de Maucombe; besides several figures in the middle-distance, who, though less conspicuous than these, nevertheless, offer the reader an example of domestic virtue; Joseph Lebas, Genestas, Benassis, Bonnet the curé, Minoret the doctor, Pillerault, David Séchard, the two Birotteaus, Chaperon the priest, Judge Popinot, Bourgeat, the Sauviats, the Tascherons, and many more. Do not all these solve the difficult literary problem which consists in making a virtuous person interesting?

It was no small task to depict the two or three thousand conspicuous types of a period; for this is, in fact, the number presented to us by each generation, and which the " Comédie Humaine " will require. This crowd of actors, of characters, this multitude of lives, needed a setting—if I may be pardoned the expression, a gallery. Hence the very natural division, as already known, into Scenes of Private Life, of Provincial Life, of Parisian, Political, Military, and Country Life. Under these six heads are classified all the studies of manners which form the history of society at large, of all its doings and movements, as our ancestors would have said. These six classes correspond, indeed, to familiar conceptions. Each has its own sense and meaning, and answers to an epoch in the life of man. I may repeat here, but very briefly, what was written by Felix Davin—a young genius snatched from literature by an early death. After being informed of my plan, he said that the Scenes of Private Life represented childhood and youth and their errors, as the Scenes of Provincial Life represented the age of passion, scheming, self-interest and ambition. Then the Scenes of Parisian Life give a picture of the tastes and vice and unbridled powers which conduce to the habits peculiar to great cities, where the extremes of good and evil meet. Each of these divisions has its local color—Paris and the Provinces—a great social antithesis which held for me immense resources.

And not man alone, but the principal events of life, fall into classes by types. There are situations which occur in every life, typical phases, and this is one of the details I most sought after. I have tried to give an idea of the different districts of our fine country. My work has its geography, as it has its genealogy and its families, its places and things, its persons and their deeds; as it has its heraldry, its nobles and commonalty, its artisans and peasants, its politicians and dandies, its army—in short, a whole world of its own.

After describing social life in these three portions, I had to delineate certain exceptional lives, which comprehend the interests of many people, or of everybody, and are in a degree outside of the general law. Hence we have Scenes of Political Life. This vast picture of society being finished and complete, was it not needful to display it in its most violent phase, beside itself, as it were, either in self-defence, or for the sake of conquest? Hence the Scenes of Military Life, as yet the most incomplete portion of my work, but for which room will be allowed in this edition, that it may form part of it when done. Finally, the Scenes of Country Life are, in a way, the evening of this long day, if I may so call the social drama. In that part are to be found the purest natures, and the application of the great principles of order, politics and morality.

Such is the foundation, full of actors, full of comedies and tragedies, on which are raised the Philosophical Studies—the second part of my work, in which the social instrument of all these effects is displayed, and the ravages of the mind are painted, feeling after feeling; the first of this series, "Wild Ass' Skin," to some extent forms a link between the Philosophical Studies and Studies of Manners, by a work of almost Oriental fancy, in which life itself is shown in a mortal struggle with the very element of all passion.

In looking forward to what remains to be done, my readers will perhaps echo what my publishers say, "Please God to spare you!" I only ask to be less tormented by men and things than I have hitherto been since I began this terrific labor. I have had this in my favor, and I thank God for it, that the talents of the time, the finest characters and the truest friends, as noble in their private lives as the former are in public life, have wrung my hand and said "courage!"

And why should I not confess that this friendship, and the

testimony here and there of persons unknown to me, have up-
held me in my career, both against myself and against unjust
attacks; against the calumny which has often persecuted me,
against discouragement, and against the too eager hopefulness,
whose utterances are misinterpreted as those of overweening
conceit? I had resolved to display stolid stoicism in the face
of abuse and insults; but on two occasions base slanders have
necessitated a reply. Though the advocates of forgiveness of
injuries may regret that I should have displayed my skill in
literary fence, there are many Christians who are of opinion
that we live in times when it is as well to show sometimes
that silence springs from generosity.

The vastness of a plan which includes both a history and a
criticism of society, an analysis of its evils, and a discussion
of its principles, authorizes me, I think, in giving my work
the title under which it now appears — "The Comédie
Humaine." Is this too ambitious? Is it not exact? That,
when it is complete, the public must pronounce.

Paris, *July*, 1842.

THE WILD ASS' SKIN

To Monsieur Savary

Member of L' Académie des Sciences

Sterne—*Tristram Shandy*, ch. cccxxi

I

THE TALISMAN.

Towards the end of the month of October, 1829, a young man entered the Palais-Royal just as the gaming-houses opened, agreeably to the law which protects a passion by its very nature easily excitable. He mounted the staircase of one of the gambling hells distinguished by the number 36, without too much deliberation.

"Your hat, sir, if you please?" a thin, querulous voice called out. A little old man, crouching in the darkness behind a railing, suddenly rose and exhibited his features, carved after a mean design.

* (1)

As you enter a gaming-house the law despoils you of your hat at the outset. Is it by way of a parable, a divine revelation? Or by exacting some pledge or other, is not an infernal compact implied? Is it done to compel you to preserve a respectful demeanor towards those who are about to gain money of you? Or must the detective who squats in our social sewers know the name of your hatter, or your own, if you happen to have written it on the lining inside? Or, after all, is the measurement of your skull required for the compilation of statistics as to the cerebral capacity of gamblers? The executive is absolutely silent on this point. But be sure of this, that though you have scarcely taken a step towards the tables, your hat no more belongs to you now than you belong to yourself. Play possesses you, your fortune, your cap, your cane, your cloak.

As you go out, it will be made clear to you, by a savage irony, that play has yet spared you something, since your property is returned. For all that, if you bring a new hat with you, you will have to pay for the knowledge that a special costume is needed for a gambler.

The evident astonishment with which the young man took a numbered tally in exchange for his hat, which was fortunately somewhat rubbed at the brim, showed clearly enough that his mind was yet untainted ; and the little old man, who had wallowed from his youth up in the furious pleasures of a gambler's life, cast a dull, indifferent glance over him, in which a philosopher might have seen wretchedness lying in the hospital, the vagrant lives of ruined folk, inquests on numberless suicides, life-long penal servitude and transportations to Guazacoalco.

His pallid, lengthy visage appeared like a haggard embodiment of the passion reduced to its simplest terms. There were traces of past anguish in its wrinkles. He supported life on the glutinous soups at Darcet's, and gambled away his meagre earnings day by day. Like some old hackney which takes no heed of the strokes of the whip, nothing could move him now. The stifled groans of ruined players, as they passed out, their mute imprecations, their stupefied faces, found him impassive. He was the spirit of play incarnate. If the young man had noticed this sorry Cerberus, perhaps he would have said, "There is only a pack of cards in that heart of his."

The stranger did not heed this warning written in flesh and blood, put there, no doubt, by Providence, who has set loathing on the threshold of all evil haunts. He walked boldly into the saloon, where the rattle of coin brought his senses under the dazzling spell of an agony of greed. Most likely he had been drawn thither by that most convincing of Jean Jacques' eloquent periods, which expresses, I think, this melancholy thought, "Yes, I can imagine that a man may take to gambling when he sees only his last shilling between him and death."

There is an illusion about a gambling saloon at night as vulgar as that of a bloodthirsty drama, and just as effective. The rooms are filled with players and onlookers, with poverty-stricken age, which drags itself thither in search of stimulation, with excited faces, and revels that began in wine, to end shortly in the Seine. The passion is there in full measure, but the great number of the actors prevents you from seeing the gambling-demon face to face. The evening is a harmony or chorus in which all take part, to which each instrument in the orchestra contributes its share. You would see there plenty of respectable people who have come in search of diversion, for which they pay as they pay for the pleasures of the theatre, or of gluttony, or they come hither as to some garret where they cheapen poignant regrets for three months to come.

Do you understand all the force and frenzy in a soul which impatiently waits for the opening of a gambling hell? Between the daylight gambler and the player at night there is the same difference that lies between a careless husband

and the lover swooning under his lady's window. Only with morning comes the real throb of the passion and the craving in its stark horror. Then you can admire the real gambler, who has neither eaten, slept, thought, nor lived, he has so smarted under the scourge of his martingale, so suffered on the rack of his desire for a game or two of cards. At that accursed hour you encounter eyes whose calmness terrifies you, faces that fascinate, glances that seem as if they had power to turn the cards over and consume them. The grandest hours of a gambling saloon are not the opening ones. If Spain has bull-fights, and Rome once had her gladiators, Paris waxes proud of her Palais-Royal, where the inevitable roulettes cause blood to flow in streams, and the public can have the pleasure of watching without fear of their feet slipping in it.

Take a quiet peep at the arena. How bare it looks! The paper on the walls is greasy to the height of your head, there is nothing to bring one reviving thought. There is not so much as a nail for the convenience of suicides. The floor is worn and dirty. An oblong table stands in the middle of the room, the tablecloth is worn by the friction of gold, but the straw-bottomed chairs about it indicate an odd indifference to luxury in the men who will lose their lives here in the quest of the fortune that is to put luxury within their reach.

This contradiction in humanity is seen wherever the soul reacts powerfully upon itself. The gallant would clothe his mistress in silks, would deck her out in soft Eastern fabrics, though he and she must lie on a truckle-bed. The ambitious dreamer sees himself at the summit of power, while he slavishly prostrates himself in the mire. The tradesman stagnates in his damp, unhealthy shop, while he builds a great mansion for his son to inherit prematurely, only to be ejected from it by law proceedings at his own brother's instance.

After all, is there a less pleasing thing in the world than a house of pleasure? Singular question! Man is always at strife with himself. His present woes give the lie to his hopes; yet he looks to a future which is not his, to indemnify him for these present sufferings; setting upon all his actions the seal of inconsequence and of the weakness of his nature. We have nothing here below in full measure but misfortune.

There were several gamblers in the room already when the young man entered. Three bald-headed seniors were lounging round the green table. Imperturbable as diplomatists, those plaster-cast faces of theirs betokened blunted sensibilities, and hearts which had long forgotten how to throb, even when a woman's dowry was the stake. A young Italian, olive-hued and dark-haired, sat at one end, with his elbows on the table, seeming to listen to the presentiments of luck that dictate a gambler's " Yes " or " No." The glow of fire and gold was on that southern face. Some seven or eight onlookers stood, by way of an audience, awaiting a drama composed of the strokes of chance, the faces of the actors, the circulation of coin, and the motion of the croupier's rake, much as a silent, motionless crowd watches the headsman in the Place de Gréve. A tall, thin man, in a threadbare coat, held a card in one hand, and a pin in the other, to mark the numbers of *red* or *black*. He seemed a modern Tantalus, with all the pleasures of his epoch at his lips, a hoardless miser drawing in imaginary gains, a sane species of lunatic who consoles himself in his misery by chimerical dreams, a man who touches peril and vice as a young priest handles the unconsecrated wafer in the white mass.

One or two experts at the game, shrewd speculators, had placed themselves opposite the bank, like old convicts, who have lost all fear of the hulks; they meant to try two or three coups, and then to depart at once with the expected gains, on which they lived. Two elderly waiters dawdled about with their arms folded, looking from time to time into the garden from the windows, as if to show their insignificant faces as a sign to passers-by.

The croupier and banker threw a ghastly and withering glance at the punters, and cried, in a sharp voice, "Make your game!" as the young man came in. The silence seemed to grow deeper as all heads turned curiously towards the new arrival. Who would have thought it? The jaded elders, the fossilized waiters, the onlookers, the fanatical Italian himself, felt an indefinable dread at sight of the stranger. Is he not wretched indeed who can excite pity here? Must he not be very helpless to receive sympathy, ghastly in appearance to raise a shudder in these places, where pain utters no cry, where wretchedness looks gay, and despair is decorous? Such thoughts as these produced a new·emotion in these torpid hearts as the young man entered. Were not executioners known to shed tears over the fair-haired, girlish heads that had to fall at the bidding of the Revolution?

The gamblers saw at a glance a dreadful mystery in the novice's face. His young features were stamped with a melancholy grace, his looks told of unsuccess and many blighted hopes. The dull apathy of the suicide had made his forehead so deadly pale, a bitter smile carved faint lines about the corners of his mouth, and there was an abandonment about him that was painful to see. Some sort of a demon sparkled in the depth of his eyes, which drooped, wearied perhaps with pleasure. Could it have been dissipation that had set its foul mark on the proud face, once pure and bright, and now brought low? Any doctor seeing the yellow circles about his eyelids, and the color in his cheeks, would have set them down to some affection of the heart or lungs, while poets would have attributed them to the havoc brought by the search for knowledge and to night-vigils by the student's lamp.

But a complaint more fatal than any disease, a disease

more merciless than genius or study, had drawn this young face, and had wrung a heart which dissipation, study, and sickness had scarcely disturbed. When a notorious criminal is taken to the convicts' prison, the prisoners welcome him respectfully, and these evil spirits in human shape, experienced in torments, bowed before an unheard-of anguish. By the depth of the wound which met their eyes, they recognized a prince among them, by the majesty of his unspoken irony, by the refined wretchedness of his garb. The frock-coat that he wore was well cut, but his cravat was on terms so intimate with his waistcoat that no one could suspect him of underlinen. His hands, shapely as a woman's, were not perfectly clean; for two days past indeed he had ceased to wear gloves. If the very croupier and the waiters shuddered, it was because some traces of the spell of innocence yet hung about his meagre, delicately-shaped form, and his scanty fair hair in its natural curls.

He looked only about twenty-five years of age, and any trace of vice in his face seemed to be there by accident. A young constitution still resisted the inroads of lubricity. Darkness and light, annihilation and existence, seemed to struggle in him, with effects of mingled beauty and terror. There he stood like some erring angel that has lost his radiance; and these emeritus-professors of vice and shame were ready to bid the novice depart, even as some toothless crone might be seized with pity for a beautiful girl who offers herself up to infamy.

The young man went straight up to the table, and, as he stood there, flung down a piece of gold which he held in his hand, without deliberation. It rolled on to the *black;* then, as strong natures can, he looked calmly, if anxiously, at the croupier, as if he held useless subterfuges in scorn.

The interest this coup awakened was so great that the old gamesters laid nothing upon it; only the Italian, inspired by a gambler's enthusiasm, smiled suddenly at some thought, and punted his heap of coin against the stranger's stake.

The banker forgot to pronounce the phrases that use and wont have reduced to an inarticulate cry—"Make your game—— The game is made —— Bets are closed !" The croupier spread out the cards, and seemed to wish luck to the new-comer, indifferent as he was to the losses or gains of those who took part in these sombre pleasures. Every bystander thought he saw a drama, the closing scene of a noble life, in the fortunes of that bit of gold; and eagerly fixed his eyes on the prophetic cards; but however closely they watched the young man, they could discover not the least sign of feeling on his cool but restless face.

"Even·! *red* wins," said the croupier officially. A dumb sort of rattle came from the Italian's throat when he saw the folded notes that the banker showered upon him, one after another. The young man only understood his calamity when the croupier's rake was extended to sweep away his last napoleon. The ivory touched the coin with a little click, as it swept it with the speed of an arrow into the heap of gold before the bank. The stranger turned pale at the lips, and softly shut his eyes, but he unclosed them again at once, and the red color returned as he affected the airs of an Englishman, to whom life can offer no new sensation, and disappeared without the glance full of entreaty for com-passion that a desperate gamester will often give the bystanders. How much can happen in a second's space; how many things depend on a throw of the die !

"That was his last cartridge, of course," said the croupier, smiling after a moment's silence, during which he picked up the coin between his finger and thumb and held it up.

"He is a cracked brain that will go and drown him-self," said a frequenter of the place. He looked round about at the other players, who all knew each other.

"Bah !" said a waiter, as he took a pinch of snuff.

"If we had but followed *his* example," said an old game-ster to the others, as he pointed out the Italian.

Everybody looked at the lucky player, whose hands shook as he counted his bank-notes.

"A voice seemed to whisper to me," he said. "The luck is sure to go against that young man's despair."

"He is a new hand," said the banker, "or he would have divided his money into three parts to give himself more chance."

The young man went out without asking for his hat; but the old watch-dog, who had noted its shabby condition, returned it to him without a word. The gambler mechanically gave up the tally, and went down-stairs whistling *Di tanti Palpiti* so feebly, that he himself scarcely heard the delicious notes.

He found himself immediately under the arcades of the Palais-Royal, reached the Rue Saint Honoré, took the direction of the Tuileries, and crossed the gardens with an undecided step. He walked as if he were in some desert, elbowed by men whom he did not see, hearing through all the voices of the crowd one voice alone—the voice of Death. He was lost in the thoughts that benumbed him at last, like the criminals who used to be taken in carts from the Palais de Justice to the Place de Grève, where the scaffold awaited them reddened with all the blood spilt there since 1793.

There is something great and terrible about suicide. Most people's downfalls are not dangerous; they are like children who have not far to fall, and cannot injure themselves; but when a great nature is dashed down, he is bound to fall from a height. He must have been raised almost to the skies; he has caught glimpses of some heaven beyond his reach. Vehement must the storms be which compel a soul to seek for peace from the trigger of a pistol.

How much young power starves and pines away in a garret for want of a friend, for lack of a woman's consolation, in the midst of millions of fellow-creatures, in the presence of a listless crowd that is burdened by its wealth! When one remembers all this, suicide looms large. Between a self-sought death and the abundant hopes whose voices call a young man to Paris, God only knows what may intervene; what contending ideas have striven within the soul; what poems have been set aside; what moans and what despair have been repressed; what abortive masterpieces and vain endeavors! Every suicide is an awful poem of sorrow. Where will you find a work of genius floating above the seas of literature that can compare with this paragraph :—

"Yesterday, at four o'clock, a young woman threw herself into the Seine from the Pont des Arts."

Dramas and romances pale before this concise Parisian phrase; so must even that old frontispiece, "The Lamentations of the glorious king of Kaërnavan, put in prison by his children," the sole remaining fragment of a lost work that drew tears from Sterne at the bare perusal—the same Sterne who deserted his own wife and family.

The stranger was beset with such thoughts as these, which passed in fragments through his mind, like tattered flags fluttering above the combat. If he set aside for a moment the burdens of consciousness and of memory, to watch the flower heads gently swayed by the breeze among the green thickets, a revulsion came over him, life struggled against the oppressive thought of suicide, and his eyes rose to the sky: gray clouds, melancholy gusts of the wind, the stormy atmosphere, all decreed that he should die.

He bent his way toward the Pont Royal, musing over the last fancies of others who had gone before him. He smiled to himself as he remembered that Lord Castlereagh had satisfied the humblest of our needs before he cut his throat, and that the academician Auger had sought for his snuff-box as he went to his death. He analyzed these extravagances, and even examined himself; for as he stood aside against the parapet to allow a porter to pass, his coat had been whitened somewhat by the contact, and he carefully brushed the dust from his sleeve, to his own surprise. He reached the middle of the arch, and looked forebodingly at the water.

"Wretched weather for drowning yourself," said a ragged old woman, who grinned at him; "isn't the Seine cold and dirty?"

His answer was a ready smile, which showed the frenzied nature of his courage; then he shivered all at once as he saw at a distance, by the door of the Tuileries, a shed with an inscription above it in letters twelve inches high: THE ROYAL HUMANE SOCIETY'S APPARATUS.

A vision of M. Dacheux rose before him, equipped by his philanthropy, calling out and setting in motion the too efficacious oars which break the heads of drowning men, if unluckily they should rise to the surface; he saw a curious crowd collecting, running for a doctor, preparing fumigations; he read the maundering paragraph in the papers, put between notes on a festivity and on the smiles of a ballet dancer; he heard the francs counted down by the prefect of police to the watermen. As a corpse, he was worth fifteen francs; but now while he lived he was only a man of talent without patrons, without friends, without a mattress to lie on, or any one to speak a word for him—a perfect social cipher, useless to a State which gave itself no trouble about him.

A death in broad daylight seemed degrading to him; he made up his mind to die at night so as to bequeath an unrecognizable corpse to a world which had disregarded the greatness of his life. He began his wanderings again, turning towards the Quai Voltaire, imitating the lagging gait of an idler seeking to kill time. As he came down the steps at the end of the bridge, his attention was drawn to the second-hand books displayed on the parapet, and he was on the point of bargaining for some. He smiled, thrust his hands philosophically into his pockets, and fell to strolling on again with a proud disdain in his manner, when he heard to his surprise some coin rattling fantastically in his pocket.

A smile of hope lit his face, and slid from his lips over his features, over his brow, and brought a joyful light to his eyes and his dark cheeks. It was a spark of happiness like one of the red dots that flit over the remains of a burnt scrap of paper; but as it is with the black ashes, so it was with his face, it became dull again when he drew out his hand and perceived only three pennies.

A little chimney-sweeper, with puffed cheeks, all black with soot, and clad in tatters, held out his hand to beg for the man's last pence.

"Ah, kind gentleman! charity, charity: for the love of St. Catherine! only a halfpenny to buy some bread!"

Two paces from the little Savoyard stood an old *pauvre honteux,** sickly and feeble, in wretched garments of ragged druggeting, who asked in a thick, muffled voice—

"Anything you like to give, monsieur; I will pray to God for you————"

But the young man turned his eyes on him, and the old beggar stopped without another word, discerning in that mournful face an abandonment of wretchedness more bitter than his own.

"Charity! charity!"

The young man threw the coins to the old man and the child, left the footway, and turned towards the houses; the harrowing sight of the Seine fretted him beyond endurance.

"May God lengthen your days!" cried the two beggars.

As he reached the shop window of a print seller, this man on the brink of death met a young woman alighting from a showy carriage. He looked in delight at her prettiness, at the pale face appropriately framed by the satin of her fashionable bonnet. Her slender form and graceful movements entranced him. Her skirt had been slightly raised as she

* Bashful beggar.

stepped to the pavement, disclosing a daintily-fitting white stocking over the delicate outlines beneath.   The young lady went into the shop and purchased albums and sets of lithographs; giving several gold coins for them, which glittered and rang upon the counter.   The young man, seemingly occupied with the prints in the window, fixed upon the fair stranger a gaze as eager as man can give, to receive in exchange an indifferent glance, such as lights by accident on a passer-by.   For him it was a leave-taking of love and of woman! but his final and strenuous questioning glance was neither understood nor felt by the slight-natured woman there; her color did not rise, her eyes did not droop.   What was it to her? one more piece of adulation, yet another sigh only prompted the delightful thought at night, "I looked rather well to-day."

The young man quickly turned to another picture, and only left it when she returned to her carriage.   The horses started off, the final vision of luxury and refinement went under an eclipse, just as that life of his would soon do also.   Slowly and sadly he followed the line of the shops, listlessly examining the specimens on view.   When the shops came to an end, he reviewed the Louvre, the Institute, the towers of Notre Dame, of the Palais, the Pont des Arts; all these public monuments seemed to have taken their tone from the heavy gray sky.

Fitful gleams of light gave a foreboding look to Paris; like a pretty woman, the city has mysterious fits of ugliness or beauty.   So the outer world seemed to be in a plot to steep this man about to die in a painful trance.   A prey to the maleficent power which acts relaxingly upon us by the fluid circulating through our nerves, his whole frame seemed gradually to experience a dissolving process.   He felt the anguish of these throes passing through him in waves, and the houses and the crowd seemed to surge to and fro in a mist before his eyes.   He tried to escape the agitation wrought in his mind by the revulsions of his physical nature, and went toward the

2

shop of a dealer in antiquities, thinking to give a treat to his senses, and to spend the interval till nightfall in bargaining over curiosities.

He sought, one might say, to regain courage and to find a stimulant, like a criminal who doubts his power to reach the scaffold. The consciousness of approaching death gave him, for the time being, the intrepidity of a duchess with a couple of lovers, so that he entered the place with an abstracted look, while his lips displayed a set smile like a drunkard's. Had not life, or rather had not death, intoxicated him? Dizziness soon overcame him again. Things appeared to him in strange colors, or as making slight movements; his irregular pulse was no doubt the cause; the blood that sometimes rushed like a burning torrent through his veins, and sometimes lay torpid and stagnant as tepid water. He merely asked leave to see if the shop contained any curiosities which he required.

A plump-faced young shopman with red hair, in an otter-skin cap, left an old peasant woman in charge of the shop—a sort of feminine Caliban, employed in cleaning a stove made marvelous by Bernard Palissy's work. This youth remarked carelessly—

"Look round, monsieur! We have nothing very remarkable here down stairs; but if I may trouble you to go up to the first floor, I will show you some very fine mummies from Cairo, some inlaid pottery, and some carved ebony —*genuine Renaissance* work, just come in, and of perfect beauty."

In the young man's fearful position this cicerone's prattle and shopman's empty talk seemed like the petty vexations by which narrow minds destroy a man of genius. But as he must even go through with it, he appeared to listen to his guide, answering him by gestures or monosyllables; but imperceptibly he arrogated the privilege of saying nothing, and gave himself up without hindrance to his closing meditations, which were appalling. He had a poet's temperament, his mind had entered by chance on a vast field; and he must see perforce the dry bones of twenty future worlds.

At a first glance the place presented a confused picture in which every achievement, human and divine, was mingled. Crocodiles, monkeys, and serpents stuffed with straw grinned at glass from church windows, seemed to wish to bite sculptured heads, to chase lacquered work, or to scramble up chandeliers. A Sèvres vase, bearing Napoleon's portrait by Mme. Jacotot, stood beside a sphinx dedicated to Sesostris. The beginnings of the world and the events of yesterday were mingled with grotesque cheerfulness. A kitchen jack leaned against a pyx, a republican sabre on a mediæval hackbut. Mme. du Barry, with a star above her head, naked, and surrounded by a cloud, seemed to look longingly out of Latour's pastel at an Indian chibook, while she tried to guess the purpose of the spiral curves that wound towards her. Instruments of death, poniards, curious pistols, and disguised weapons had been flung down pell-mell among the paraphernalia of daily life; porcelain tureens, Dresden plates, translucent cups from China, old salt-cellars, comfit-boxes belonging to feudal times. A carved ivory ship sped full sail on the back of a motionless tortoise.

The Emperor Augustus remained unmoved and imperial with an air-pump thrust into one eye. Portraits of French sheriffs and Dutch burgomasters, phlegmatic now as when in life, looked down pallid and unconcerned on the chaos of past ages below them.

Every land of earth seemed to have contributed some stray fragment of its learning, some example of its art. Nothing seemed lacking to this philosophical kitchen-midden, from a redskin's calumet, a green and golden slipper from the seraglio, a Moorish yataghan, a Tartar idol, to the soldier's tobacco pouch, to the priest's ciborium, and the plumes that once adorned a throne. This extraordinary combination was rendered yet more bizarre by the accidents of lighting, by a multitude of confused reflections of various hues, by the sharp contrast of blacks and whites. Broken cries seemed to reach the ear, unfinished dramas seized upon the imagination, smothered lights caught the eye. A thin coating of invisible dust covered all the multitudinous corners and convolutions of these objects of various shapes which gave highly picturesque effects.

First of all, the young man compared the three galleries which civilization, cults, divinities, masterpieces, dominions, carousals, sanity, and madness had filled to repletion, to a mirror with numerous facets, each depicting a world. After this first hazy idea he would fain have selected his pleasures, but by dint of using his eyes, thinking and musing, a fever began to possess him, caused perhaps by the gnawing pain of hunger. The spectacle of so much existence, individual or national, to which these pledges bore witness, ended by numbing his senses—the purpose with which he entered the shop was fulfilled. He had left the real behind, and had climbed gradually up to an ideal world; he had attained to the enchanted palace of ecstasy, whence the universe appeared to him by fragments and in shapes of flame, as once the future blazed out before the eyes of St. John in Patmos.

A crowd of sorrowing faces, beneficent and appalling, dark and luminous, far and near, gathered in numbers, in myriads, in whole generations. Egypt, rigid and mysterious, arose from her sands in the form of a mummy swathed in black bandages; then the Pharaohs swallowed up nations, that they might build themselves a tomb; and he beheld Moses and the Hebrews and the desert, and a solemn antique world. Fresh and joyous, a marble statue spoke to him from a twisted column of the pleasure-loving myths of Greece and Ionia. Ah! who would not have smiled with him to see, against the earthen, red background, the brown-faced maiden dancing with gleeful reverence before the god Priapus, wrought in the fine clay of an Etruscan vase? The Latin queen caressed her chimera.

The whims of imperial Rome were there in life, the bath was disclosed, the toilette of a languid Julia, dreaming, waiting for her Tibullus. Strong with the might of Arabic spells, the head of Cicero evoked memories of a free Rome, and unrolled before him the scrolls of Titus Livius. The young man beheld *Senatus Populusque Romanus;* consuls, lictors, togas with purple fringes; the fighting in the Forum, the angry people, passed in review before him like the cloudy faces of a dream.

Then Christian Rome predominated in his vision. A painter had laid heaven open; he beheld the Virgin Mary wrapped in a golden cloud among the angels, shining more brightly than the sun, receiving the prayers of sufferers, on whom this second Eve Regenerate smiles pityingly. At the touch of a mosaic, made of various lavas from Vesuvius and Etna, his fancy fled to the hot tawny south of Italy. He was present at Borgia's orgies, he roved among the Abruzzi, sought for Italian love intrigues, grew ardent over pale faces and dark, almond-shaped eyes. He shivered over midnight adventures, cut short by the cool thrust of a jealous blade, as he saw a mediæval dagger with a hilt wrought like lace, and spots of rust like splashes of blood upon it.

India and its religions took the shape of the idol with his peaked cap of fantastic form, with little bells, clad in silk and gold. Close by, a mat, as pretty as the bayadere who once lay upon it, still gave out a faint scent of sandal wood. His fancy was stirred by a goggle-eyed Chinese monster, with mouth awry and twisted limbs, the invention of a people who, grown weary of the monotony of beauty, found an indescribable pleasure in an infinite variety of ugliness. A salt-cellar from Benvenuto Cellini's workshop carried him back to the Renaissance at its height, to the time when there was no restraint on art or morals, when torture was the sport of sovereigns; and from their councils, churchmen with courtesans' arms about them issued decrees of chastity for simple priests.

On a cameo he saw the conquests of Alexander, the massacres of Pizarro in a matchlock, and religious wars disorderly, fanatical, and cruel, in the shadows of a helmet. Joyous pictures of chivalry were called up by a suit of Milanese armor, brightly polished and richly wrought; a paladin's eyes seemed to sparkle yet under the visor.

This sea of inventions, fashions, furniture, works of art and fiascos, made for him a poem without end. Shapes and colors and projects all lived again for him, but his mind received no clear and perfect conception. It was the poet's task to complete the sketches of the great master, who had scornfully mingled on his palette the hues of the numberless vicissitudes of human life. When the world at large at last released him, when he had pondered over many lands, many epochs, and various empires, the young man came back to the life of the individual. He impersonated fresh characters, and turned his mind to details, rejecting the life of nations as a burden too overwhelming for a single soul.

Yonder was a sleeping child, modeled in wax, a relic of Ruysch's collection, an enchanting creation which brought back the happiness of his own childhood. The cotton garment of a Tahitian maid next fascinated him; he beheld the primitive life of nature, the real modesty of naked chastity, the joys of an idleness natural to mankind, a peaceful fate by a slow river of sweet water under a plantain tree that bears its pleasant manna without the toil of man. Then all at once he became a corsair, investing himself with the terrible poetry that Lara has given to the part: the thought came at the sight of the mother-of-pearl tints of a myriad of sea-shells, and grew as he saw madrepores redolent of the sea-weeds and the storms of the Atlantic.

The sea was forgotten again at a distant view of exquisite

miniatures; he admired a precious missal in manuscript, adorned with arabesques in gold and blue. Thoughts of peaceful life swayed him; he devoted himself afresh to study and research, longing for the easy life of the monk, devoid alike of cares and pleasures; and from the depths of his cell he looked out upon the meadows, woods, and vineyards of his convent. Pausing before some work of Teniers, he took for his own the helmet of the soldier or the poverty of the artisan; he wished to wear a smoke-begrimed cap with these Flemings, to drink their beer and join their game at cards, and smiled upon the comely plumpness of a peasant woman. He shivered at a snowstorm by Mieris; he seemed to take part in Salvator Rosa's battle-piece; he ran his fingers over a tomahawk from Illinois, and felt his own hair rise as he touched a Cherokee scalping-knife. He marveled over the rebec that he set in the hands of some lady of the land, drank in the musical notes of her ballad, and in the twilight by the Gothic arch above the hearth he told his love in a gloom so deep that he could not read his answer in her eyes.

He caught at all delights, at all sorrows; grasped at existence in every form; and endowed the phantoms conjured up from that inert and plastic material so liberally with his own life and feelings, that the sound of his own footsteps reached him as if from another world, or as the hum of Paris reaches the towers of Notre Dame.

He ascended the inner staircase which led to the first floor, with its votive shields, panoplies, carved shrines, and figures on the wall at every step. Haunted by the strangest shapes, by marvelous creations belonging to the borderland betwixt life and death, he walked as if under the spell of a dream. His own existence became a matter of doubt to him; he was neither wholly alive nor dead, like the curious objects about him. The light began to fade as he reached the show-rooms, but the treasures of gold and silver heaped up there scarcely seemed to need illumination from without. The most extravagant whims of prodigals, who have run through millions to perish in garrets, had left their traces here in this vast bazaar of human follies. Here, beside a writing desk, made at the cost of 100,000 francs, and sold for a hundred pence, lay a lock with a secret worth a king's ransom. The human race was revealed in all the grandeur of its wretchedness; in all the splendor of its infinite littleness. An ebony table that an artist might worship, carved after Jean Goujon designs, in years of toil, had been purchased perhaps at the price of firewood. Precious caskets, and things that fairy hands might have fashioned, lay there in heaps like rubbish.

"You must have the worth of millions here!" cried the young man as he entered the last of an immense suite of rooms, all decorated and gilded by eighteenth century artists.

"Thousands of millions, you might say," said the florid shopman; "but you have seen nothing as yet. Go up to the third floor, and you shall see!"

The young man followed his guide to a fourth gallery, where one by one there passed before his wearied eyes several pictures by Poussin, a magnificent statue by Michael Angelo, enchanting landscapes by Claude Lorraine, a Gerard Dow (like a stray page from Sterne), Rembrandts, Murillos, and pictures by Velasquez, as dark and full of color as a poem of Byron's; then came classic bas-reliefs, finely-cut agates, wonderful cameos! Works of art upon works of art, till the craftsman's skill palled on the mind, masterpiece after masterpiece till art itself became hateful at last and enthusiasm died. He came upon a Madonna by Raphael, but he was tired of Raphael; a figure by Correggio never received the glance it demanded of him. A priceless vase of antique porphyry carved round about with pictures of the most grotesquely wanton of Roman divinities, the pride of some Corinna, scarcely drew a smile from him.

. The ruins of fifteen hundred vanished years oppressed him; he sickened under all this human thought; felt bored by all this luxury and art. He struggled in vain against the constantly renewed fantastic shapes that sprang up from under his feet, like children of some sportive demon.

Are not fearful poisons set up in the soul by a swift concentration of all her energies, her enjoyments, or ideas; as modern chemistry, in its caprice, repeats the action of creation by some gas or other? Do not many men perish under the shock of the sudden expansion of some moral acid within them?

"What is there in that box?" he inquired, as he reached a large closet—final triumph of human skill, originality, wealth, and splendor, in which there hung a large, square mahogany coffer, suspended from a nail by a silver chain.

"Ah, monsieur keeps the key of it," said the stout assistant mysteriously. "If you wish to see the portrait, I will gladly venture to tell him."

"Venture!" said the young man; "then is your master a prince?"

"I don't know what he is," the other answered. Equally astonished, each looked for a moment at the other. Then construing the young man's silence as an order, the apprentice left him alone in the closet.

Have you never launched into the immensity of time and space as you read the geological writings of Cuvier? Carried by his fancy, have you hung as if suspended by a magician's wand over the illimitable abyss of the past? When the fossil bones of animals belonging to civilizations before the Flood are turned up in bed after bed and layer upon layer of the quarries of Montmartre or among the schists of the Ural range, the soul receives with dismay a glimpse of millions of peoples forgotten by feeble human memory and unrecognized by permanent divine tradition, peoples whose ashes cover our globe with two feet of earth that yields bread to us and flowers.

Is not Cuvier the great poet of our era? Byron has given

admirable expression to certain moral conflicts, but our immortal naturalist has reconstructed past worlds from a few bleached bones; has rebuilt cities, like Cadmus, with monsters' teeth; has animated forests with all the secrets of zoölogy gleaned from a piece of coal; has discovered a giant population from the footprints of a mammoth. These forms stand erect, grow large, and fill regions commensurate with their giant size. He treats figures like a poet; a nought set beside a seven by him produces awe.

He can call up nothingness before you without the phrases of a charlatan. He searches a lump of gypsum, finds an impression in it, says to you, "Behold!" All at once marble takes an animal shape, the dead come to life, the history of the world is laid open before you. After countless dynasties of giant creatures, races of fish and clans of molluscs, the race of man appears at last as the degenerate copy of a splendid model, which the Creator has perchance destroyed. Emboldened by his gaze into the past, this petty race, children of yesterday, can overstep chaos, can raise a psalm without end, and outline for themselves the story of the Universe in an Apocalypse that reveals the past. After the tremendous resurrection that took place at the voice of this man, the little drop in the nameless Infinite, common to all the spheres, that is ours to use, and that we call Time, seems to us a pitiable moment of life. We ask ourselves the purpose of our triumphs, our hatreds, our loves, overwhelmed as we are by the destruction of so many past universes, and whether it is worth while to accept the pain of life in order that hereafter we may become an intangible speck. Then we remain as if dead, completely torn away from the present till the *valet de chambre* comes in and says, "*Madame la comtesse* answers that she is expecting *monsieur.*"

All the wonders which had brought the known world before the young man's mind wrought in his soul much the same feeling of dejection that besets the philosopher investigating unknown creations. He longed more than ever for death as he flung himself back in a curule chair and let his eyes wander across the illusions composing a panorama of the past. The pictures seemed to light up, the Virgin's heads smiled on him, the statues seemed alive. Everything danced and swayed around him, with a motion due to the gloom and the tormenting fever that racked his brain; each monstrosity grimaced at him, while the portraits on the canvas closed their eyes for a little relief. Every shape seemed to tremble and start, and to leave its place gravely or flippantly, gracefully or awkwardly, according to its fashion, character, and surroundings.

A mysterious Sabbath began, rivalling the fantastic scenes witnessed by Faust upon the Brocken. But these optical illusions, produced by weariness, over-strained eyesight, or the accidents of twilight, could not alarm the young man. The terrors of life had no power over a soul grown familiar with the terrors of death. He even gave himself up, half-amused by its bizarre eccentricities, to the influence of this moral galvanism; its phenomena, closely connected with his last thoughts, assured him that he was still alive. The silence about him was so deep that he embarked once more in dreams that grew gradually darker and darker as if by magic, as the light slowly faded. A last struggling ray from the sun lit up rosy answering lights. He raised his head and saw a skeleton dimly visible, with its skull bent doubtfully to one side, as if to say, "The dead will none of thee as yet."

He passed his hand over his forehead to shake off the drowsiness, and felt a cold breath of air as an unknown furry something swept past his cheeks. He shivered. A muffled clatter of the windows followed; it was a bat, he fancied, that had given him this chilly sepulchral caress. He could yet dimly see for a moment the shapes that surrounded him, by the vague light in the west; then all these inanimate objects were blotted out in uniform darkness. Night and the hour of death had suddenly come. Thenceforward, for a while, he lost consciousness of the things about him ; he was either buried in deep meditation, or sleep overcame him, brought on by weariness or by the stress of those many thoughts that lacerated his heart.

Suddenly he thought that an awful voice called him by name ; it was like some feverish nightmare, when at a step the dreamer falls headlong over into an abyss, and he trembled. He closed his eyes, dazzled by bright rays from a red circle of light that shone out from the shadows. In the midst of the circle stood a little old man who turned the light of a lamp upon him, yet he had not heard him enter, nor move, nor speak. There was something magical about the apparition. The boldest man, awakened in such a way, would have felt alarm at the sight of this figure, which might have issued from some sarcophagus hard by.

A curiously youthful look in the unmoving eyes of the spectre forbade the idea of anything supernatural ; but for all that, in the brief space between his dreaming and waking life, the young man's judgment remained philosophically suspended, as Descartes claims. He was, in spite of himself, under the influence of an unaccountable hallucination, a mystery that our pride rejects, and that our imperfect science vainly tries to solve.

Imagine a short old man, thin and spare, in a long black velvet gown girded round him by a thick silk cord. His long white hair escaped on either side of his face from under a black velvet cap which closely fitted his head and made a formal setting for his countenance. His gown enveloped his body like a winding-sheet, so that all that was left visible was a narrow bleached human face. But for the wasted arm, thin as a draper's wand, which held aloft the lamp that cast all its light upon him, the face would have seemed to hang in mid-air. A gray pointed beard concealed the chin of this fantastical appearance, and gave him the look of one of those

A LITTLE OLD MAN TURNED THE LIGHT OF A LAMP
UPON HIM.

Jewish types which serve artists as models for Moses. His lips were so thin and colorless that it needed a close inspection to find the lines of his mouth at all in the pallid face. His great wrinkled brow and hollow bloodless cheeks, the inexorably stern expression of his small green eyes that no longer possessed eyebrows or lashes, might have convinced the young man that Gerard Dow's "Money Changer" had come down from his frame. The craftiness of an inquisitor, revealed in those curving wrinkles and creases that wound about his temples, indicated a profound knowledge of life. There was no deceiving this man, who seemed to possess a power of detecting the secrets of the most wary heart.

The wisdom and the moral codes of every people seemed gathered up in his passive face, just as all the productions of the globe had been heaped up in his dusty show-rooms. He seemed to possess the tranquil luminous vision of some god before whom all things are open, or the haughty power of a man who knows all things.

With two strokes of the brush a painter could have so altered the expression of this face, that what had been a serene representation of the Eternal Father should change to the sneering mask of a Mephistopheles; for though sovereign power was revealed by the forehead, mocking folds lurked about the mouth. He must have sacrificed all the joys of earth, as he had crushed all human sorrows beneath his potent will. The man at the brink of death shivered at the thought of the life led by this spirit, so solitary and remote from our world; joyless, since he had no one illusion left; painless, because pleasure had ceased to exist for him. There he stood, motionless and serene as a star in a bright mist. His lamp lit up the obscure closet, just as his green eyes, with their quiet malevolence, seemed to shed a light on the moral world.

This was the strange spectacle that startled the young man's returning sight, as he shook off the dreamy fancies and thoughts of death that had lulled him. An instant of dismay, a momentary return to belief in nursery tales, may be forgiven him, seeing that his senses were obscured. Much thought had wearied his mind, and his nerves were exhausted with the strain of the tremendous drama within him, and by the scenes that had heaped on him all the horrid pleasures that a piece of opium can produce.

But this apparition had appeared in Paris, on the Quai Voltaire, and in the nineteenth century; the time and place made sorcery impossible. The idol of French scepticism had died in the house just opposite, the disciple of Gay-Lussac and Arago, who had held the charlatanism of intellect in contempt. And yet the young man submitted himself to the influence of an imaginative spell, as all of us do at times, when we wish to escape from an inevitable certainty, or to tempt the power of Providence. So some mysterious apprehension of a strange force made him tremble before the old man with the lamp. All of us have been stirred in the same way by the sight of Napoleon, or of some other great man, made illustrious by his genius or by fame.

"You wish to see Raphael's portrait of Jesus Christ, monsieur?" the old man asked politely. There was something metallic in the clear, sharp ring of his voice.

He set the lamp upon a broken column, so that all its light might fall on the brown case.

At the sacred names of Christ and Raphael the young man showed some curiosity. The merchant, who no doubt looked for this, pressed a spring, and suddenly the mahogany panel slid noiselessly back in its groove, and discovered the canvas to the young man's admiring gaze. At sight of this deathless creation, he forgot his fancies in the show-rooms and the freaks of his dreams, and became himself again, The old man became a being of flesh and blood, very much alive, with nothing chimerical about him, and took up his existence at once upon solid earth.

The sympathy and love, and the gentle serenity in the divine face, exerted an instant sway over the younger spectator. Some influence falling from heaven bade cease the burning torment that consumed the marrow of his bones. The head of the Saviour of mankind seemed to issue from among the shadows represented by a dark background; an aureole of light shone out brightly from his hair; an impassioned belief seemed to glow through him, and to thrill every feature. The word of life had just been uttered by those red lips, the sacred sounds seemed to linger still in the air; the spectator besought the silence for those captivating parables, hearkened for them in the future, and had to turn to the teachings of the past. The untroubled peace of the divine eyes, the comfort of sorrowing souls, seemed an interpretation of the Evangel. The sweet triumphant smile revealed the secret of the Catholic religion, which sums up all things in the precept, "Love one another." This picture breathed the spirit of prayer, enjoined forgiveness, overcame self, caused sleeping powers of good to waken. For this work of Raphael's had the imperious charm of music; you were brought under the spell of memories of the past; his triumph was so absolute that the artist was forgotten. The witchery of the lamplight heightened the wonder; the head seemed at times to flicker in the distance, enveloped in cloud.

"I covered the surface of that picture with gold-pieces," said the merchant carelessly.

"And now for death!" cried the young man, awakened from his musings. His last thought had recalled his fate to him, as it led him imperceptibly back from the forlorn hopes to which he clung.

"Ah, ha! then my suspicions were well founded!" said the other, and his hands held the young man's wrists in a grip like that of a vise.

The young man smiled wearily at his mistake, and said gently—

"You, sir, have nothing to fear; it is not your life, but my own that is in question —— But why should I hide a harmless fraud?" he went on, after a look at the anxious old man. "I came to see your treasure to while away the time till night should come and I could drown myself decently. Who would grudge this last pleasure to a poet and a man of science?"

While he spoke, the jealous merchant watched the haggard face of his pretended customer with keen eyes. Perhaps the mournful tones of his voice reassured him, or he also read the dark signs of fate in the faded features that had made the gamblers shudder; he released his hands, but with a touch of caution, due to the experience of some hundred years at least, he stretched his arm out to a sideboard as if to steady himself, took up a little dagger and said—

"Have you been a supernumerary clerk of the Treasury for three years without receiving any perquisites?"

The young man could scarcely suppress a smile as he shook his head.

"Perhaps your father has expressed his regret for your birth a little too sharply? Or have you disgraced yourself?"

"If I meant to be disgraced, I should live."

"You have been hissed perhaps at the Funambules? Or you have had to compose couplets to pay for your mistress' funeral? Do you want to be cured of the gold fever? Or to be quit of the spleen? For what blunder is your life a forfeit?"

"You must not look among the common motives that impel suicides for the reason of my death. To spare myself the task of disclosing my unheard-of sufferings, for which language has no name, I will tell you this—that I am in the deepest, most humiliating, and most cruel trouble, and," he went on in proud tones that harmonized ill with the words just uttered, "I have no wish to beg for either help or sympathy."

"Eh! eh!"

The two syllables which the old man pronounced resembled the sound of a rattle.   Then he went on thus:

"Without compelling you to entreat me, without making you blush for it, and without giving you so much as a French centime, a para from the Levant, a German heller, a Russian kopeck, a Scottish farthing, a single obolus or sestercius from the ancient world, or one piastre from the new, without offering you anything whatever in gold, silver, or copper, notes or drafts, I will make you richer, more powerful, and of more consequence than a constitutional king."

The young man thought that the old man must be in his dotage, and waited in bewilderment without venturing to reply.

"Turn round," said the merchant, suddenly catching up the lamp in order to light up the opposite wall ; "look at that leathern skin," he went on.

The young man rose abruptly, and showed some surprise at the sight of a piece of shagreen which hung on the wall behind his chair.   It was only about the size of a fox's skin, but it seemed to fill the deep shadows of the place with such brilliant rays that it looked like a small comet, an appearance at first sight inexplicable.   The young sceptic went up to this so-called talisman, which was to rescue him from his woes, with a scoffing phrase in his thoughts.   Still a harmless curiosity led him to bend over it and look at it from all points of view, and he soon found out the cause of its singular brilliancy. The dark grain of the leather had been so carefully burnished and polished, the striped markings of the graining were so sharp and clear, that every particle of the surface of the bit of Oriental leather was in itself a focus which concentrated the light, and reflected it vividly.

He accounted for this phenomenon categorically to the old man, who only smiled meaningly by way of answer.   His superior smile led the young scientific man to fancy that he himself had been deceived by some imposture.   He had no

3

wish to carry one more puzzle to his grave, and hastily turned
the skin over, like some child eager to find out the mysteries
of a new toy.

"Ah," he cried, "here is the mark of a seal which they
call in the East the Signet of Solomon."

"So you know that then," asked the merchant. His pecu-
liar method of laughter, two or three quick breathings
through the nostrils, said more than any words however elo-
quent.

"Is there anybody in the world simple enough to believe
in that idle fancy?" said the young man, nettled by the spite-
fulness of the silent chuckle. "Don't you know," he con-
tinued, "that the superstitions of the East have perpetuated
the mystical form and the counterfeit characters of the symbol,
which represents a mythical dominion? I have no more laid
myself open to a charge of credulity in this case, than if I
had mentioned sphinxes or griffins, whose existence mythology
in a manner admits."

"As you are an Orientalist," replied the other, "perhaps
you can read that sentence."

He held the lamp close to the talisman, which the young
man held towards him, and pointed out some characters
inlaid in the surface of the wonderful skin, as if they had
grown on the animal to which it once belonged.

"I must admit," said the young man, "that I have no
idea how the letters could be engraved so deeply on the skin
of a wild ass." And he turned quickly to the tables strewn
with curiosities, and seemed to look for something.

"What is it that you want?" asked the old man.

"Something that will cut the leather, so that I can see
whether the letters are printed or inlaid."

The old man held out his stiletto. The young man took
it and tried to cut the skin above the lettering; but when
he had removed a thin shaving of leather from them, the
characters still appeared below, so clear and so exactly like

the surface impression, that for a moment he was not sure that he had cut anything away after all.

"The craftsmen of the Levant have secrets known only to themselves," he said, half in vexation, as he eyed the characters of this Oriental sentence.

"Yes," said the old man, "it is better to attribute it to man's agency than to God's."

The mysterious words were thus arranged :—

لو ملكتنى ملكت الكل

ولكن عمرك ملكى

واراد الله هكذا

اطلب وستننال مطالبك

ولكن قسن مطالبك على عمرك

وهى هاهنا

فبكل مرامك استنسنزل ايامك

أتريد فى

الله يجيبك

آمين

Or, as it runs in English :—

POSSESSING ME THOU SHALT POSSESS ALL THINGS.
BUT THY LIFE IS MINE, FOR GOD HAS SO WILLED IT.
WISH, AND THY WISHES SHALL BE FULFILLED ;
BUT MEASURE THY DESIRES, ACCORDING
TO THE LIFE THAT IS IN THEE.
THIS IS THY LIFE,
WITH EACH WISH I MUST SHRINK
EVEN AS THY OWN DAYS.
WILT THOU HAVE ME? TAKE ME.
GOD WILL HEARKEN UNTO THEE.
SO BE IT !

"So you read Sanskrit fluently," said the old man. "You have been in Persia perhaps, or in Bengal?"

"No, sir," said the stranger, as he felt the emblematical skin curiously. It was almost as rigid as a sheet of metal.

The old merchant set the lamp back again upon the column, giving the other a look as he did so. "He has given up the notion of dying already," the glance said with phlegmatic irony.

"Is it a jest, or is it an enigma?" asked the young man.

The other shook his head and said soberly—

"I don't know how to answer you. I have offered this talisman with its terrible powers to men with more energy in them than you seem to me to have; but though they laughed at the questionable power it might exert over their futures, not one of them was ready to venture to conclude the fateful contract proposed by an unknown force. I am of their opinion, I have doubted and refrained, and——"

"Have you never even tried its power?" interrupted the young stranger.

"Tried it!" exclaimed the old man. "Suppose that you were on the column in the Place Vendome, would you try flinging yourself into space? Is it possible to stay the course of life? Has a man ever been known to die by halves? Before you came here, you had made up your mind to kill yourself, but all at once a mystery fills your mind, and you think no more about death. You child! Does not any one day of your life afford mysteries more absorbing? Listen to me. I saw the licentious days of the Regency. I was like you, then, in poverty; I have begged my bread; but for all that, I am now a centenarian with a couple of years to spare, and a millionaire to boot. Misery was the making of me, ignorance has made me learned. I will tell you in a few words the great secret of human life. By two instinctive processes man exhausts the springs of life within him. Two verbs cover all the forms which these two causes of death may take—'To will and to have your will.' Between these two limits of human activity the wise have discovered an intermediate formula, to which I owe my good fortune and long life. 'To will' consumes us, and 'To have our will' destroys us, but 'To know' steeps our feeble organisms in perpetual calm. In me Thought has destroyed Will, so that Power is relegated to the ordinary functions of my economy. In a word, it is not in the heart which can be broken, nor in the senses that become deadened, but it is in the brain that cannot waste away and survives everything else, that I have set my life. Moderation has kept mind and body unruffled. Yet I have seen the whole world. I have learned all languages, lived after every manner. I have loaned a Chinaman money, taking his father's corpse as a pledge, slept in an Arab's tent on the security of his bare word, signed contracts in every capital of Europe, and left my gold without hesitation in savage wigwams. I have attained everything, because I have known how to despise all things.

"My one ambition has been to see. Is not sight in a manner insight? And to have knowledge or insight, is not that to have instinctive possession? To be able to discover the very substance of fact and to unite its essence to our essence? Of material possession what abides with you but an idea? Think, then, how glorious must be the life of a man who can stamp all realities upon his thought, place the springs of happiness within himself, and draw thence uncounted pleasures in idea, unsoiled by earthly stains. Thought is a key to all treasures; the miser's gains are ours without his cares. Thus I have soared above this world, where my enjoyments have been intellectual joys. I have reveled in the contemplation of seas, peoples, forests, and mountains! I have seen all things, calmly, and without weariness; I have set my desires on nothing; I have waited in expectation of everything. I have walked to and fro in the world as in a garden round about my own dwelling. Troubles, loves, ambitions, losses, and sorrows, as men call them, are for me ideas, which I transmute into waking dreams; I express and transpose instead of feeling them; instead of permitting them to prey upon my life, I dramatize and expand them; I divert myself with them as if they were romances which I could read by the power of vision within me. As I have never overtaxed my constitution, I still enjoy robust health; and as my mind is endowed with all the force that I have not wasted, this head of mine is even better furnished than my galleries. The true millions lie here," he said, striking his forehead. "I spend delicious days in communings with the past; I summon before me whole countries, places, extents of sea, the fair faces of history. In my imaginary seraglio I have all the women I have never possessed. Your wars and revolutions come up before me for judgment. What is a feverish fugitive admiration for some more or less brightly colored piece of flesh and blood; some more or less rounded human form; what are all the disasters that wait on your erratic whims, compared with the magnificent power of conjuring up the whole world within your soul, compared with the immeasurable joys of movements, unstrangled by the cords of time, unclogged by the fetters of space; the joys of beholding all things, of comprehending all things, of leaning over the parapet of the world to question the other spheres, to hearken to the voice of God? There," he burst out, vehemently, "there are To Will and To have your Will, both together," he pointed to the bit of shagreen; "there are your social ideas, your immoderate desires, your excesses, your pleasures that end in death, your sorrows that quicken the pace of life, for pain is perhaps but a violent pleasure. Who could determine the point where pleasure becomes pain, where pain is still a pleasure? Is not the utmost brightness of the ideal world soothing to us, while the lightest shadows of the physical world annoy? Is not knowledge the secret of wisdom? And what is folly but a riotous expenditure of Will or Power?"

"Very good, then, a life of riotous excess for me!" said the young man, pouncing upon the piece of shagreen.

"Young man, beware!" cried the other with incredible vehemence.

"I had resolved my existence into thought and study," the young man replied; "and yet they have not even supported me. I am not to be gulled by a sermon worthy of Swedenborg, nor by your Oriental amulet, nor yet by your charitable endeavors to keep me in a world wherein existence is no longer possible for me. —— Let me see, now," he added, clutching the talisman convulsively, as he looked at the old man, "I wish for a royal banquet, a carouse worthy of this century, which, it is said, has brought everything to perfection! Let me have young boon companions, witty, unwarped by prejudice, merry to the verge of madness! Let one wine succeed another, each more biting and perfumed than the last, and strong enough to bring about three days of delirium! Passionate women's forms should grace that night! I would be borne away to unknown regions beyond the confines of this world by the car and four-winged steeds of a frantic and uproarious orgie. Let us ascend to the skies, or plunge ourselves in the mire. I do not know if one soars or sinks at such moments, and I do not care! Next, I bid this enigmatical power to concentrate all delights for me in one single joy. Yes, I must comprehend every pleasure of earth and heaven in the final embrace that is to kill me. Therefore, after the wine, I wish to hold high festival to Priapus, with songs that might rouse the dead, and kisses without end; the sound of them should pass like the crackling of flame through Paris, should revive the heat of youth and passion in husband and wife, even in hearts of seventy years."

A laugh burst from the little old man. It rang in the young man's ears like an echo from hell, and tyrannously cut him short. He said no more.

"Do you imagine that my floors are going to open suddenly, so that luxuriously-appointed tables may rise through them, and guests from another world? No, no, young madcap. You have entered into the compact now, and there is an end of. it. Henceforward, your wishes will be accurately fulfilled, but at the expense of your life. The compass of your days, visible in that skin, will contract according to the strength and number of your desires, from the least to the most extravagant. The Brahmin from whom I had this skin once explained to me that it would bring about a mysterious connection between the fortunes and the wishes of its possessor. Your first wish is a vulgar one, which I could fulfil, but I leave that to the issues of your new existence. After all, you were wishing to die ; very well, your suicide is only put off for a time."

The young man was surprised and irritated because the singular old man persisted in not taking him seriously. A half philanthropic intention peeped so clearly forth from his last jesting observation, that he exclaimed—

" I shall soon see, sir, if any change comes over my fortunes in the time it will take to cross the width of the quay. But I should like us to be quits for such a momentous service ; that is, if you are not laughing at an unlucky wretch, so I wish that you may fall in love with an opera-dancer. You would understand the pleasures of intemperance then, and might perhaps grow lavish of the wealth that you have husbanded so philosophically."

He went out without heeding the old man's heavy sigh, went back through the galleries and down the staircase, followed by the stout assistant who vainly tried to light his passage ; he fled with the haste of a robber caught in the act. Blinded by a kind of delirium, he did not even notice the unexpected flexibility of the piece of shagreen, which coiled itself up, pliant as a glove in his excited fingers, till it would go into the pocket of his coat, where he mechanically thrust it. As he rushed out of the door into the street, he ran up against three young men who were passing arm in arm.

"Brute!"

"Idiot!"

Such were the gratifying expressions exchanged between them.

"Why, it is Raphael!"

"Good! we were looking for you."

"What! it is you, then?"

These three friendly exclamations quickly followed the insults, as the light of a street lamp, flickering in the wind, fell upon the astonished faces of the group.

"My dear fellow, you must come with us!" said the young man that Raphael had all but knocked down.

"What is all this about?"

"Come along, and I will tell you the history of it as we go."

By fair means or foul, Raphael must go along with his friends towards the Pont des Arts; they surrounded him, and linked him by the arm among their merry band.

"We have been after you for about a week," the speaker went on. "At your respectable hotel *de Saint Quentin*, where, by the way, the sign with the alternate black and red letters cannot be removed, and hangs out just as it did in the time of Jean Jacques, that Leonarda of yours told us that you were off into the country. For all that, we certainly did not look like duns, creditors, sheriff's officers, or the like. But no matter! Rastignac had seen you the evening before at the Bouffons; we took courage again, and made it a point of honor to find out whether you were roosting in a tree in the Champs Elysées, or in one of those philanthropic abodes where the beggars sleep on a twopenny rope, or if, more lucky, you were bivouacking in some boudoir or other. We could not find you anywhere. Your name was not in the jailer's registers at St. Pelagie nor at La Force! Government

departments, *cafes*, libraries, lists of prefects' names, news-
paper offices, restaurants, greenrooms—to cut it short, every
lurking place in Paris, good or bad, has been explored in the
most expert manner.   We bewailed the loss of a man endowed
with such genius, that one might look to find him either at
Court or in the common jails.   We talked of canonizing you
as a hero of July, and, upon my word, we regretted you ! ' '

   As he spoke, the friends were crossing the Pont des Arts.
Without listening to them, Raphael looked at the Seine, at
the clamoring waves that reflected the lights of Paris.   Above
that river, in which but now he had thought to fling himself,
the old man's prediction had been fulfilled, the hour of his
death had been already put back by fate.

   " We really regretted you," said his friend, still pursuing
his theme.   " It was a question of a plan in which we in-
cluded you as a superior person, that is to say, somebody who
can put himself above other people.   The constitutional
thimble-rig is carried on to-day, dear boy, more seriously than
ever.   The infamous monarchy, displaced by the heroism of
the people, was a sort of drab, you could laugh and revel with
her ; but La Patrie is a shrewish and virtuous wife, and willy-
nilly you must take her prescribed endearments.   Then be-
sides, as you know, authority passed over from the Tuileries
to the journalists, at the time when the Budget changed its
quarters and went from the Faubourg Saint Germain to the
Chaussee d'Antin.   But this you may not know, perhaps.
The Government, that is, the aristocracy of lawyers and bank-
ers who represent the country to-day, just as the priests used
to do in the time of the monarchy, has felt the necessity of
mystifying the worthy people of France with a few new words
and old ideas, like philosophers of every school, and all strong
intellects ever since time began.   So now Royalist-national
ideas must be inculcated, by proving to us that it is far better
to pay twelve hundred million francs thirty-three centimes to
La Patrie, represented by Messieurs Such-and-Such, than to

pay eleven hundred million francs nine centimes to a king who used to say *I* instead of *we*. In a word, a journal, with two or three hundred thousand francs, good, at the back of it, has just been started, with a view to making an opposition paper to content the discontented, without prejudice to the national government of the citizen-king. We scoff at liberty as at despotism now, and at religion or incredulity quite impartially. And since, for us, 'our country' means a capital where ideas circulate and are sold at so much a line, a succulent dinner every day, and the play at frequent intervals, where profligate women swarm, where suppers last on into the next day, and light loves are hired by the hour like cabs ; and since Paris will always be the most adorable of all countries, the country of joy, liberty, wit, pretty women, *mauvais sujets*,* and good wine ; where the truncheon of authority never makes itself disagreeably felt, because one is so close to those who wield it—we, therefore, sectaries of the god Mephistopheles, have engaged to whitewash the public mind, to give fresh costumes to the actors, to put a new plank or two in the Government booth, to doctor doctrinaires, and warm up old Republicans, to touch up the Bonapartists a bit, and revictual the Centre ; provided that we are allowed to laugh in secret at both kings and peoples, to think one thing in the morning and another at night, and to lead a merry life *à la* Panurge, or to recline upon soft cushions, like the Orientals.

"The sceptre of this burlesque and macaronic kingdom," he went on, "we have reserved for you ; so we are taking you straightway to a dinner given by the founder of the said newspaper, a retired banker, who, at a loss to know what to do with his money, is going to buy some brains with it. You will be welcomed as a brother, we shall hail you as king of these free lances who will undertake anything ; whose perspicacity discovers the intentions of Austria, England, or Russia, before either Russia, Austria, or England have formed any.

* Good-for-nothings.

Yes, we will invest you with the sovereignty of those puissant
intellects which give to the world its Mirabeaus, Talleyrands,
Pitts, and Metternichs—all the clever Crispins who treat the
destinies of a kingdom as gamblers' stakes, just as ordinary
men play dominoes for *kirschenwasser*.   We have given you
out to be the most undaunted champion who ever wrestled in
a drinking-bout at close quarters with the monster called
Carousal, who all bold spirits wish to try a fall with ; we have
gone so far as to say that you have never yet been worsted.
I hope you will not make liars of us.   Taillefer, our amphi-
tryon, has undertaken to surpass the circumscribed saturnalias
of the petty modern Lucullus.   He is rich enough to infuse
pomp into trifles, and style and charm into dissipation. ————
Are you listening, Raphael?" asked the orator, interrupting
himself.

"Yes," answered the young man, less surprised by the ac-
complishment of his wishes than by the natural manner in
which the events had come about.

He could not bring himself to believe in magic, but he
marveled at the accidents of human fate.

"Yes, you say, just as if you were thinking of your grand-
father's demise," remarked one of his neighbors.

"Ah !" cried Raphael, " I was thinking, my friends, that
we are in a fair way to become very great scoundrels," and there
was an ingenuousness in his tones that set these writers, the
hope of young France, in a roar.   " So far our blasphemies
have been uttered over our cups ; we have passed our judg-
ments on life while drunk, and taken men and affairs in an
after-dinner frame of mind.   We were innocent of action ;
we were bold in words.   But now we are to be branded
with the hot iron of politics ; we are going to enter the con-
vict's prison and to drop our illusions.   Although one has no
belief left, except in the devil, one may regret the paradise
of one's youth and the age of innocence, when we devoutly
offered the tip of our tongue to some good priest for the con-

secrated wafer of the sacrament. Ah, my good friends, our first peccadilloes gave us so much pleasure because the consequent remorse set them off and lent a keen relish to them; but nowadays——''

"Oh! now," said the first speaker, "there is still left——"

"What?" asked another.

"Crime——"

"There is a word as high as the gallows and deeper than the Seine," said Raphael.

"Oh, you don't understand me; I mean political crime. Since this morning, a conspirator's life is the only one I covet. I don't know that the fancy will last over to-morrow, but to-night at least my gorge rises at the anæmic life of our civilization and its railroad evenness. I am seized with a passion for the miseries of the retreat from Moscow, for the excitements of the Red Corsair, or for a smuggler's life. I should like to go to Botany Bay, as we have no Chartreux left us here in France; it is a sort of infirmary reserved for little Lord Byrons, who, having crumpled up their lives like a serviette after dinner, have nothing left to do but to set their country ablaze, blow their own brains out, plot for a republic, or clamor for a war——"

"Emile," Raphael's neighbor called eagerly to the speaker, "on my honor, but for the revolution of July I would have taken orders, and gone off down into the country somewhere to lead the life of an animal, and——"

"And you would have read your Breviary through every day."

"Yes."

"You are a coxcomb."

"Why we read the newspapers as it is!"

"Not bad that for a journalist! But hold your tongue, we are going through a crowd of subscribers. Journalism, look you, is the religion of modern society, and has even gone a little further."

" What do you mean ?"

" Its pontiffs are not obliged to believe in it any more than the people are."

Chatting thus, like good fellows who have known their *De Viris illustribus* for years past, they reached a mansion in the Rue Joubert.

Emile was a journalist who had acquired more reputation by dint of doing nothing than others had derived from their achievements. A bold, caustic, and powerful critic, he possessed all the qualities that his defects permitted. An outspoken giber, he made numberless epigrams on a friend to his face, but would defend him if absent with courage and loyalty. He laughed at everything, even at his own career. Always impecunious, he yet lived, like all men of his calibre, plunged in unspeakable indolence. He would fling some word containing whole volumes in the teeth of folk who could not put a syllable of sense into their books. He lavished promises that he never fulfilled ; he made a pillow of his luck and reputation, on which he slept, and ran the risk of waking up to old age in a workhouse. A steadfast friend to the gallows foot, a cynical swaggerer with a child's simplicity, a worker only from necessity or caprice.

" In the language of Maître Alcofribas, we are about to make famous a piece of good cheer," he remarked to Raphael as he pointed out the flower-stands that made a perfumed forest of the staircase.

" I like a vestibule to be well warmed and richly carpeted," Raphael said. " Luxury in the peristyle is not common in France. I feel as if life had begun anew here."

"And up above we are going to drink and make merry once more, my dear Raphael. Ah ! yes," he went on, " and I hope we are going to come off conquerors, too, and walk over everybody else's head."

As he spoke, he jestingly pointed to the guests. They were entering a large room which shone with gilding and lights, and there all the younger men of note in Paris welcomed them. Here was one who had just revealed fresh powers; his first picture vied with the glories of imperial art. There, another, who but yesterday had launched forth a volume, an acrid book filled with a sort of literary arrogance, which opened up new ways to the modern school. A sculptor, not far away, with vigorous power visible in his rough features, was chatting with one of those unenthusiastic scoffers who can either see excellence anywhere or nowhere, as it happens. Here, the cleverest of our caricaturists, with mischievous eyes and bitter tongue, lay in wait for epigrams to translate into pencil strokes; there stood the young and audacious writer, who distilled the quintessence of political ideas better than any other man, or compressed the work of some prolific writer as he held him up to ridicule; he was talking with the poet whose works would have eclipsed all the writings of the time if his ability had been as strenuous as his hatreds. Both were trying not to say the truth while they kept clear of lies, as they exchanged flattering speeches. A famous musician administered soothing consolation in a rallying fashion to a young politician who had just fallen, quite unhurt, from his rostrum. Young writers who lacked style stood beside other young writers who lacked ideas, and authors of political prose by prosaic poets.

At the sight of all these incomplete beings, a simple Saint Simonian, ingenuous enough to believe in his own doctrine, charitably paired them off, designing, no doubt, to convert them into monks of his order. A few men of science mingled in the conversation, like nitrogen in the atmosphere, and several *vaudevillistes* shed rays like the sparkling diamonds that give neither light nor heat. A few paradox-mongers, laughing up their sleeves at any folk who embraced their likes or dislikes in men or affairs, had already begun a two-edged policy, conspiring against all systems, without committing themselves to any side. Then there was the self-appointed critic who admires nothing, and will blow his nose in the middle of a *cavatina* at the Bouffons, who applauds before any one else begins, and contradicts every one who says what he himself was about to say; he was there giving out the sayings of wittier men for his own. Of all the assembled guests, a future lay before some five; ten or so should acquire a fleeting renown; as for the rest, like all mediocrities, they might apply to themselves the famous falsehood of Louis XVIII., Union and oblivion.

The anxious jocularity of a man who is expending two thousand crowns sat on their host. His eyes turned impatiently towards the door from time to time, seeking one of his guests who kept him waiting. Very soon a stout little person appeared, who was greeted by a complimentary murmur; it was the notary who had invented the newspaper that very morning. A valet-de-chambre in black opened the doors of a vast dining-room, whither every one went without ceremony, and took his place at an enormous table.

Raphael took a last look round the room before he left it. His wish had been realized to the full. The rooms were adorned with silk and gold. Countless wax tapers set in handsome candelabra lit up the slightest details of gilded friezes, the delicate bronze sculpture, and the splendid colors of the furniture. The sweet scent of rare flowers, set in stands tastefully made of bamboo, filled the air. Everything, even the curtains, was pervaded by elegance without pretension, and there was a certain imaginative charm about it all which acted like a spell on the mind of a needy man.

"An income of a hundred thousand livres a year is a very nice beginning of the catechism, and a wonderful assistance to putting morality into our actions," he said, sighing. "Truly my sort of virtue can scarcely go afoot, and vice means, to my thinking, a garret, a threadbare coat, a gray hat in winter time, and sums owing to the porter. I should like to live in the lap of luxury a year, or six months, no matter! And then afterwards, die. I should have known, exhausted, and consumed a thousand lives at any rate."

"Why, you are taking the tone of a stockbroker in good luck," said Emile, who overheard him. "Pooh! your riches would be a burden to you as soon as you found that they would spoil your chances of coming out above the rest of us. Hasn't the artist always kept the balance true between the poverty of riches and the riches of poverty? And isn't struggle a necessity to some of us? Look out for your digestion, and only look," he added, with a mock-heroic gesture, "at the majestic, thrice holy, and edifying appearance of this amiable capitalist's dining-room. That man has in reality only made his money for our benefit. Isn't he a kind of sponge of the polyp order, overlooked by naturalists, which should be carefully squeezed before he is left for his heirs to feed upon? There is style, isn't there, about those bas-reliefs that adorn the walls? And the lustres, and the pictures, what luxury well carried out! If one may believe those who envy him, or who know, or think they know, the origins of his life, then this man got rid of a German and some others—his best friend for one, and the mother of that friend, during the Revolution. Could you house crimes under the venerable Taillefer's silvering locks? He looks to me a very worthy man. Only see how the silver sparkles, and is every glittering ray like the stab of a dagger to him? ——— Let us go in, one might as well believe in Mahomet. If common report speaks truth, here are thirty men of talent, and good fellows too, prepared to dine off the flesh and blood of a whole family; ——— and here are we ourselves, a pair of youngsters full of open-hearted enthusiasm, and we shall be partakers in his guilt. I have a mind to ask our capitalist whether he is a respectable character. ——— "

"No, not now," cried Raphaël, "but when he is dead drunk; we shall have had our dinner then."

The two friends sat down laughing. First of all, by a

4

glance more rapid than a word, each paid his tribute of admiration to the splendid general effect of the long table, white as a bank of freshly-fallen snow, with its symmetrical line of covers, crowned with their pale golden rolls of bread. Rainbow colors gleamed in the starry rays of light reflected by the glass; the lights of the tapers crossed and recrossed each other indefinitely; the dishes covered with their silver domes whetted both appetite and curiosity.

Few words were spoken. Neighbors exchanged glances as the Madeira circulated. Then the first course appeared in all its glory; it would have done honor to the late Cambacérès, Brillat-Savarin would have celebrated it. The wines of Bordeaux and Burgundy, white and red, were royally lavished. This first part of the banquet might have been compared in every way to a rendering of some classical tragedy. The second act grew a trifle noisier. Every guest had had a fair amount to drink, had tried various grades at his pleasure, so that as the remains of the magnificent first course were removed, tumultuous discussions began; a pale brow here and there began to flush, sundry noses took a purpler hue, faces lit up, and eyes sparkled.

While intoxication was only dawning, the conversation did not overstep the bounds of civility; but banter and *bon mots* slipped by degrees from every tongue; and then slander began to rear its little snake's head, and spoke in dulcet tones; a few shrewd ones here and there gave heed to it, hoping to keep their heads. So the second course found their minds somewhat heated. Every one ate as he spoke, spoke while he ate, and drank without heeding the quantity of the liquor, the wine was so biting, the bouquet so fragrant, the example around so infectious. Taillefer made a point of stimulating his guests, and plied them with the formidable wines of the Rhone, with fierce Tokay, and heady old Roussillon.

The champagne, impatiently expected and lavishly poured

out, was a scourge of fiery sparks to these men, released like posthorses from some mail-coach by a relay ; they let their spirits gallop away into the wilds of argument to which no one listened, began to tell stories which had no auditors, and repeatedly asked questions to which no answer was made. Only the loud voice of wassail could be heard, a voice made up of a hundred confused clamors, which rose and grew like a *crescendo* of Rossini's. Insidious toasts, swagger, and challenges followed.

Each renounced any pride in his own intellectual capacity, in order to vindicate that of hogsheads, casks, and vats ; and each made noise enough for two. A time came when the footmen smiled, while their masters all talked at once. A philosopher would have been interested, doubtless, by the singularity of the thoughts expressed, a politician would have been amazed by the incongruity of the methods discussed in that mêlée of words or doubtfully luminous paradoxes, where truths, grotesquely caparisoned, met in conflict across the uproar of brawling judgments, of arbitrary decisions and folly, much as bullets, shells, and grapeshot are hurled across a battlefield.

It was at once a volume and a picture. Every philosophy, religion, and moral code differing so greatly in every latitude, every government, every great achievement of the human intellect fell before a scythe as long as Time's own ; and you might have found it hard to decide whether it was wielded by Gravity intoxicated, or by Inebriation grown sober and clear-sighted. Borne away by a kind of tempest, their minds, like the sea raging against the cliffs, seemed ready to shake the laws which confine the ebb and flow of civilizations ; unconsciously fulfilling the will of God, who has suffered evil and good to abide in nature, and reserved the secret of their continual strife to Himself. A frantic travesty of debate ensued, a Walpurgis-revel of intellects. Between the dreary jests of these children of the

Revolution over the inauguration of a newspaper, and the talk of the joyous gossips at Gargantua's birth, stretched the gulf that divides the nineteenth century from the sixteenth. Laughingly they had begun the work of destruction, and our journalists laughed amid the ruins.

"What is the name of that young man over there?" said the notary, indicating Raphäel. "I thought I heard some one call him Valentin."

"What stuff is this?" said Emile, laughing; "plain Valentin, say you? Raphael *de* Valentin, if you please. We bear an eagle or, on a field sable, with a silver crown, beak, and claws gules, and a fine motto: NON CECIDIT ANIMUS. We are no foundling child, but a descendant of the Emperor Valens, of the stock of the Valentinois, founders of the cities of Valence in France, and Valencia in Spain, rightful heirs to the Empire of the East. If we suffer Mahmoud on the throne of Byzantium, it is out of pure condescension. and for lack of funds and soldiers."

With a fork flourished above Raphael's head, Emile outlined a crown upon it. The notary bethought himself a moment, but soon fell to drinking again, with a gesture peculiar to himself; it was quite impossible, it seemed to say, to secure in his clientèle the cities of Valence and Byzantium, the Emperor Valens, Mahmoud, and the house of Valentinois.

"Should not the destruction of those ant-hills, Babylon, Tyre, Carthage, and Venice, each crushed beneath the foot of a passing giant, serve as a warning to man, vouchsafed by some mocking power?" said Claude Vignon, who must play the Bossuet, as a sort of purchased slave, at the rate of fivepence a line.

"Perhaps Moses, Sylla, Louis XI., Richelieu, Robespierre, and Napoleon were but the same men who cross our civilizations now and again, like a comet across the sky," said a disciple of Ballanche.

" Why try to fathom the designs of Providence ? " said
Canalis, maker of ballads.

" Come, now," said the man who set up for a critic,
" there is nothing more elastic in the world than your Prov-
idence."

" Well, sir, Louis XIV. sacrificed more lives over digging the
foundations of the Maintenon's aqueducts, than the Conven-
tion expended in order to assess the taxes justly, to make one
law for everybody, and one nation of France, and to establish
the rule of equal inheritance," said Massol, whom the lack
of a syllable before his name had made a Republican.

" Are you going to leave our heads on our shoulders ? "
asked Moreau (of the Oise), a substantial farmer. " You,
sir, who took blood for wine just now ? "

" Where is the use ? Aren't the principles of social order
worth some sacrifices, sir ? "

" Hi ! Bixiou ! What's-his-name, the Republican, con-
siders a landowner's head a sacrifice ! " said a young man to
his neighbor.

" Men and events count for nothing," said the Republican,
following out his theory in spite of hiccoughs ; " in politics,
as in philosophy, there are only principles and ideas."

" What an abomination ! Then you would ruthlessly put
your friends to death for a shibboleth ? "

" Eh, sir ! the man who feels compunction is your thorough
scoundrel, for he has some notion of virtue ; while Peter the
Great and the Duke of Alva were embodied systems, and the
pirate Monbard an organization."

" But can't society rid itself of your systems and organiza-
tions ? " said Canalis.

" Oh, granted ! " cried the Republican.

" That stupid Republic of yours makes me feel queasy.
We sha'n't be able to carve a capon in peace, because we
shall find the agrarian law inside it."

" Ah, my little Brutus, stuffed with truffles, your principles

are all right enough.   But you are like my valet, the rogue is
so frightfully possessed with a mania for property that if I
left him to clean my clothes after his fashion, he would soon
clean me out."

"Crass idiots!" replied the Republican, "you are for
setting a nation straight with tooth-picks.   To your way of
thinking, justice is more dangerous than thieves."

"Oh, dear!" cried the attorney Desroches.

"Aren't they a bore with their politics!" said the notary
Cardot.   "Shut up!   That's enough of it.   There is no knowl-
edge nor virtue worth shedding a drop of blood for.   If Truth
were brought into liquidation, we might find her insolent."

"It would be much less trouble, no doubt, to amuse our-
selves with evil, rather than dispute about good.   Moreover,
I would give all the speeches made for forty years past at the
Tribune for a trout, for one of Perrault's tales or Charlet's
sketches."

"Quite right!   Hand me the asparagus.   Because, after
all, liberty begets anarchy, anarchy leads to despotism, and
despotism back again to liberty.   Millions have died without
securing a triumph for any one system.   Is not that the
vicious circle in which the whole moral world revolves?   Man
believes that he has reached perfection, when in fact he has
but re-arranged matters."

"Oh! oh!" cried Cursy, the *vaudevilliste;* "in that case,
gentlemen, here's to Charles X., the father of liberty."

"Why not?" asked Emile.   "When law becomes des-
potic, morals are relaxed, and *vice versa.*"

"Let us drink to the imbecility of authority, which gives us
such an authority over imbeciles!" said the banker.

"Napoleon left us glory, at any rate, my good friend!"
exclaimed a naval officer who had never left Brest.

"Glory is a poor bargain; you buy it dear, and it will not
keep.   Does not the egotism of the great take the form of
glory, just as for nobodies it is their own well-being?"

"You are very fortunate, sir——"

"The first inventor of ditches must have been a weakling, for society is only useful to the puny. The savage and the philosopher, at either extreme of the moral scale, hold property in equal horror."

"All very fine!" said Cardot; "but if there were no property, there would be no documents to draw up."

"These green peas are excessively delicious !"

"And the *curé* was found dead in his bed in the morning. —— "

"Who is talking about death? Pray don't trifle, I have an uncle."

"Could you bear his loss with resignation?"

"No question."

"Gentlemen, listen to me! How TO KILL AN UNCLE. Silence ! (Cries of "Hush! hush!") In the first place, take an uncle, large and stout, seventy years old at least, they are the best uncles. (Sensation.) Get him to eat a *paté de foie gras*, any pretext will do."

"Ah, but my uncle is a thin, tall man, and very niggardly and abstemious."

"That sort of uncle is a monster; he misappropriates existence."

"Then," the speaker on uncles went on, "tell him, while he is digesting it, that his banker has failed."

"How if he bears up?"

"Let loose a pretty girl on him."

"And if——?" asked the other, with a shake of the head.

"Then he wouldn't be an uncle—an uncle is a gay dog by nature."

"Malibran has lost two notes in her voice."

"No, sir, she has not."

"Yes, sir, she has."

"Oh, ho ! No and yes, is not the sum-up of all religious,

political, or literary dissertations? Man is a clown dancing on the edge of an abyss."

"You would make out that I am a fool."

"On the contrary, you cannot make me out."

"Education, there's a pretty piece of tomfoolery. M. Heineffettermach estimates the number of printed volumes at more than a thousand millions; and a man cannot read more than a hundred and fifty thousand in his lifetime. So, just tell me what that word *education* means. For some it consists in knowing the names of Alexander's horse, of the dog Bérécillo, of the Seigneur d'Accords, and in ignorance of the man to whom we owe the discovery of rafting and the manufacture of porcelain. For others it is the knowledge how to burn a will and live respected, be looked up to and popular, instead of stealing a watch with half-a-dozen aggravating circumstances, after a previous conviction, and so perishing, hated and dishonored, in the Place de Grève."

"Will Nathan's work live?"

"He has very clever collaborators, sir."

"Or Canalis'?"

"He is a great man; let us say no more about him."

"You are all drunk!"

"The conseqnence of a Constitution is the immediate stultification of intellects. Art, science, public works, everything, is consumed by a horribly egotistic feeling, the leprosy of the time. Three hundred of your bourgeoisie, set down on benches, will only think of planting poplars. Tyranny does great things lawlessly, while Liberty will scarcely trouble herself to do petty ones lawfully."

"Your reciprocal instruction will turn out counters in human flesh," broke in an Absolutist. "All individuality will disappear in a people brought to a dead level by education."

"For all that, is not the aim of society to secure happiness to each member of it?" asked the Saint-Simonian.

"If you had an income of fifty thousand livres, you would not think much about the people. If you are smitten with a tender passion for the race, go to Madagascar; there you will find a nice little nation all ready to Saint-Simonize, classify, and cork up in your phials, but here every one fits into his niche like a peg in a hole. A porter is a porter, and a blockhead is a fool, without a college of fathers to promote them to those positions."

"You are a Carlist."

"And why not?" Despotism pleases me; it implies a certain contempt for the human race. I have no animosity against kings, they are so amusing. Is it nothing to sit enthroned in a room, at a distance of thirty million leagues from the sun?"

"Let us once more take a broad view of civilization," said the man of learning who, for the benefit of the inattentive sculptor, had opened a discussion on primitive society and autochthonous races. "The vigor of a nation in its origin was in a way physical, unitary, and crude; then as aggregations increased, government advanced by a decomposition of the primitive rule, more or less skilfully managed. For example, in remote ages national strength lay in theocracy, the priest held both sword and censer; a little later there were two priests, the pontiff and the king. To-day our society, the latest word of civilization, has distributed power according to the number of combinations, and we come to the forces called business, thought, money, and eloquence. Authority thus divided is steadily approaching a social dissolution, with interest as its one opposing barrier. We depend no longer on either religion or physical force, but upon intellect. Can a book replace the sword? Can discussion be a substitute for action? That is the question."

"Intellect has made an end of everything," cried the Carlist. "Come, now! Absolute freedom has brought about national suicides; their triumph left them as listless as an English millionaire."

"Won't you tell us something new? You have made fun of authority of all sorts to-day, which is every bit as vulgar as denying the existence of God. So you have no belief left, and the century is like an old Sultan worn out by debauchery! Your Byron, in short, sings of crime and its emotions in a final despair of poetry."

"Don't you know," replied Bianchon, quite drunk by this time, "that a dose of phosphorus more or less makes the man of genius or the scoundrel, a clever man or an idiot, a virtuous person or a criminal?"

"Can any one treat of virtue thus?" cried Cursy. "Virtue, the subject of every drama at the theatre, the *dénoument* of every play, the foundation of every court of law."

"Be quiet, you ass. You are an Achilles for virtue, without his heel," said Bixiou.

"Some drink!"

"What will you bet that I will drink a bottle of champagne like a flash, at one pull?"

"What a flash of wit!"

"Drunk as lords," muttered a young man gravely, trying to give some wine to his waistcoat.

"Yes, sir; real government is the art of ruling by public opinion."

"Opinion? That is the most vicious jade of all. According to you moralists and politicians, the laws you set up are always to go before those of nature, and opinion before conscience. You are right and wrong both. Suppose society bestows down pillows on us, that benefit is made up for by the gout; and justice is likewise tempered by red-tape, and colds accompany Cashmere shawls."

"Wretch!" Emile broke in upon the misanthrope, "how can you slander civilization here at table, up to the eyes in wines and exquisite dishes? Eat away at that roebuck with gilded horns and feet, and do not carp at your mother."

"Is it any fault of mine if Catholicism puts a million deities in a sack of flour, that Republics will end in a Napoleon, that monarchy dwells between the assassination of Henry IV. and the trial of Louis XVI., and Liberalism produces La Fayettes?"

"Didn't you embrace him in July?"

"No."

"Then hold your tongue, you sceptic."

"Sceptics are the most conscientious of men."

"They have no conscience."

"What are you saying? They have two a piece, at least."

"So you want to discount heaven, a thoroughly commercial notion. Ancient religions were but the unchecked development of physical pleasure, but we have developed a soul and expectations; some advance has been made."

"What can you expect, my friends, of a century filled with politics to repletion?" asked Nathan. "What befell "The History of the King of Bohemia and his Seven Castles" a most entrancing conception? —— "

"I say," the would-be critic cried down the whole length of the table, "the phrases might have been drawn at haphazard from a hat, 'twas a work written 'down to Charenton.'"

"You are a fool!"

"And you are a rogue!"

"Oh! oh!"

"Ah! ah!"

"They are going to fight."

"No, they aren't."

"You will find me to-morrow, sir."

"This very moment," Nathan answered.

"Come, come, you pair of fire-eaters."

"You are another!" said the prime mover in the quarrel.

"They can hardly stand on their legs."

"Ah, I can't stand upright, perhaps," said the pugnacious Nathan, straightening himself up like a stag-beetle about to fly.

He stared stupidly round the table, then completely exhausted by the effort, sank back into his chair, and mutely hung his head.

"Would it not have been nice," the critic said to his neighbor, "to fight about a book I have neither read nor seen?"

"Emile, look out for your coat, your neighbor is growing pale," said Bixiou.

"Kant? Yet another ball flung out for fools to sport with, sir! Materialism and spiritualism are a fine pair of battle-dores with which charlatans in long gowns keep a shuttle-cock a-going. Suppose that God is everywhere, as Spinoza says, or that all things proceed from God, as says St. Paul. —— the nincompoops, the door shuts or opens, but isn't the movement the same? Does the fowl come from the egg, or the egg from the fowl? —— Just hand me some duck —— and there, you have all science."

"Simpleton!" cried the man of science, "your problem is settled by fact!"

"What fact?"

"Professors' chairs were not made for philosophy, but philosophy for professors' chairs. Put on a pair of spectacles and read the budget."

"Thieves!"

"Nincompoops!"

"Knaves!"

"Gulls!"

"Where but in Paris will you find such a ready and rapid exchange of thought?" cried Bixiou, in a deep, bass voice.

"Bixiou! Act a classical farce for us! Come, now!"

"Would you like me to depict the nineteenth century?"

"Silence!"

"Pay attention!"

" Clap a muffle on your trumpets ! "

" Shut up, you Turk ! "

" Give him some wine, and let that fellow keep quiet."

" Now, then, Bixiou ! "

The artist buttoned his black coat to the collar, put on yellow gloves, and began to burlesqne the *Revue des Deux Mondes* by acting a squinting old lady; but the uproar drowned his voice, and no one heard a word of the satire. Still, if he did not catch the spirit of the century, he represented the *Revue* at any rate, for his own intentions were not very clear to him.

Dessert was served as if by magic. A huge epergne of gilded bronze from Thomire's studio overshadowed the table. Tall statuettes, which a celebrated artist had endued with ideal beauty according to conventional European notions, sustained and carried pyramids of strawberries, pines, fresh dates, golden grapes, clear-skinned peaches, oranges brought from Setubal by steamer, pomegranates, Chinese fruit ; in short, all the surprises of luxury, miracles of confectionery, the most tempting dainties, and choicest delicacies. The coloring of this epicurean work of art was enhanced by the splendors of porcelain, by sparkling outlines of gold, by the chasing of the vases. Poussin's landscapes, copied on Sèvres ware, were crowned with graceful fringes of moss, green, translucent and fragile as ocean weeds.

The revenue of a German prince would not have defrayed the cost of this arrogant display. Silver and mother-of-pearl, gold and crystal, were lavished afresh in new forms ; but scarcely a vague idea of this almost Oriental fairyland penetrated eyes now heavy with wine, or crossed the delirium of intoxication. The fire and fragrance of the wines acted like potent philtres and magical fumes, producing a kind of mirage in the brain, binding feet, and weighing down hands. The pyramids of fruit were ransacked, voices grew thicker, the clamor increased. Words were no longer distinct, glasses

flew in pieces, senseless peals of laughter broke out. Cursy
snatched up a horn and struck up a flourish on it. It acted
like a signal given by the devil. Yells, hisses, songs, cries,
and groans went up from the maddened crew. You might
have smiled to see men, light-hearted by nature, grow tragical
as Crébillon's dramas, and pensive as a sailor in a coach.
Hard-headed men blabbed secrets to the inquisitive, who were
long passed heeding them. Saturnine faces were wreathed in
smiles worthy of a pirouetting dancer. Claude Vignon
shuffled about like a bear in a cage. Intimate friends began
to fight.

Animal likenesses, so curiously traced by physiologists, in
human faces, came out in gestures and behavior. A book lay
open for a Bichat if he had repaired thither fasting and col-
lected. The master of the house, knowing his condition, did
not dare to stir, but encouraged his guests' extravagances
with a fixed grimacing smile, meant to be hospitable and
appropriate. His large face, turning from blue and red to a
purple shade terrible to see, partook of the general commo-
tion by movements like the heaving and pitching of a brig.

"Now, did you murder them?" Emile asked him.

"Capital punishment is going to be abolished, they say, in
favor of the Revolution of July?" answered Taillefer, raising
his eyebrows with drunken sagacity.

"Don't they rise up before you in dreams at times?"
Raphael persisted.

"There's a statute of limitations," said the murderer—
Crœsus.

"And on his tombstone," Emile began, with a sardonic
laugh, "the stonemason will carve, 'Passer-by, accord a
tear, in memory of one that's here.' Oh," he continued,
"I would cheerfully pay a hundred sous to any mathematician
who would prove the existence of hell to me by an algebraical
equation."

He flung up a coin and cried—

"Heads for the existence of God!"

"Don't look!" Raphael cried, pouncing upon it. "Who knows? Suspense is so pleasant."

"Unluckily," Emile said, with burlesque melancholy, "I can see no halting-place between the unbeliever's arithmetic and the papal *Pater noster.* Pshaw! let us drink. Clink glasses was, I believe, the oracular answer of the Epicureans and final conclusion of Pantagruel."

"We owe our arts and monuments to the *Pater noster*, and our knowledge, too, perhaps; and a still greater benefit— modern government—whereby a vast and teeming society is wondrously represented by some five hundred intellects. It neutralizes opposing forces and gives free play to CIVILIZA- TION, that Titan queen who has succeeded the ancient terrible figure of the KING, that sham Providence, reared by man between himself and heaven. In the face of such achieve- ments atheism seems like a barren skeleton. What do you say?"

"I am thinking of the seas of blood shed by Catholicism," Emile replied, quite unimpressed. "It has drained our hearts and veins dry to make a mimic deluge. No matter! Every man who thinks must range himself beneath the banner of Christ, for He alone has consummated the triumph of spirit over matter; He alone has revealed to us, like a poet, an interme- diate world that separates us from the Deity."

"Believest thou?" asked Raphael, with an unaccountable drunken smile. "Very good; we must not commit ourselves; so we will drink the celebrated toast, *Diis ignotis !*"

And they drained the chalice filled up with science, car- bonic acid gas, perfumes, poetry, and incredulity.

"If the gentlemen will go to the drawing-room, coffee is ready for them," said the major-domo.

There was scarcely one of those present whose mind was not floundering by this time in the delights of chaos, where every spark of intelligence is quenched, and the body, set free from its tyranny, gives itself up to the frenetic joys of liberty. Some who had arrived at the apogee of intoxication were dejected, as they painfully tried to arrest a single thought which might assure them of their own existence; others, deep in the heavy morasses of indigestion, denied the possibility of movement. The noisy and the silent were oddly assorted.

For all that, when new joys were announced to them by the stentorian tones of the servant, who spoke on his master's behalf, they all rose, leaning upon, dragging or carrying one another. But on the threshold of the room the entire crew paused for a moment, motionless, as if fascinated. The intemperate pleasures of the banquet seemed to fade away at this titillating spectacle, prepared by their amphitryon to appeal to the most sensual of their instincts.

Beneath the shining wax-lights in a golden chandelier, round about a table inlaid with gilded metal, a group of women, whose eyes shone like diamonds, suddenly met the stupefied stare of the revelers. Their toilettes were splendid, but less magnificent than their beauty, which eclipsed the other marvels of this palace. A light shone from their eyes, bewitching as those of sirens, more brilliant and ardent than the blaze that streamed down upon the snowy marble, the delicately carved surfaces of bronze, and lit up the satin sheen of the tapestry. The contrasts of their attitudes and the slight movements of their heads, each differing in character and nature of attraction, set the heart afire. It was like a thicket, where blossoms mingled with rubies, sapphires, and coral; a combination of gossamer scarves that flickered like beacon-lights; of black ribbons about snowy throats; of gorgeous turbans and demurely enticing apparel. It was a seraglio that appealed to every eye, and fulfilled every fancy. Each form posed to admiration was scarcely concealed by the folds of cashmere, and half-hidden, half-revealed, by transparent gauze and diaphanous silk. The little slender feet were eloquent, though the fresh red lips uttered no sound.

Demure and fragile-looking girls, pictures of maidenly innocence, with a semblance of conventual unction about their heads, were there like apparitions that a breath might dissipate. Aristocratic beauties with haughty glances; languid, flexible, slender, and complaisant, bent their heads as though there were royal protectors still in the market. An Englishwoman seemed like a spirit of melancholy—some coy, pale, shadowy form among Ossian's mists, or a type of remorse flying from crime. The Parisienne was not wanting in all her beauty that consists in an indescribable charm; armed with her irresistible weakness, vain of her costume and her wit, pliant and hard, a heartless, passionless siren that yet can create factitious treasures of passion and counterfeit emotion.

Italians shone in the throng, serene and self-possessed in their bliss; handsome Normans, with splendid figures; women of the south, with black hair and well-shaped eyes. Lebel might have summoned together all the fair women of Versailles, who since morning had perfected all their wiles and now came like a troop of Oriental women, bidden by the slave merchant to be ready to set out at dawn. They stood disconcerted and confused about the table, huddled together in a murmuring group like bees in a hive. The combination of timid embarrassment with coquettishness and a sort of expostulation was the result either of calculated effect or spontaneous modesty. Perhaps a sentiment of which women are never utterly divested prescribed to them the cloak of modesty to heighten and enhance the charms of wantonness. So the venerable Taillefer's designs seemed on the point of collapse; for these unbridled natures were subdued from the very first by the majesty with which woman is invested. There was a murmur of admiration, which vibrated like a soft musical note. Wine had not taken love for traveling companion; instead of violent tumult of passions, the guests thus taken by surprise, in a moment of weakness, gave themselves up to luxurious raptures of delight.

5

Artists obeyed the voice of poetry which constrains them, and studied with pleasure the different delicate tints of these chosen examples of beauty. Sobered by a thought perhaps due to some emanation from a bubble of carbonic acid in the champagne, a philosopher shuddered at the misfortunes which had brought these women, once perhaps worthy of the truest devotion, to this. Each one doubtless could have unfolded a cruel tragedy. Infernal tortures followed in the train of most of them, and they drew after them faithless men, broken vows, and pleasures atoned for in wretchedness. Polite advances were made by the guests, and conversations began, as varied in character as the speakers. They broke up into groups. It might have been a fashionable drawing-room where ladies and young girls offer after dinner the assistance that coffee, liqueurs, and sugar afford to diners who are struggling in the toils of a perverse digestion. But in a little while laughter broke out, the murmur grew, and voices were raised. The saturnalia, subdued for a moment, threatened at times to renew itself. The alternations of sound and silence bore a distant resemblance to a symphony of Beethoven's.

The two friends, seated on a silken divan, were first approached by a tall, well-proportioned girl of stately bearing; her features were irregular, but her face was striking and vehement in expression, and impressed the mind by the vigor of its contrasts. Her dark hair fell in luxuriant curls, with which some hand seemed to have played havoc already, for the locks fell lightly over the splendid shoulders that thus attracted attention. The long brown curls half hid her queenly throat, though where the light fell upon it, the delicacy of its fine outlines was revealed. Her warm and vivid coloring was set off by the dead white of her complexion. Bold and ardent glances came from under the long eyelashes; the damp, red, half-open lips challenged a kiss. Her frame was strong but compliant; with a bust and arms strongly developed, as in figures drawn by the Caracci, she yet seemed active and elastic, with a panther's strength and suppleness, and in the same way the energetic grace of her figure suggested fierce pleasures.

But though she might romp perhaps and laugh, there was something terrible in her eyes and her smile. Like a pythoness possessed by the demon, she inspired awe rather than pleasure. All changes, one after another, flashed like lightning over every mobile feature of her face. She might captivate a jaded fancy, but a young man would have feared her. She was like some colossal statue fallen from the height of a Greek temple, so grand when seen afar, too roughly hewn to be seen anear. And yet, in spite of all, her terrible beauty could have stimulated exhaustion; her voice might charm the deaf; her glances might put life into the bones of the dead; and therefore Emile was vaguely reminded of one of Shakespeare's tragedies—a wonderful maze, in which joy groans, and there is something wild even about love, and the magic of forgiveness and the warmth of happiness succeed to cruel storms of rage. She was a siren that can both kiss and devour; laugh like a devil, or weep as angels can. She could concentrate in one instant all a woman's powers of attraction in a single effort (the sighs of melancholy and the charms of maiden's shyness alone excepted), then in a moment rise in fury like a nation in revolt, and tear herself, her passion, and her lover in pieces.

Dressed in red velvet, she trampled under her reckless feet the stray flowers fallen from other heads, and held out a salver to the two friends, with careless hands. The white arms stood out in bold relief against the velvet. Proud of her beauty; proud (who knows?) of her corruption, she stood like a queen of pleasure, like an incarnation of enjoyment; the enjoyment that comes of squandering the accumulations of three generations; that scoffs at its progenitors, and makes merry over a corpse; that will dissolve pearls and wreck thrones, turn old men into boys, and make young men prematurely old; enjoyment only possible to giants weary of their power, tormented by reflection, or for whom strife has become a plaything.

" What is your name ? " asked Raphael.

" Aquilina."

" Out of *Venice Preserved !* " exclaimed Emile.

" Yes," she answered. " Just as a pope takes a new name when he is exalted above all other men, I, too, took another name when I raised myself above women's level."

" Then have you, like your patron saint, a terrible and noble lover, a conspirator, who would die for you ? " cried Emile eagerly—this gleam of poetry had aroused his interest.

" Once I had," she answered. " But I had a rival, too, in La Guillotine. I have worn something red about me ever since, lest any happiness should carry me away."

" Oh, if you are going to get her on to the story of those four lads of La Rochelle, she will never get to the end of it. That's enough, Aquilina. As if every woman could not bewail some lover or other, though not every one has the luck to lose him on the scaffold, as you have done. I would a great deal sooner see a lover of mine in a trench at the back of Clamart than in a rival's arms."

All this in the gentlest and most melodious accents, and pronounced by the prettiest, gentlest, and most innocent-looking little person that a fairy wand ever drew from an enchanted eggshell. She had come up noiselessly, and they became aware of a slender, dainty figure, charmingly timid blue eyes, and white transparent brows. No *ingénue* among the naiads, a truant from her river spring, could have been shyer, whiter, more ingenuous than this young girl, seemingly about sixteen years old, ignorant of evil and of the storms of life, and fresh from some church in which she must have prayed the angels to call her to heaven before the time. Only in Paris are such natures as this to be found, concealing depths of depravity behind a fair mask, and the most artificial vices beneath a brow as young and fair as an opening flower.

At first the angelic promise of those soft lineaments misled the friends. Raphael and Emile took the coffee which she poured into the cups brought by Aquilina, and began to talk with her. In the eyes of the two poets she soon became transformed into some sombre allegory of I know not what aspect of human life. She opposed to the vigorous and ardent expression of her commanding acquaintance a revelation of heartless corruption and voluptuous cruelty. Heedless enough to perpetrate a crime, hardy enough to feel no misgivings; a pitiless demon that wrings larger and kinder natures with torments that it is incapable of knowing, that simpers over a traffic in love, sheds tears over a victim's funeral, and beams with joy over the reading of the will. A poet might have admired the magnificent Aquilina; but the winning Euphrasia must be repulsive to every one—the first was the soul of sin; the second, sin without a soul in it.

"I should dearly like to know," Emile remarked to this pleasing being, "if you ever reflect upon your future?"

"My future!" she answered with a laugh. "What do you mean by my future? Why should I think about something that does not exist as yet? I never look before or behind. Isn't one day at a time more than I can concern myself with as it is? And besides, the future, as we know, means the hospital."

"How can you foresee a future in the hospital, and make no effort to avert it?"

"What is there so alarming about the hospital?" asked the terrific Aquilina. "When we are neither wives nor mothers, when old age draws black stockings over our limbs, sets wrinkles on our brows, withers up the woman in us, and darkens the light in our lover's eyes, what could we need when that comes to pass? You would look on us then as mere human clay; we with our habiliments shall be for you like so much mud—worthless, lifeless, crumbling to pieces, going about with the rustle of dead leaves. Rags or the daintiest finery will be as one to us then ; the ambergris of the boudoir will breathe an odor of death and dry bones ; and suppose there is a heart there in that mud, not one of you but would make mock of it, not so much as a memory will you spare to us. Is not our existence precisely the same whether we live in a fine mansion with lap-dogs to tend, or sort rags in a workhouse ? Does it make much difference whether we shall hide our gray heads beneath lace or a hand-kerchief striped with blue and red ; whether we sweep a crossing with a birch broom, or the steps of the Tuileries with satins ; whether we sit beside a gilded hearth, or cower over the ashes in a red earthen pot ; whether we go to the opera or look on in the Place de Grève ? "

" *Aquilina mia*, you have never shown more sense than in this depressing fit of yours," Euphrasia remarked. "Yes, cashmere, point d'Alençon, perfumes, gold, silks, luxury, everything that sparkles, everything pleasant, belongs to youth alone. Time alone may show us our folly, but good fortune will acquit us. You are laughing at me," she went on, with a malicious glance at the friends ; "but am I not right ? I would sooner die of pleasure than of illness. I am not afflicted with a mania for perpetuity, nor have I a great veneration for human nature, such as God has made it. Give me millions, and I would squander them ; I should not keep one centime for the year to come. Live to be charming and have power, that is the decree of my every heart-beat. Society sanctions my life ; does it not pay for my extrava-gances ? Why does Providence pay me every morning my income, which I spend every evening ? Why are hospitals built for us ? And Providence did not put good and evil on either hand for us to select what tires and pains us. I should be very foolish if I did not amuse myself."

" And how about others ? " asked Emile.

" Others ? Oh, well, they must manage for themselves. I

prefer laughing at their woes to weeping over my own. I defy any man to give me the slightest uneasiness."

"What have you suffered to make you think like this?" asked Raphael.

"I myself have been forsaken for an inheritance," she said, striking an attitude that displayed all her charms; and yet I had worked night and day to keep my love! I am not to be gulled by any smile or vow, and I have set myself to make one long entertainment of my life."

"But does not happiness come from the soul within?" cried Raphael.

"It may be so," Aquilina answered; "but is it nothing to be conscious of admiration, of flattery; to triumph over other women, even over the most virtuous, humiliating them before our beauty and our splendor? Not only so; one day of our life is worth ten years of middle-class existence, and so it is all summed up."

"Is not a woman hateful without virtue?" Emile said to Raphael.

Euphrasia's glance was like a viper's, as she said with an irony in her voice that cannot be rendered—

"Virtue! we leave that to deformity and to ugly women. What would the poor things be without it?"

"Hush, be quiet," Emile broke in, "Don't talk about something you have never known."

"That I have never known!" Euphrasia answered. "You give yourself for life to some person you abominate; you must bring up children who will neglect you, who wound your very heart, and you must say, 'Thank you!' for it; and these are the virtues you prescribe to women. And that is not enough. By way of requiting her self-denial, you must come and add to her sorrows by trying to lead her astray; and though you are rebuffed, she is compromised. A nice life! How far better to keep one's freedom, to follow one's inclinations in love, and die young."

"Have you no fear of the price to be paid some day for all this?"

"Even then," she said, "instead of mingling pleasures and troubles, my life will consist of two separate parts—a youth of happiness is secure, and there may come a hazy, uncertain old age, during which I can suffer at my leisure."

"She has never loved," came in the deep tones of Aquilina's voice. "She never went a hundred leagues to drink in one look and a denial with untold raptures. She has not hung her own life on a thread, nor tried to stab more than one man to save her sovereign lord, her king, her divinity. Love, for her, meant a fascinating colonel."

"Here she is with her La Rochelle," Euphrasia made answer. "Love comes like the wind, no one knows whence. And, for that matter, if one of those brutes had once fallen in love with you, you would hold sensible men in horror."

"Brutes are put out of the question by the Code," said the tall, sarcastic Aquilina.

"I thought you had more kindness for the army," laughed Euphrasia.

"How happy they are in their power of dethroning their reason in this way," Raphael exclaimed.

"Happy!" asked Aquilina, with a dreadful look, and a smile full of pity and terror, "Ah, you do not know what it is to be condemned to a life of pleasure, with your dead hidden in your heart."

A moment's consideration of the rooms was like a foretaste of Milton's Pandemonium. The faces of those still capable of drinking were a hideous blue tint, from burning draughts of punch. Mad dances were kept up with wild energy, excited laughter and outcries broke out like the explosion of fireworks. The boudoir and a small adjoining room were strewn like a battlefield with the insensible and incapable. Wine, pleasure, and dispute had heated the atmosphere. Wine and love, delirium and unconsciousness possessed them, and were written upon all faces, upon the furniture; were expressed by the surrounding disorder, and brought light films over the vision of those assembled, so that the air seemed full of intoxicating vapor. A glittering dust arose, as in the luminous paths made by a ray of sunlight, the most bizarre forms flitted through it, grotesque struggles were seen athwart it. Groups of interlaced figures blended with the white marbles, the noble masterpieces of sculpture that adorned the rooms.

Though the two friends yet preserved a sort of fallacious clearness in their ideas and voices, a feeble appearance and faint thrill of animation, it was yet almost impossible to distinguish what was real among the fantastic absurdities before them, or what foundation there was for the impossible pictures that passed unceasingly before their weary eyes. The strangest phenomena of dreams beset them, the lowering heavens, the fervid sweetness caught by faces in our visions, and unheard-of agility under a load of chains,—all these so vividly, that they took the pranks of the orgy about them for the freaks of some nightmare in which all movement is silent, and cries never reach the ear. The *valet de chambre* succeeded just then, after some little difficulty, in drawing his master into the ante-chamber to whisper to him—

"The neighbors are all at their windows, complaining of the racket, sir."

"If noise alarms them, why don't they lay down straw before their doors?" was Taillefer's rejoinder.

Raphael's sudden burst of laughter was so unseasonable and abrupt, that his friend demanded the reason of his unseemly hilarity.

"You will hardly understand me," he replied. "In the first place, I must admit that you stopped me on the Quai Voltaire just as I was about to throw myself into the Seine, and you would like to know, no doubt, my motives for dying. And when I proceed to tell you that by an almost miraculous

chance the most poetic memorials of the material world had
but just then been summed up for me as a symbolical inter-
pretation of human wisdom ; whilst at this minute the remains
of all the intellectual treasures ravaged by us at table are com-
prised in these two women, the living and authentic types of
folly, would you be any the wiser? Our profound apathy
towards men and things supplied the half-tones in a crudely
contrasted picture of two theories of life so diametrically
opposed. If you were not drunk, you might perhaps catch a
gleam of philosophy in this.''

"And if you had not both feet on that fascinating Aquilina,
whose heavy breathing suggests an analogy with the sounds
of a storm about to burst,'' replied Emile, absently engaged
in the harmless amusement of winding and unwinding Eu-
phrasia's hair, "you would be ashamed of your inebriated
garrulity. Both your systems can be packed in a phrase, and
reduced to a single idea. The mere routine of living brings
a stupid kind of wisdom with it, by blunting our intelligence
with work ; and on the other hand, a life passed in the limbo
of the abstract or in the abysses of the moral world, produces
a sort of wisdom run mad. The conditions may be summed
up in brief; we may extinguish emotion, and so live to old
age, or we may choose to die young as martyrs to contending
passions. And yet this decree is at variance with the tem-
peraments with which we were endowed by the bitter jester
who modeled all creatures.''

"Idiot!'' Raphael burst in. "Go on epitomizing your-
self after that fashion, and you will fill volumes. If I at-
tempted to formulate those two ideas clearly, I might as well
say that man is corrupted by the exercise of his wits, and
purified by ignorance. You are calling the whole fabric of
society to account. But whether we live with the wise or
perish with the fool, isn't the result the same sooner or later?
And have not the prime constituents of the quintessence of

both systems been before expressed in a couple of words—
Carymary, carymara."

"You make me doubt the existence of a God, for your stupidity is greater than His power," said Emile. "Our beloved Rabelais summed it all up in a shorter word than your *Carymary, carymara;* from his 'Perhaps' Montaigne derived his own 'What do I know?' After all, this last word of moral science is scarcely more than the cry of Pyrrhus set betwixt good and evil, or Buridan's ass between the two measures of oats. But let this everlasting question alone, resolved to-day by a 'Yes' and a 'No.' What experience did you look to find by a jump into the Seine? Were you jealous of the hydraulic machine on the Pont Nôtre Dame?"

"Ah, if you but knew my history."

"Pooh," said Emile; "I did not think you could be so commonplace; that remark is hackneyed. Don't you know that every one of us claims to have suffered as no other ever did?"

"Ah!" Raphael sighed.

"What a mountebank art thou with thy 'Ah!' Look here, now! Does some disease of mind or body, by contracting your muscles, bring back of a morning the wild horses that tear you in pieces at night, as with Damiens once upon a time? Were you driven to sup off your own dog in a garret, uncooked and without salt? Have your children ever cried, 'I am hungry?' Have you sold your mistress' hair to hazard the money at play? Have you ever drawn a sham bill of exchange on a fictitious uncle at a sham address, and feared lest you should not be in time to take it up? Come now, I am attending! If you were going to drown yourself for some woman, or by way of a protest, or out of sheer dulness, I disown you. Make your confession, and no lies! I don't at all want a historical memoir. And, above all things, be as concise as your clouded intellect permits; I am as critical as a professor, and as sleepy as a woman at her vespers."

"You silly fool!" said Raphael. "When has not suffering been keener for a more susceptible nature? Some day when science has attained to a pitch that enables us to study the natural history of hearts, when they are named and classified in genera, sub-genera, and families; into crustaceæ, fossils, saurians, infusoria, or whatever it is,—then, my dear fellow, it will be ascertained that there are natures as tender and fragile as flowers, that are broken by the slight bruises that some stony hearts do not even feel——."

"For pity's sake, spare me thy exordium," said Emile, as, half plaintive, half amused, he took Raphael's hand.

A WOMAN WITHOUT A HEART.

AFTER a moment's silence, Raphael said with a careless gesture—

"Perhaps it is an effect of the fumes of punch—I really cannot tell—this clearness of mind that enables me to comprise my whole life in a single picture, where figures and hues, lights, shades, and half-tones are faithfully rendered. I should not have been so surprised at this poetical play of imagination if it were not accompanied with a sort of scorn for my past joys and sorrows. Seen from afar, my life appears to contract by some mental process. That long, slow agony of ten years' duration can be brought to memory to-day in some few phrases, in which pain is resolved into a mere idea, and pleasure becomes a philosophical reflection. Instead of feeling things, I weigh and consider them——"

"You are as tiresome as the explanation of an amendment," cried Emile.

"Very likely," said Raphael submissively. "I spare you the first seventeen years of my life for fear of abusing a listener's patience. Till that time, like you and thousands of others, I had lived my life at school or the Lyceum, with its imaginary troubles and genuine happinesses, which are so pleasant to look back upon. Our jaded palates still crave that Lenten fare, so long as we have not tried it afresh. It was a pleasant life, with the tasks that we thought so contemptible, but which taught us application for all that."

"Let the drama begin," said Emile, half-plaintively, half-comically.

"When I left school," Raphael went on, with a gesture that claimed the right of speaking, "my father submitted me

to a strict discipline ; he installed me in a room near his own
study, and I had to rise at five in the morning and be in bed
by nine at night.   He meant me to take my law studies seri-
ously.   I attended the schools, and read with an advocate as
well ; but my lectures and work were so narrowly circum-
scribed by the laws of time and space, and my father required
such a strict account of my doings, at dinner, that——"

"What is this to me?" asked Emile.

" The devil take you ! " said Raphael.   " How are you to
enter into my feelings if I do not relate the facts that insensi-
bly shaped my character, made me timid, and prolonged the
period of youthful simplicity?   In this manner I cowered
under as strict a despotism as a monarch's till I came of age.
To depict the tedium of my life, it will be perhaps enough to
portray my father for you.   He was tall, thin, and slight,
with a hatchet face, and pale complexion ; a man of few
words, fidgety as an old maid, exacting as a senior clerk.
His paternal solicitude hovered over my merriment and gleeful
thoughts, and seemed to cover them with a leaden pall.   Any
effusive demonstration on my part was received by him as a
childish absurdity.   I was far more afraid of him than I had
been of any of our masters at school.

"I seem to see him before me at this moment.   In his
chestnut-brown frock-coat he looked like a red herring
wrapped up in the cover of a pamphlet, and he held him-
self as erect as an Easter candle.   But I was fond of my father,
and at heart he was right enough.   Perhaps we never hate
severity when it has its source in greatness of character and
pure morals, and is skilfully tempered with kindness.   My
father, it is true, never left me a moment to myself, and only
when I was twenty years old gave me so much as ten francs
of my own, ten knavish prodigals of francs, such a hoard as
I had long vainly desired, which set me a-dreaming of unutter-
able felicity ; yet, for all that, he sought to procure relaxations
for me.   When he had promised me a treat months **before-**

hand, he would take me to Les Bouffons, or to a concert or ball, where I hoped to find a mistress. A mistress! that meant independence. But bashful and timid as I was, knowing nobody, and ignorant of the dialect of drawing-rooms, I always came back as awkward as ever, and swelling with unsatisfied desires, to be put in harness like a troop horse next day by my father, and to return with morning to my advocate, the Palais de Justice, and the law. To have swerved from the straight course which my father had mapped out for me would have drawn down his wrath upon me; at my first delinquency, he threatened to ship me off as a cabin-boy to the Antilles. A dreadful shiver ran through me if I had ventured to spend a couple of hours in some pleasure party.

"Imagine the most wandering imagination and passionate temperament, the tenderest soul and most artistic nature, dwelling continually in the presence of the most flint-hearted, atrabilious, and frigid man on earth; think of me as a young girl married to a skeleton, and you will understand the life whose curious scenes can only be a hearsay tale to you; the plans for running away that perished at the sight of my father, the despair soothed by slumber, the dark broodings charmed away by music. I breathed my sorrows forth in melodies. Beethoven or Mozart would keep my confidences sacred. Nowadays, I smile at recollections of the scruples which burdened my conscience at that epoch of innocence and virtue.

"If I set foot in a restaurant, I gave myself up for lost; my fancy led me to look on a café as a disreputable haunt, where men lost their characters and embarrassed their fortunes; as for engaging in play, I had not the money to risk. Oh, if I needed to send you to sleep, I would tell you about one of the most frightful pleasures of my life, one of those pleasures with fangs that bury themselves in the heart, as the branding-iron enters the convict's shoulder. I was at a ball at the house of the Duc de Navarreins, my father's cousin. But to

make my position the more perfectly clear, you must know
that I wore a threadbare coat, ill-fitting shoes, a tie fit for a
stableman, and a soiled pair of gloves.   I shrank into a corner
to eat ices and watch the pretty faces at my leisure.   My
father noticed me.   Actuated by some motive that I did not
fathom, so dumbfounded was I by this act of confidence, he
handed me his keys and purse to keep.   Ten paces away some
men were gambling.   I heard the rattling of gold; I was
twenty years old; I longed to be steeped for one whole day
in the follies of my time of life.   It was a license of the im-
agination that would find a parallel neither in the freaks of
courtesans, nor in the dreams of young girls.   For a year
past I had beheld myself well dressed, in a carriage, with a
pretty woman by my side, playing the great lord, dining at
Véry's, deciding not to go back home till the morrow; but
was prepared for my father with a plot more intricate than
the Marriage of Figaro, which he could not possibly have
unraveled.   All this bliss would cost, I estimated, fifty crowns.
Was it not the artless idea of playing truant that still had
charms for me?

"I went into a small adjoining room, and when alone
counted my father's money with smarting eyes and trembling
fingers—a hundred crowns!   The joys of my escapade rose
before me at the thought of the amount; joys that flitted
about me like Macbeth's witches around their caldron; joys
how alluring! how thrilling! how delicious!   I became a
deliberate rascal.   I heeded neither my tingling ears nor
the violent beating of my heart, but took out two twenty-franc
pieces that I seem to see yet.   The dates had been erased,
and Bonaparte's head simpered upon them.   After I had
put back the purse in my pocket, I returned to a gaming-table
with the two pieces of gold in the palms of my damp hands,
prowling about the players like a sparrow-hawk round a coop
of chickens.   Tormented by inexpressible terror, I flung a
sudden clairvoyant glance round me, and feeling quite sure

that I was seen by none of my acquaintances, betted on a stout, jovial little man, heaping upon his head more prayers and vows than are put up during two or three storms at sea. Then with an intuitive scoundrelism, or Machiavelism, surprising in one of my age, I went and stood in the door, and looked about me in the rooms, though I saw nothing; for both mind and eyes hovered about that fateful green cloth.

" That evening fixes the date of a first observation of a physiological kind; to it I owe a kind of insight into certain mysteries of our double nature that I have since been enabled to penetrate. I had my back turned on the table where my future felicity lay at stake, a felicity but so much the more intense that it was criminal. Between me and the players stood a wall of onlookers some five deep, who were chatting; the murmur of voices drowned the clinking of gold, which mingled in the sounds sent up by this orchestra; yet, despite all obstacles, I distinctly heard the words of the two players by a gift accorded to the passions, which enables them to annihilate time and space. I saw the points they made; I knew which of the two turned up the king as well as if I had actually seen the cards; at a distance of ten paces, in short, the fortunes of play blanched my face.

" My father suddenly went by, and then I knew what the Scripture meant by ' The Spirit of God passed before his face.' I had won. I slipped through the crowd of men who had gathered about the players with the quickness of an eel escaping through a broken mesh in a net. My nerves thrilled with joy instead of anguish. I felt like some criminal on the way to torture released by a chance meeting with the king. It happened that a man with a decoration found himself short by forty francs. Uneasy eyes suspected me; I turned pale, and drops of perspiration stood on my forehead. I was well punished, I thought, for having robbed my father. Then the kind little stout man said, in a voice like an angel's surely, 'All these gentlemen have paid their stakes,' and put down

6

the forty francs himself. I raised my head in triumph upon
the players. After I had returned the money I had taken
from it to my father's purse, I left my winnings with that
honest and worthy gentleman, who continued to win. As
soon as I found myself possessed of a hundred and sixty
francs, I wrapped them up in my handkerchief, so that they
could neither move nor rattle on the way back; and I played
no more.

"'What were you doing at the card-table?' said my father
as we stepped into the carriage.

"'I was looking on,' I answered, trembling.

"'But it would have been nothing out of the common if
you had been prompted by self-love to put some money down
on the table. In the eyes of men of the world you are quite
old enough to assume the right to commit such follies. So I
should have pardoned you, Raphael, if you had made use of
my purse.'

"I did not answer. When we reached home, I returned
the keys and the money to my father. As he entered his
study, he emptied out his purse on the mantelpiece, counted
the money, and turned to me with a kindly look, saying,
with more or less long and significant pauses between each
phrase—

"'My boy, you are very nearly twenty now. I am satis-
fied with you. You ought to have an allowance, if only to
teach you how to lay it out, and to gain some acquaintance
with everyday business. Henceforward I shall let you have
a hundred francs each month. Here is your first quarter's
income for this year,' he added, fingering a pile of gold, as if
to make sure that the amount was correct. 'Do what you
please with it.'

"I confess that I was ready to fling myself at his feet, to
tell him that I was a thief, a scoundrel, and, worse than all, a
liar! But a feeling of shame held me back. I went up to
him for an embrace, but he gently pushed me away.

"'You are a man now, my child,' he said. 'What I have just done was a very proper and simple thing, for which there is no need to thank me. If I have any claim to your gratitude, Raphael,' he went on in a kind but dignified way, 'it is because I have preserved your youth from the evils that destroy young men in Paris. We will be two friends henceforth. In a year's time you will be a doctor of law. Not without some hardship and privation you have acquired the sound knowledge and the love of, and application to, work that is indispensable to public men. You must learn to know me, Raphael. I do not want to make either an advocate or a notary of you, but a statesman, who shall be the pride of our humble house. Good-night,' he added.

"From that day my father took me fully into confidence. I was an only son ; and, ten years before, I had lost my mother. In time past my father, the head of a historic family remembered even now in Auvergne, had come to Paris to fight against his evil star, dissatisfied at the prospect of tilling the soil, with his useless sword by his side. He was endowed with the shrewdness that gives the men of the south of France a certain ascendancy when energy goes with it. Almost unaided, he made a position for himself near the fountain of power. The Revolution brought a reverse of fortune, but he had managed to marry an heiress of good family, and, in the time of the Empire, appeared to be on the point of restoring to our house its ancient splendor.

"The Restoration, while it brought back considerable property to my mother, was my father's ruin. He had formerly purchased several estates abroad, conferred by the Emperor on his generals ; and now for ten years he struggled with liquidators, diplomatists, and Prussian and Bavarian courts of law, over the disputed possession of these unfortunate endowments. My father plunged me into the intricate labyrinths of law proceedings on which our future depended. We might be compelled to return the rents, as well as the proceeds arising from sales of timber made during the years 1814 to 1817; in that case my mother's property would have barely saved our credit. So it fell out that the day on which my father in a fashion emancipated me, brought me under a most galling yoke. I entered on a conflict like a battlefield; I must work day and night; seek interviews with statesmen, surprise their convictions, try to interest them in our affairs, and gain them over, with their wives and servants, and their very dogs; and all this abominable business had to take the form of pretty speeches and polite attentions. Then I knew the mortifications that had left their blighting traces on my father's face. For about a year I led outwardly the life of a man of the world, but enormous labors lay beneath the surface of gadding about, and eager efforts to attach myself to influential kinsmen, or to people likely to be useful to us. My relaxations were lawsuits, and memorials still furnished the staple of my conversation. Hitherto my life had been blameless, from the sheer impossibility of indulging the desires of youth; but now I became my own master, and in dread of involving us both in ruin by some piece of negligence, I did not dare to allow myself any pleasure or expenditure.

"While we are young, and before the world has rubbed off the delicate bloom from our sentiments, the freshness of our impressions, the noble purity of conscience which will never allow us to palter with evil, the sense of duty is very strong within us, the voice of honor clamors within us, and we are open and straightforward. At that time I was all these things. I wished to justify my father's confidence in me. But lately I would have stolen a paltry sum from him, with secret delight; but now that I shared the burden of his affairs, of his name and of his house, I would secretly have given up my fortune and my hopes for him, as I was sacrificing my pleasures, and even have been glad of the sacrifice! So when Mde. Villèle exhumed, for our special benefit, an imperial decree concerning forfeitures, and had ruined us, I authorized the sale of my property, only retaining an island in the middle of the Loire, where my mother was buried. Perhaps arguments and evasions, philosophical, philanthropic, and political considerations would not fail me now, to hinder the perpetration of what my solicitor termed a folly; but at one-and-twenty, I repeat, we are all aglow with generosity and affection. The tears that stood in my father's eyes were to me the most splendid of fortunes, and the thought of those tears has often soothed my sorrow. Ten months after he had paid his creditors, my father died of grief; I was his idol, and he had ruined me! The thought killed him. Towards the end of the autumn of 1826, at the age of twenty-two, I was the sole mourner at his graveside—the grave of my father and my earliest friend. Not many young men have found themselves alone with their thoughts as they followed a hearse, or have seen themselves lost in crowded Paris, and without money or prospects. Orphans rescued by public charity have at any rate the future of the battlefield before them, and find a shelter in some institution and a father in the government or in the agent of the King. I had nothing.

"Three months later, an agent made over to me eleven hundred and twelve francs, the net proceeds of the winding up of my father's affairs. Our creditors had driven us to sell our furniture. From my childhood I had been used to set a high value on the articles of luxury about us, and I could not help showing my astonishment at the sight of this meagre balance.

"'Oh, rococo, all of it!' said the auctioneer. A terrible word that fell like a blight on the sacred memories of my childhood, and dispelled my earliest illusions, the dearest of all. My entire fortune was comprised in this account rendered, my future lay in a linen bag with eleven hundred and twelve francs in it, human society stood before me in the person of an auctioneer's clerk, who kept his hat on while he spoke. Jonathas, an old servant who was much attached to me, and whom my mother had formerly pensioned with an annuity of four hundred francs, spoke to me as I was leaving the house that I had so often gaily left for a drive in my childhood.

"'Be very economical, Monsieur Raphael!'

The good fellow was crying.

"Such were the events, dear Emile, that ruled my destinies, moulded my character, and set me, while still young, in an utterly false social position," said Raphael after a pause. "Family ties, weak ones, it is true, bound me to a few wealthy houses, but my own pride would have kept me aloof from them if contempt and indifference had not shut their doors to me in the first place. I was related to people who were very influential, and who lavished their patronage on strangers; but I found neither relations nor patrons in them. Continually circumscribed in my affections, they recoiled upon me. Unreserved and simple by nature, I must have appeared frigid and sophisticated. My father's discipline had destroyed all confidence in myself. I was shy and awkward; I could not believe that my opinion carried any weight whatever; I took no pleasure in myself; I thought myself ugly, and was ashamed to meet my own eyes. In spite of the inward voice that must be the stay of a man with anything in him, in all his struggles, the voice that cries, 'Courage! Go forward!' in spite of sudden revelations of my own strength in my solitude; in spite of the hopes that thrilled me as I compared new works, that the public admired so much, with the schemes that hovered in my brain,—in spite of all this, I had a childish mistrust of myself.

"An overweening ambition preyed upon me; I believed that I was meant for great things, and yet I felt myself to be nothing. I had need of other men, and I was friendless. I found I must make my way in the world, where I was quite alone, and bashful, rather than afraid.

"All through the year in which, by my father's wish, I threw myself into the whirlpool of fashionable society, I came away with an inexperienced heart, and fresh in mind. Like every grown child, I sighed in secret for a love affair. I met, among young men of my own age, a set of swaggerers who held their heads high, and talked about trifles as they seated themselves without a tremor beside women who inspired awe in me. They chattered nonsense, sucked the heads of their canes, gave themselves affected airs, appropriated the fairest women, and laid, or pretended that they had laid their heads on every pillow. Pleasure, seemingly, was at their beck and call; they looked on the most virtuous and prudish as an easy prey, ready to surrender at a word, at the slightest impudent gesture or insolent look. I declare, on my soul and conscience, that the attainment of power, or of a great name in literature, seemed to me an easier victory than a success with some young, witty, and gracious lady of high degree.

"So I found the tumult of my heart, my feelings, and my creeds all at variance with the axioms of society. I had plenty of audacity in my character, but none in my manner. Later, I found out that women did not like to be implored. I have from afar adored many a one to whom I devoted a soul proof against all tests, a heart to break, energy that shrank from no sacrifice and from no torture; *they* accepted fools whom I would not have engaged as hall porters. How often, mute and motionless, have I not admired the lady of my dreams, swaying in the dance; given up my life in thought to one eternal caress, expressed all my hopes in a look, and laid before her, in my rapture, a young man's love, which should outstrip all fables. At some moments I was ready to barter my whole life for one single night. Well, as I could never find a listener for my impassioned proposals, eyes to rest my own upon, a heart made for my heart, I lived on in all the sufferings of impotent force that consumes itself; lacking either opportunity or courage or experience. I despaired, maybe, of making myself understood, or I feared to be understood but too well; and yet the storm within me was ready to burst at every chance courteous look. In spite of my readiness to take the semblance of interest in look or word for a tenderer solicitude, I dared neither to speak nor to be silent seasonably. My words grew insignificant, and my silence stupid, by sheer stress of emotion. I was too ingenuous, no doubt, for that artificial life, led by candle-light, where every thought is expressed in conventional phrases, or by words that fashion dictates; and not only so, I had not learned how to employ speech that says nothing, and silence that says a great deal. In short, I concealed the fires that consumed me, and with such a soul as women wish to find, with all the elevation of soul that they long for, and a mettle that fools plume themselves upon, all women have been cruelly treacherous to me.

" So in my simplicity I admired the heroes of this set when they bragged about their conquests, and never suspected them of lying. No doubt it was a mistake to wish for a love that springs for a word's sake; to expect to find in the heart of a vain, frivolous woman, greedy for luxury and intoxicated with vanity, the great sea of passion that surged tempestuously in my own breast. Oh! to feel that you were born to love, to make some woman's happiness, and yet to find not one, not even a noble and courageous Marceline, not so much as an old marquise! Oh! to carry a treasure in your wallet, and not find even some child, or inquisitive young girl, to admire it! In my despair I often wished to kill myself."

" Finely tragical to-night! " cried Emile.

"Let me pass sentence on my life," Raphael answered. " If your friendship is not strong enough to bear with my elegy, if you cannot put up with half an hour's tedium for my sake, go to sleep! But, then, never ask again for the reason of the suicide that hangs over me, that comes nearer and calls to me, that I bow myself before. If you are to judge a man, you must know his secret thoughts, sorrows, and feelings; to know merely the outward events of a man's life would only serve to make a chronological table—a fool's notion of history."

Emile was so much struck with the bitter tones in which these words were spoken, that he began to pay close attention to Raphael, whom he watched with a bewildered expression.

" Now," continued the speaker, " all these things that be-fell me appear in a new light. The sequence of events that I once thought so unfortunate created the splendid powers of which, later, I became so proud. If I may believe you, I possess the power of readily expressing my thoughts, and I could take a forward place in the great field of knowledge ; and is not this the result of scientific curiosity, of excessive application, and a love of reading which possessed me from the age of seven till my entry on life? The very neglect in which I was left, and the consequent habits of self-repression and self-concentration ; did not these things teach me how to consider and reflect? Nothing in me was squandered in obedience to the exactions of the world, which humble the proudest soul and reduce it to a mere husk ; and was it not this very fact that refined the emotional part of my nature till it became the perfected instrument of a loftier purpose than passionate desires? I remember watching the women who mistook me with all the insight of contemned love.

" I can see now that my natural sincerity must have been displeasing to them ; women, perhaps, even require a little hypocrisy. And I, who in the same hour's space am alter-nately a man and a child, frivolous and thoughtful, free from bias and brimful of superstition, and oftentimes myself as much a woman as any of them ; how should they do other-wise than take my simplicity for cynicism, my innocent can-dor for impudence? They found my knowledge tiresome ; my feminine languor, weakness. I was held to be listless and incapable of love or of steady purpose ; a too active imagination, that curse of poets, was no doubt the cause. My silence was idiotic ; and as I dare say I alarmed them by my efforts to please, women one and all have condemned me. With tears and mortification, I bowed before the decision of the world ; but my distress was not barren. I determined to revenge myself on society ; I would dominate the feminine intellect, and so have the feminine soul at my mercy ; all eyes should be fixed upon me, when the servant at the door announced my name. I had determined from my childhood that I would be a great man ; I said with André Chénier, as I struck my forehead, ' There is something underneath that ! ' I felt, I believed, the thought within me that I must express, the system I must establish, the knowledge I must interpret.

" Let me pour out my follies, dear Emile ; to-day I am barely twenty-six years old, certain of dying unrecognized, and I have never been the lover of the woman I dreamed of possessing. Have we not all of us, more or less, believed in the reality of a thing because we wished it ? I would never have a young man for my friend who did not place himself in dreams upon a pedestal, weave crowns for his head, and have complaisant mistresses. I myself would often be a general, nay, emperor ; I have been a Byron, and then a nobody. After this sport on these pinnacles of human achievement, I became aware that all the difficulties and steeps of life were yet to face. My exuberant self-esteem came to my aid ; I had that intense belief in my destiny, which perhaps amounts to genius in those who will not permit themselves to be distracted by contact with the world, as sheep that leave their wool on the briars of every thicket they pass by. I meant to cover myself with glory, and to work in silence for the mistress I hoped to have one day. Woman for me was resolved into a single type, and this woman I hoped to meet in the first that met my eyes ; but in each and all I saw a queen, and as queens must make the first advances to their lovers, they must draw near to me—to me, so sickly, shy, and poor. For her, who should take pity on me, my heart held in store such gratitude over and beyond love, that I had worshipped her her whole life long. Later, my observations have taught me bitter truths.

"In this way, dear Emile, I ran the risk of remaining companionless for good. The incomprehensible bent of women's minds appears to lead them to see nothing but the weak points in a clever man, and the strong points of a fool. They feel the liveliest sympathy with the fool's good qualities, which perpetually flatter their own defects; while they find the man of talent hardly agreeable enough to compensate for his shortcomings. All capacity is a sort of intermittent fever, and no woman is anxious to share in its discomforts only; they look to find in their lovers the wherewithal to gratify their own vanity. It is themselves that they love in us! But the artist, poor and proud, along with his endowment of creative power, is furnished with an aggressive egotism! Everything about him is involved in I know not what whirlpool of his ideas, and even his mistress must gyrate along with them. How is a woman, spoilt with praise, to believe in the love of a man like that? Will she go to seek him out? That sort of a lover has not the leisure to sit beside a sofa and give himself up to the sentimental simperings that women are so fond of, and on which the false and unfeeling pride themselves. He cannot spare the time from his work, and how can he afford to humble himself and go a masquerading? I was ready to give my life once and for all, but I could not degrade it in detail. Besides, there is something indescribably paltry in a stockbroker's tactics, who runs on errands for some insipid affected woman; all this disgusts an artist. Love in the abstract is not enough for a great man in poverty; he has need of its utmost devotion. The frivolous creatures who spend their lives in trying on cashmeres, or make themselves into clothespegs to hang the fashions from, exact the devotion which is not theirs to give; for them, love means the pleasure of ruling and not of obeying. She who is really a wife, one in heart, flesh, and bone, must follow wherever he leads, in whom her life, her strength, her pride, and happiness are centred. Ambitious men need those Oriental women whose whole thought is given to the study of their requirements; for unhappiness means for them the incompatibility of their means with their desires. But I, who took myself for a man of genius, must needs feel attracted by these very she-coxcombs. So, as I cherished ideas so different from those generally received; as I wished to scale the heavens without a ladder, was possessed of wealth that could not circulate, and of knowledge so wide and so imperfectly arranged and digested that it overtaxed my memory; as I had neither relations nor friends in the midst of this lonely and ghastly desert, a desert of paving stones, full of animation, life, and thought, wherein every one is worse than inimical, indifferent to wit, I made a very natural, if foolish, resolve, which required such unknown impossibilities, that my spirits rose. It was as if I had laid a wager with myself, for I was at once the player and the cards.

"This was my plan. The eleven hundred francs must keep life in me for three years—the time I allowed myself in which to bring to light a work which should draw attention to me, and make me either a name or a fortune. I exulted at the thought of living on bread and milk, like a hermit in the Thebaid, while I plunged into the world of books and ideas, and so reached a lofty sphere beyond the tumult of Paris, a sphere of silent labor where I would entomb myself like a chrysalis to await a brilliant and splendid new birth. I imperiled my life in order to live. By reducing my requirements to real needs and the barest necessaries, I found that three hundred and sixty-five francs sufficed for a year of penury; and, in fact, I managed to exist on that slender sum, so long as I submitted to my own claustral discipline."

"Impossible!" cried Emile.

I CANNOT RECOLLECT PAYING FOR WATER: I WENT OUT
TO FETCH IT EVERY MORNING.

"I lived for nearly three years in that way," Raphael answered, with a kind of pride. "Let us reckon it out. Three *sous* for bread, two for milk, and three for cold meat, kept me from dying of hunger, and my mind in a state of peculiar lucidity. I have observed, as you know, the wonderful effects produced by diet upon the imagination. My lodgings cost me three *sous* daily; I burnt three *sous* more in oil at night; I did my own housework, and wore flannel shirts so as to reduce the laundress' bill to two *sous* per day. The money I spent yearly in coal, if divided up, never cost more than two *sous* for each day. I had three years' supply of clothing, and I only dressed when going out to some library or public lecture. These expenses, all told, only amounted to eighteen *sous*, so two were left over for emergencies. I cannot recollect, during that long period of toil, either crossing the Pont des Arts, or paying for water; I went out to fetch it every morning from the fountain in the Place Saint Michel, at the corner of the Rue de Grès. Oh, I wore my poverty proudly. A man urged on towards a fair future walks through life like an innocent person to his death; he feels no shame about it.

"I would not think of illness. Like Aquilina, I faced the hospital without terror. I had not a moment's doubt of my health, and besides, the poor can only take to their beds to die. I cut my own hair till the day when an angel of love and kindness— But I do not want to anticipate the state of things that I shall reach later. You must simply know that I lived with one grand thought for a mistress, a dream, an illusion which deceives us all more or less at first. To-day I laugh at myself, at that self, holy perhaps and heroic, which is now no more. I have since had a closer view of society and the world, of our manners and customs, and see the dangers of my innocent credulity and the superfluous nature of my fervent toil. Stores of that sort are quite useless to aspirants for fame. Light should be the baggage of seekers after fortune!

"Ambitious men spend their youth in rendering themselves

worthy of patronage; it is their great mistake. While the foolish creatures are laying in stores of knowledge and energy, so that they shall not sink under the weight of responsible posts that recede from them, schemers come and go who are wealthy in words and destitute of ideas, astonish the ignorant, and creep into the confidence of those who have a little knowledge. While the first kind study, the second march ahead; the one sort is modest, and the other impudent; the man of genius is silent about his own merit, but these schemers make a flourish of theirs, and they are bound to get on. It is so strongly to the interest of men in office to believe in ready-made capacity, and in brazen-faced merit, that it is downright childish of the learned to expect material rewards. I do not seek to paraphrase the commonplace moral, the song of songs that obscure genius is forever singing; I want to come, in a logical manner, by the reason of the frequent successes of mediocrity. Alas! study shows us such a mother's kindness that it would be a sin perhaps to ask any other reward of her than the pure and delightful pleasures with which she sustains her children.

"Often I remember soaking my bread in milk, as I sat by the window to take the fresh air, while my eyes wandered over a view of roofs—brown, gray, or red, slated or tiled, and covered with yellow or green mosses. At first the prospect may have seemed monotonous, but I very soon found peculiar beauties in it. Sometimes at night, streams of light through half-closed shutters would light up and color the dark abysses of this strange landscape. Sometimes the feeble lights of the street lamps sent up yellow gleams through the fog, and in each street dimly outlined the undulations of a crowd of roofs, like billows in a motionless sea. Very occasionally, too, a face appeared in this gloomy waste; above the flowers in some skyey garden I caught a glimpse of an old woman's crooked angular profile as she watered her nasturtiums; or, in a crazy attic window, a young girl, fancying herself quite alone as she dressed herself—a view of nothing more than a fair fore-head and long tresses held above her by a pretty white arm.

" I liked to see the short-lived plant-life in the gutters—poor weeds that a storm soon washed away. I studied the mosses, with their colors revived by showers, or transformed by the sun into a brown velvet that fitfully caught the light. Such things as these formed my recreations—the passing poetic moods of daylight, the melancholy mists, sudden gleams of sunlight, the silence and the magic of night, the mysteries of dawn, the smoke wreaths from each chimney; every chance event, in fact, in my curious world became familiar to me. I came to love this prison of my own choosing. This level Parisian prairie of roofs, beneath which lay populous abysses, suited my humor, and harmonized with my thoughts.

" Sudden descents into the world from the divine height of scientific meditation are very exhausting; and, besides, I had apprehended perfectly the bare life of the cloister. When I made up my mind to carry out this new plan of life, I looked for quarters in the most out-of-the-way parts of Paris. One evening, as I returned home to the Rue des Cordiers from the Place de l'Estrapade, I saw a girl of fourteen playing with a battledore at the corner of the Rue de Cluny; her winsome ways and laughter amused the neighbors. September was not yet over; it was warm and fine, so that women sat chatting before their doors as if it were a fête-day in some country town. At first I watched the charming expression of the girl's face and her graceful attitudes, her pose fit for a painter. It was a pretty sight. I looked about me, seeking to under-stand this blithe simplicity in the midst of Paris, and saw that the street was a blind alley and but little frequented. I re-membered that Jean Jacques had once lived here, and looked up the Hôtel Saint-Quentin. Its dilapidated condition awakened hopes of a cheap lodging, and I determined to enter.

" I found myself in a room with a low ceiling; the candles, in classic-looking copper candlesticks, were set in a row under

each key.   The predominating cleanliness of the room made
a striking contrast to the usual state of such places.   This one
was as neat as a bit of *genre;* there was a charming trimness
about the blue coverlet, the cooking pots and furniture.   The
mistress of the house rose and came to me.   She seemed to be
about forty years of age ; sorrows had left their traces on her
features, and weeping had dimmed her eyes.   I deferentially
mentioned the amount I could pay ; it seemed to cause her
no surprise ; she sought out a key from the row, went up to
the attics with me, and showed me a room that looked out on
the neighboring roofs and courts ; long poles with linen dry-
ing on them hung out of the window.

"Nothing could be uglier than this garret, awaiting its
scholar, with its dingy yellow walls and odor of poverty.
The roofing fell in a deep slope, and the sky was visible
through chinks in the tiles.   There was room for a bed, a
table, and a few chairs, and beneath the highest point of the
roof my piano could stand.   Not being rich enough to fur-
nish this cage (that might have been one of the *Piombi* of
Venice), the poor woman had never been able to let it ; and
as I had saved from the recent sale the furniture that was in
a fashion peculiarly mine, I very soon came to terms with my
landlady, and moved in on the following day.

"For three years I lived in this airy sepulchre, and worked
unflaggingly day and night ; and so great was the pleasure,
that study seemed to me the fairest theme and the happiest
solution of life.   The tranquillity and peace that a scholar
needs is something as sweet and exhilarating as love.   Un-
speakable joys are showered on us by the exertion of our
mental faculties ; the quest of ideas, and the tranquil contem-
plation of knowledge ; delights indescribable, because purely
intellectual and impalpable to our senses.   So we are obliged
to use material terms to express the mysteries of the soul.
The pleasure of striking out in some lonely lake of clear
water, with forests, rocks, and flowers around, and the soft

stirring of the warm breeze,—all this would give to those who knew them not a very faint idea of the exultation with which my soul bathed itself in the beams of an unknown light, hearkened to the awful and uncertain voice of inspiration, as vision upon vision poured from some unknown source through my throbbing brain.

"No earthly pleasure can compare with the divine delight of watching the dawn of an idea in the space of abstractions, as it rises like the morning sun; an idea that, better still, attains gradually like a child to puberty and man's estate. Study lends a kind of enchantment to all our surroundings. The wretched desk covered with brown leather at which I wrote, my piano, bed, and arm-chair, the old wall-paper and furniture, seemed to have for me a kind of life in them, and to be humble friends of mine and mute partakers of my destiny. How often have I confided my soul to them in a glance! A warped bit of beading often met my eyes, and suggested new developments,—a striking proof of my system, or a felicitous word by which to render my all but inexpressible thought. By sheer contemplation of the things about me I discerned an expression and a character in each. If the setting sun happened to steal in through my narrow window, they would take new colors, fade or shine, grow dull or gay, and always amaze me with some new effect. These trifling incidents of a solitary life, which escape those preoccupied with outward affairs, make the solace of prisoners. And what was I but the captive of an idea, imprisoned in my system, but sustained also by the prospect of a brilliant future? At each obstacle that I overcame, I seemed to kiss the soft hands of a woman with a fair face, a wealthy, well-dressed woman, who should some day say softly, while she caressed my hair—

"'Poor angel, how thou hast suffered!'

"I had undertaken two great works—one a comedy that in a very short time must bring me wealth and fame, and an entry into those circles whither I wished to return, to exercise

7

the royal privilege of a man of genius. You all saw nothing in that masterpiece but the blunder of a young man fresh from college, a babyish fiasco. Your jokes clipped the wings of a throng of illusions, which have never stirred since within me. You, dear Emile, alone brought soothing to the deep wounds that others had made in my heart. You alone will admire my 'Theory of the Will.' I devoted most of my time to that long work, for which I studied Oriental languages, physiology and anatomy. If I do not deceive myself, my labors will complete the task begun by Mesmer, Lavater, Gale, and Bichat, and open up new paths in science.

"There ends that fair life of mine, the daily sacrifice, the unrecognized silkworm's toil, that is, perhaps, its own sole recompense. Since attaining years of discretion, until the day when I finished my 'Theory,' I observed, learned, wrote, and read unintermittingly; my life was one long imposition, as schoolboys say. Though by nature effeminately attached to Oriental indolence, sensual in tastes, and a wooer of dreams, I worked incessantly, and refused to taste any of the enjoyments of Parisian life. Though a glutton, I became abstemious; and loving exercise and sea voyages as I did, and haunted by the wish to visit many countries, still child enough to play at ducks and drakes with pebbles over a pond, I led a sedentary life with a pen in my fingers. I liked talking, but I went to sit and mutely listen to professors who gave public lectures at the Library or the museum. I slept upon my solitary pallet like a Benedictine brother, though woman was my one chimera, a chimera that fled from me as I wooed it! In short, my life has been a cruel contradiction, a perpetual cheat. After that, judge a man!

"Sometimes my natural propensities broke out like a fire long smothered. I was debarred from the women whose society I desired, stripped of everything and lodged in an artist's garret, and by a sort of mirage or calenture I was surrounded by captivating mistresses. I drove through the streets of Paris, lolling on the soft cushions of a fine equipage. I plunged into dissipation, into corroding vice, I desired and possessed everything, for fasting had made me light-headed like the tempted St. Anthony. Slumber, happily, would put an end at last to these devastating trances; and on the morrow science would beckon me, smiling, and I was faithful to her. I imagine that women reputed virtuous must often fall a prey to these insane tempests of desire and passion, which rise in us in spite of ourselves. Such dreams have a charm of their own; they are something akin to evening gossip round the winter fire, when one sets out for some voyage in China. But what becomes of virtue during these delicious excursions, when fancy overleaps all difficulties?

"During the first ten months of seclusion I led the life of poverty and solitude that I have described to you; I used to steal out unobserved every morning to buy my own provisions for the day; I tidied my room; I was at once master and servant, and played the Diogenes with incredible spirit. But afterwards, while my hostess and her daughter watched my ways and behavior, scrutinized my appearance and divined my poverty, there could not but be some bonds between us; perhaps because they were themselves so very poor. Pauline, the charming child, whose latent and unconscious grace had, in a manner, brought me there, did me many services that I could not well refuse. All women fallen on evil days are sisters; they speak a common language; they have the same generosity—the generosity that possesses nothing, and so is lavish of its affection, of its time, and of its very self.

"Imperceptibly Pauline took me under her protection, and would do things for me. No kind of objection was made by her mother, whom I even surprised mending my linen; she blushed for the charitable occupation. In spite of myself, they took charge of me, and I accepted their services.

"In order to understand the peculiar condition of my

mind, my preoccupation with work must be remembered, the
tyranny of ideas, and the instinctive repugnance that a man
who leads an intellectual life must ever feel for the material
details of existence.   Could I well repulse the delicate atten-
tions of Pauline, who would noiselessly bring me my frugal
repast, when she noticed that I had taken nothing for seven
or eight hours? She had the tact of a woman and the inven-
tiveness of a child ; she would smile as she would make sign
to me that I must not see her.   Ariel glided under my roof
in the form of a sylph who foresaw every want of mine.

"One evening Pauline told me her story with touching
simplicity.   Her father had been a major in the horse grena-
diers of the imperial guard.   He had been taken prisoner by
the Cossacks, at the passage of the Beresina ; and when
Napoleon later on proposed an exchange, the Russian authori-
ties made search for him in Siberia in vain ; he had escaped
with a view of reaching India, and since then Mme. Gaudin,
my landlady, could hear no news of her husband.   Then
came the disasters of 1814 and 1815 ; and, left alone and
without resource, she had decided to let furnished lodgings in
order to keep herself and her daughter.

"She always hoped to see her husband again.   Her great-
est trouble was about her daughter's education ; the Princess
Borghese was her Pauline's godmother ; and Pauline must not
be unworthy of the fair future promised by her imperial pro-
tectress.   When Mme. Gaudin confided to me this heavy
trouble that preyed upon her, she said with sharp pain in her
voice, 'I would give up the property and the scrap of paper
that makes Gaudin a baron of the empire, and all our rights
to the endowment of Wistchnau, if only Pauline could be
brought up at Saint-Denis!'   Her words struck me ; now I
could show my gratitude for the kindnesses expended on me
by the two women ; all at once the idea of offering to finish
Pauline's education occurred to me ; and the offer was made
and accepted in the most perfect simplicity.   In this way I

came to have some hours of recreation. Pauline had natural aptitude ; she learned so quickly that she soon surpassed me at the piano. As she became accustomed to think aloud in my presence, she unfolded all the sweet refinements of a heart that was opening itself out to life, as some flower-cup opens slowly to the sun. She listened to me, pleased and thoughtful, letting her dark velvet eyes rest upon me with a half-smile in them ; she repeated her lessons in soft and gentle tones, and showed childish glee when I was satisfied with her. Her mother grew more and more anxious every day to shield the young girl from every danger (for all the beauty promised in early life was developing in the crescent moon), and was glad to see her spend whole days indoors in study. My piano was the only one she could use, and while I was out she practised on it. When I came home, Pauline would be in my room, in her shabby dress, but her slightest movement revealed her slender figure in its attractive grace, in spite of the coarse materials that she wore. As with the heroine of the fable of ' Peau d'Ane,' a dainty foot peeped out of the clumsy shoes. But all her wealth of girlish beauty was as lost upon me. I had laid commands upon myself to see a sister only in Pauline. I dreaded lest I should betray her mother's faith in me. I admired the lovely girl as if she had been a picture, or as the portrait of a dead mistress ; she was at once my child and my statue. For me, another Pygmalion, the maiden with the hues of life and the living voice was to become a form of inanimate marble. I was very strict with her, but the more I made her feel my pedagogue's severity, the more gentle and submissive she grew.

" If a generous feeling strengthened me in my reserve and self-restraint, prudent considerations were not lacking beside. Integrity of purpose cannot, I think, fail to accompany integrity in money matters. To my mind, to become insolvent or to betray a woman is the same sort of thing. If you love a young girl, or allow yourself to be beloved by her, a contract is implied, and its conditions should be thoroughly understood. We are free to break with the woman who sells herself, but not with the young girl who has given herself to us and does not know the extent of her sacrifice. I must have married Pauline, and that would have been madness. Would it not have given over that sweet girlish heart to terrible misfortunes? My poverty made its selfish voice heard, and set an iron barrier between that gentle nature and mine. Besides, I am ashamed to say, that I cannot imagine love in the midst of poverty. Perhaps this is a vitiation due to that malady of mankind called civilization; but a woman in squalid poverty would exert no fascination over me, were she attractive as Homer's Galatea, the fair Helen.

"Ah, *vive l'amour!* But let it be in silk and cashmere, surrounded with the luxury which so marvelously embellishes it; for is it not perhaps itself a luxury? I enjoy making havoc with an elaborate erection of scented hair; I like to crush flowers, to disarrange and crease a smart toilette at will. A bizarre attraction lies for me in burning eyes that blaze through a lace veil, like flame through cannon smoke. My way of love would be to mount by a silken ladder, in the silence of a winter night. And what bliss to reach, all powdered with snow, a perfumed room, with hangings of painted silk, to find a woman there, who likewise shakes away the snow from her; for what other name can be found for the white muslin wrappings that vaguely define her, like some angel form issuing from a cloud! And then I wish for furtive joys, for the security of audacity. I want to see once more that woman of mystery, but let it be in the throng, dazzling, unapproachable, adored on all sides, dressed in laces and ablaze with diamonds, laying her commands upon every one; so exalted above us that she inspires awe, and none dares to pay his homage to her.

"She gives me a stolen glance, amid her court, a look that exposes the unreality of all this; that resigns for me the world and all men in it ! Truly I have scorned myself for a passion for a few yards of lace, velvet, and fine lawn, and the hairdresser's feats of skill ; a love of wax-lights, a carriage and a title, a heraldic coronet painted on window panes, or engraved by a jeweler; in short, a liking for all that is adventitious and least womanly in woman. I have scorned and reasoned with myself, but all in vain.

" A woman of rank with her subtle smile, her high-born air, and self-esteem captivates me. The barriers she erects between herself and the world awaken my vanity, a good half of love. There would be more relish for me in bliss that all others envied. If my mistress does nothing that other women do, and neither lives nor conducts herself like them, wears a cloak that they cannot attain, breathes a perfume of her own, then she seems to rise far above me. The further she rises from earth, even in the earthlier aspects of love, the fairer she becomes for me.

" Luckily for me we have had no queen in France these twenty years, for I should have fallen in love with her. A woman must be wealthy to acquire the manners of a princess. What place had Pauline among these far-fetched imaginings? Could she bring me the love that is death, that brings every faculty into play, the nights that are paid for by life? We hardly die, I think, for an insignificant girl who gives herself to us; and I could never extinguish these feelings and poet's dreams within me. I was born for an inaccessible love, and fortune has overtopped my desire.

" How often have I set satin shoes on Pauline's tiny feet, confined her form, slender as a young poplar, in a robe of gauze, and thrown a loose scarf about her as I saw her tread the carpets in her mansion and led her out to her splendid carriage ! In such guise I should have adored her. I endowed her with all the pride she lacked, stripped her of her virtues, her natural simple charm, and frank smile, in order to plunge her heart in our Styx of depravity and make it invulnerable,

load her with our crimes, make of her the fantastical doll of
our drawing-rooms, the frail being who lies a-bed in the
morning and comes to life again at night with the dawn of
tapers.   Pauline was fresh-hearted and affectionate—I would
have had her cold and formal.

"In the last days of my frantic folly, memory brought
Pauline before me, as it brings the scene of our childhood,
and made me pause to muse over past delicious moments that
softened my heart.   I sometimes saw her, the adorable girl
who sat quietly sewing at my table, wrapped in her medita-
tions ; the faint light from my window fell upon her and was
reflected back in silvery rays from her thick black hair ; some-
times I heard her young laughter, or the rich tones of her
young voice singing some canzonet that she composed without
effort.   And often my Pauline seemed to grow greater, as
music flowed from her, and her face bore a striking resem-
blance to the noble one that Carlo Dolci chose for the type of
Italy.   My cruel memory brought her back athwart the dissi-
pations of my existence, like a remorse, or a symbol of purity.
But let us leave the poor child to her own fate.   Whatever
her troubles may have been, at any rate I protected her from
menacing tempest—I did not drag her down into my hell.

"Until last winter I led the uneventful studious life of
which I have given you some faint picture.   In the earliest
days of December, 1829, I came across Rastignac, who, in
spite of the shabby condition of my wardrobe, linked his arm
in mine, and inquired into my affairs with a quite brotherly
interest.   Caught by his engaging manner, I gave him a
brief account of my life and hopes ; he began to laugh, and
treated me as a mixture, of a man of genius and a fool.   His
Gascon accent and knowledge of the world, the easy life his
clever management procured for him, all produced an irresist-
ible effect upon me.   I should die an unrecognized failure in
a hospital, Rastignac said, and be buried in a pauper's grave.
He talked of charlatanism.   Every man of genius was a

charlatan, he plainly showed me in that pleasant way of his that makes him so fascinating. He insisted that I must be out of my senses, and would be my own death, if I lived on alone in the Rue des Cordiers. According to him I ought to go into society, to accustom people to the sound of my name, and to rid myself of the simple title of 'Monsieur' which sits but ill on a great man in his lifetime.

" ' Those who know no better,' he cried, 'call this sort of business *scheming,* and moral people condemn it for a "dissipated life." We need not stop to look at what people think, but see the results. You work, you say? Very good, but nothing will ever come of that. Now, I am ready for anything and fit for nothing. As lazy as a lobster very likely: but I succeed everywhere. I go out into society, I push myself forward, the others make way before me; I brag and am believed; I incur debts which somebody else pays! Dissipation, dear boy, is a methodical policy. The life of a man who deliberately runs through his fortune often becomes a business speculation; his friends, his pleasures, patrons, and acquaintances are his capital. Suppose a merchant runs a risk of a million for twenty years, he can neither sleep, eat, nor amuse himself; he is brooding over his million; it makes him run about all over Europe; he worries himself, goes to the devil in every way that man has invented. Then comes a liquidation, such as I have seen myself, which very often leaves him penniless and without a reputation or a friend. The spendthrift, on the other hand, takes life as a serious game, and sees his horses run. He loses his capital, perhaps, but he stands a chance of being nominated Receiver-General, of making a wealthy marriage, or of an appointment as attaché to a minister or an ambassador; and he has his friends left and his name, and he never wants money. He knows the standing of everybody, and uses every one for his own benefit. Is this logical, or am I a madman after all? Haven't you there all the moral of the comedy that goes on every day in this world? Your work is completed,' he went on after a pause; 'you are immensely clever! Well, you have only arrived at my starting-point. Now, you had better look after its success yourself; it is the surest way. You will make allies in every clique, and secure applause beforehand. I mean to go halves in your glory myself; I shall be the jeweler who set the diamonds in your crown. Come here to-morrow evening, by way of a beginning. I will introduce you to a house where all Paris goes, all *our* Paris, that is—the Paris of exquisites, millionaires, celebrities, all the folk who talk gold like Chrysostom. When they have taken up a book, that book becomes the fashion; and if it is something really good for once, they will have declared it to be a work of genius without knowing it. If you have any sense, my dear fellow, you will insure the success of your " Theory," by a better understanding of the theory of success. To-morrow evening you shall go to see that queen of the moment—the beautiful Countess Fœdora.'

" 'I have never heard of her.' . . .

" 'You Hottentot!' laughed Rastignac; 'you do not know Fœdora? A great match with an income of nearly eighty thousand livres, who has taken a fancy to nobody, or else no one has taken a fancy to her. A sort of feminine enigma, a half-Russian Parisienne, or a half-Parisian Russian. All the romantic productions that never get published are brought out at her house; she is the handsomest woman in Paris, and the most gracious! You are not even a Hottentot; you are something between the Hottentot and the beast. Good-bye till to-morrow.'

" He swung round on his heel and made off without waiting for any answer. It never occurred to him that a reasoning being could refuse an introduction to Fœdora. How can the fascination of a name be explained? FŒDORA haunted me like some evil thought, with which you seek to come to terms. A voice said in me, ' You are going to see Fœdora!'

In vain I reasoned with that voice, saying that it lied to me; all my arguments were defeated by the name 'Fœdora.' Was not the name, and even the woman herself, the symbol of all my desires, and the object of my life?

"The name called up recollections of the conventional glitter of the world, the upper world of Paris with its brilliant fêtes and the tinsel of its vanities. The woman brought before me all the problems of passion on which my mind continually ran. Perhaps it was neither the woman nor the name, but my own propensities, that sprang up within me and tempted me afresh. Here was the Countess Fœdora, rich and loveless, proof against the temptations of Paris; was not this woman the very incarnation of my hopes and visions? I fashioned her for myself, drew her in fancy, and dreamed of her. I could not sleep that night; I became her lover; I overbrimmed a few hours with a whole lifetime—a lover's lifetime; the experience of its prolific delights burned me.

"The next day I could not bear the tortures of delay; I borrowed a novel, and spent the whole day over it, so that I could not possibly think nor keep account of the time till night. Fœdora's name echoed through me even as I read, but only as a distant sound: though it could be heard, it was not troublesome. Fortunately, I owned a fairly creditable black coat and a white waistcoat; of all my fortune there now remained about thirty francs, which I had distributed about among my clothes and in my drawers, so as to erect between my whims and the spending of a five-franc piece a thorny barrier of search, and an adventurous peregrination round my room. While I was dressing, I dived about for my money in an ocean of papers. This scarcity of specie will give you some idea of the value of that squandered upon gloves and cab-hire; a month's bread disappeared at one fell swoop. Alas! money is always forthcoming for our caprices; we only grudge the cost of things that are useful or necessary. We recklessly fling gold to an opera-dancer, and haggle with a tradesman whose hungry family must wait for the settlement of our bill. How many men are there that wear a coat that costs a hundred francs, carry a diamond in the head of their cane, and dine for twenty-five *sous* for all that !   It seems as though we could never pay enough for the pleasures of vanity.

"Rastignac, punctual to his appointment, smiled at the transformation, and joked about it.   On the way he gave me benevolent advice as to my conduct with the countess ; he described her as mean, vain, and suspicious ; but though mean, she was ostentatious, her vanity was transparent, and her mistrust good-humored.

"'You know I am pledged,' he said, 'and what I should lose, too, if I tried a change in love.   So my observation of Fœdora has been quite cool and disinterested, and my remarks must have some truth in them.   I was looking to your future when I thought of introducing you to her; so mind very carefully what I am about to say.   She has a terrible memory.   She is clever enough to drive a diplomatist wild ; she would know it at once if he spoke the truth.   Between ourselves, I fancy that her marriage was not recognized by the Emperor, for the Russian ambassador began to smile when I spoke of her ; he does not receive her either, and only bows very coolly if he meets her in the Bois.   For all that, she is in Madame de Serizy's set, and visits Mesdames de Nucingen and de Restaud.   There is no cloud over her here in France ; the Duchesse de Carigliano, the most strait-laced maréchale in the whole Bonapartist coterie, often goes to spend the summer with her at her country house.   Plenty of young fops, sons of peers of France, have offered her a title in exchange for her fortune, and she has politely declined them all.   Her susceptibilities, may be, are not to be touched by anything less than a count.   Aren't you a marquis?   Go ahead if you fancy her.   This is what you may call "receiving your instructions.'"

"His raillery made me think that Rastignac wished to

joke and excite my curiosity, so that I was in a paroxysm of my extemporized passion by the time that we stopped before a peristyle full of flowers. My heart beat and my color rose as we went up the great carpeted staircase, and I noticed about me all the studied refinements of English comfort; I was infatuatedly *bourgeois;* I forgot my origin and all my personal and family pride. Alas! I had just left a garret, after three years of poverty, and I could not just then set the treasures there acquired above such trifles as these. Nor could I rightly estimate the worth of the vast intellectual capital which turns to riches at the moment when opportunity comes within our reach, opportunity that does not overwhelm, because study has prepared us for the struggles of public life.

"I found a woman of about twenty-two years of age; she was of average height, was dressed in white, and held a feather fire-screen in her hand; a group of men stood around her. She rose at the sight of Rastignac, and came towards us with a gracious smile and a musically-uttered compliment, prepared no doubt beforehand, for me. Our friend had spoken of me as a rising man, and his clever way of making the most of me had procured me this flattering reception. I was confused by the attention which every one paid to me; but Rastignac had luckily mentioned my modesty. I was brought in contact with scholars, men of letters, ex-ministers, and peers of France. The conversation, interrupted awhile by my coming, was resumed. I took courage, feeling that I had a reputation to maintain, and, without abusing my privilege, I spoke when it fell to me to speak, trying to state the questions at issue in words more or less profound, witty or trenchant, and I made a certain sensation. Rastignac was a prophet for the thousandth time in his life. As soon as the gathering was large enough to restore freedom to individuals, he took my arm, and we went round the rooms.

"'Don't look as if you were too much struck by the princess,' he said, 'or she will guess your object in coming to visit her.'

"The rooms were furnished in excellent taste. Each apartment had a character of its own, as in wealthy English houses; and the silken hangings, the style of the furniture, and the ornaments, even the most trifling, were all subordinated to the original idea. In a gothic boudoir the doors were concealed by tapestried curtains, and the paneling by hangings; the clock and the pattern of the carpet were made to harmonize with the gothic surroundings. The ceiling, with its carved cross-beams of brown wood, was full of charm and originality; the panels were beautifully wrought; nothing disturbed the general harmony of the scheme of decoration, not even the windows with their rich colored glass. I was surprised by the extensive knowledge of decoration that some artist had brought to bear on a little modern room, it was so pleasant and fresh, and not heavy, but subdued with its dead gold hues. It had all the vague sentiment of a German ballad; it was a retreat fit for some romance of 1827, perfumed by the exotic flowers set in their stands. Another apartment in the suite was a gilded reproduction of the Louis Quatorze period, with modern paintings on the walls in odd but pleasant contrast.

"'You would not be so badly lodged,' was Rastignac's slightly sarcastic comment. 'It is captivating, isn't it?' he added, smiling as he sat down. Then suddenly he rose, and led me by the hand into a bedroom, where the softened light fell upon the bed under its canopy of muslin and white watered silk—a couch for a young fairy betrothed to one of the genii.

"'Isn't it wantonly bad taste, insolent and unbounded coquetry,' he said, lowering his voice, 'that allows us to see this throne of love? She gives herself to no one, and anybody may leave his card here. If I were not committed, I should like to see her at my feet all tears and submission.'

" ' Are you so certain of her virtue ? '

" ' The boldest and even the cleverest adventurers among us acknowledge themselves defeated, and continue to be her lovers and devoted friends. Isn't that woman a puzzle ? '

" His words seemed to intoxicate me ; I had jealous fears already of the past. I leaped for joy, and hurried back to the Countess, whom I had seen in the gothic boudoir. She stopped me by a smile, made me sit beside her, and talked about my work, seeming to take the greatest interest in it, and all the more when I set forth my theories amusingly, instead of adopting the formal language of a professor for their explanation. It seemed to divert her to be told that the human will was a material force like steam ; that in the moral world nothing could resist its power if a man taught himself to concentrate it, to economize it, and to project continually its fluid mass in given directions upon other souls. Such a man, I said, could modify all things relatively to man, even the peremptory laws of nature. The questions Fœdora raised showed a certain keenness of intellect. I took a pleasure in deciding some of them in her favor, in order to flatter her ; then I confuted her feminine reasoning with a word, and roused her curiosity by drawing her attention to an every-day matter—to sleep, a thing so apparently commonplace that in reality it is an insoluble problem for science. The Countess sat in silence for a moment when I told her that our ideas were complete organic beings, existing in an invisible world, and influencing our destinies ; and for witnesses I cited the opinions of Descartes, Diderot, and Napoleon, who had directed, and still directed, all the currents of the age.

" So I had the honor of amusing this woman ; she asked me to come to see her when she left me, giving me *les grandes entrées*, in the language of the court. Whether it was by dint of substituting polite formulas for genuine expressions of feeling, a commendable habit of mine, or because Fœdora hailed in me a coming celebrity, an addition to her learned

menagerie; for some reason I thought I had pleased her. I
called all my previous physiological studies and knowledge of
woman to my aid, and minutely scrutinized this singular
person and her ways all the evening. I concealed myself
in the embrasure of a window, and sought to discover her
thoughts from her bearing. I studied the tactics of the
mistress of the house, as she came and went, sat and chatted,
beckoned to this one or that, asked questions, listened to
the answers, as she leaned against the frame of the door;
I detected a languid charm in her movements, a grace in
the flutterings of her dress, remarked the nature of the feel-
ings she so powerfully excited, and became very incredulous
as to her virtue. If Fœdora would none of love to-day, she
had had strong passions at some time; past experience of
pleasure showed itself in the attitudes she chose in conversa-
tion, in her coquettish way of leaning against the panel be-
hind her, she seemed scarcely able to stand alone, and yet
ready for flight from too bold a glance. There was a kind of
eloquence about her lightly folded arms, which, even for
benevolent eyes, breathed sentiment. Her fresh red lips
sharply contrasted with her brilliantly pale complexion. Her
brown hair brought out all the golden color in her eyes, in
which blue streaks mingled as in Florentine marble; their ex-
pression seemed to increase the significance of her words.
A studied grace lay in the charms of her bodice. Perhaps a
rival might have found the lines of the thick eyebrows, which
almost met, a little hard; or found a fault in the almost in-
visible down that covered her features. I saw the signs of
passion everywhere, written on those Italian eyelids, on the
splendid shoulders worthy of the Venus of Milo, on her
features, in the darker shade of down above a somewhat thick
under-lip. She was not merely a woman, but a romance.
The whole blended harmony of lines, the feminine luxuriance
of her frame, and its passionate promise, were subdued by a
constant inexplicable reserve and modesty at variance with

everything else about her. It needed an observation as keen as my own to detect such signs as these in her character. To explain myself more clearly, there were two women in Fœdora, divided perhaps by the line between head and body; the one, the head alone, seemed to be susceptible, and the other phlegmatic. She prepared her glance before she looked at you, something unspeakably mysterious, some inward convulsion seemed revealed by her glittering eyes.

"So, to be brief, either my imperfect moral science had left me a good deal to learn in the moral world, or a lofty soul dwelt in the Countess, lent to her face those charms that fascinated and subdued us, and gave her an ascendancy only the more complete because it comprehended a sympathy of desire.

"I went away completely enraptured with this woman, dazzled by the luxury around her, gratified in every faculty of my soul—noble and base, good and evil. When I felt myself so excited, eager, and elated, I thought I understood the attraction that drew thither those artists, diplomatists, men in office, those stock-jobbers encased in triple brass. They came, no doubt, to find in her society the delirious emotion that now thrilled through every fibre in me, throbbing through my brain, setting the blood a-tingle in every vein, fretting even the tiniest nerve. And she had given herself to none, so as to keep them all. A woman is a coquette so long as she knows not love.

"'Well,' I said to Rastignac, 'they married her, or sold her, perhaps, to some old man, and recollections of her first marriage have caused her aversion for love.'

"I walked home from the Faubourg St. Honoré, where Fœdora lived. Almost all the breadth of Paris lies between her mansion and the Rue des Cordiers, but the distance seemed short, in spite of the cold. And I was to lay siege to Fœdora's heart, in winter, and a bitter winter, with only thirty francs in my possession, and such a distance as that lay between us! Only a poor man knows what such a passion costs in cab-hire, gloves, linen, tailor's bills, and the like. If the Platonic stage lasts a little too long, the affair grows ruinous. As a matter of fact, there is many a Lauzun among students of law, who find it impossible to approach a lady-love living on a first floor. And I, sickly, thin, poorly dressed, wan and pale as any artist convalescent after a work, how could I compete with other young men, curled, handsome, smart, outcravating Croatia; wealthy men, equipped with tilburys, and armed with assurance?

"'Bah, death or Fœdora!' I cried, as I went round by a bridge; 'my fortune lies in Fœdora.'

"That gothic boudoir and Louis Quatorze salon came before my eyes. I saw the Countess again in her white dress with its large graceful sleeves, and all the fascinations of her form and movements. These pictures of Fœdora and her luxurious surroundings haunted me even in my bare, cold garret, when at last I reached it, as disheveled as any naturalist's wig. The contrast suggested evil counsel; in such a way crimes are conceived. I cursed my honest, self-respecting poverty, my garret where such teeming fancies had stirred within me. I trembled with fury, I reproached God, the devil, social conditions, my own father, the whole universe, indeed, with my fate and my misfortunes. I went hungry to bed, muttering ludicrous imprecations, but fully determined to win Fœdora. Her heart was my last ticket in the lottery, my fortune depended upon it.

"I spare you the history of my earlier visits, to reach the drama the sooner. In my efforts to appeal to her, I essayed to engage her intellect and her vanity on my side; in order to secure her love, I gave her any quantity of reasons for increasing her self-esteem; I never left her in a state of indifference; women like emotions at any cost, I gave them to her in plenty; I would rather have had her angry with me than indifferent.

"At first, urged by a strong will and a desire for her love, I assumed a little authority, but my own feelings grew stronger and mastered me; I relapsed into truth, I lost my head, and fell desperately in love.

"I am not very sure what we mean by the word love in our poetry and talk, but I know that I have never found in all the ready rhetorical phrases of Jean Jacques Rousseau, in whose room perhaps I was lodging; nor among the feeble inventions of two centuries of our literature, nor in any picture that Italy has produced, a representation of the feelings that expanded all at once in my double nature. The view of the lake of Bienne, some music of Rossini's, the Madonna of Murillo now in the possession of General Soult, Lescombat's letters, a few sayings scattered through collections of anecdotes; but most of all the prayers of religious ecstatics, and passages in our fables—these things alone have power to carry me back to the divine heights of my first love.

"Nothing expressed in human language, no thought reproducible in color, marble, sound, or articulate speech, could ever render the force, the truth, the completeness, the suddenness with which love awoke in me. To speak of art is to speak of illusion. Love passes through endless transformations before it passes forever into our existence and makes it glow with its own color of flame. The process is imperceptible, and baffles the artist's analysis. Its moans and complaints are tedious to an uninterested spectator. One would need to be very much in love to share the furious transports of Lovelace, as one reads 'Clarissa Harlowe.' Love is like some fresh spring, that leaves its cresses, its gravel bed and flowers, to become first a stream and then a river, changing its aspect and its nature as it flows to plunge itself in some boundless ocean, where restricted natures only find monotony, and where great souls are engulfed in endless contemplation.

"How can I dare to describe the hues of fleeting emotions, the nothings beyond all price, the spoken accents that beggar language, the looks that hold more than all the wealth of poetry? Not one of the mysterious scenes that draw us insensibly nearer and nearer to a woman, but has depths in it which can swallow up all the poetry that ever was written. How can the inner life and mystery that stirs in our souls penetrate through our glozes, when we have not even words to describe the visible and outward mysteries of beauty? What enchantment steeped me for how many hours in unspeakable rapture, filled with the sight of her! What made me happy? I know not. That face of hers overflowed with light at such times; it seemed in some way to glow with it; the outlines of her face, with the scarcely perceptible down on its delicate surface, shone with a beauty belonging to the far-distant horizon that melts into the sunlight. The light of day seemed to caress her as she mingled in it; rather it seemed that the light of her eyes was brighter than the daylight itself; or some shadow passing over that fair face made a kind of change there, altering its hues and its expression. Some thought would often seem to glow on her white brows; her eyes appeared to dilate, and her eyelids trembled; a smile rippled over her features: the living coral of her lips grew full of meaning as they closed and unclosed; an indistinguishable something in her hair made brown shadows on her fair temples: in each new phase Fœdora spoke. Every slight variation in her beauty made a new pleasure for my eyes, disclosed charms my heart had never known before; I tried to read a separate emotion or a hope in every change that passed over her face. This mute converse passed between soul and soul, like sound and answering echo; and the short-lived delights then showered upon me have left indelible impressions behind. Her voice would cause a frenzy in me that I could hardly understand. I could have copied the example of some prince of Lorraine, and held a live coal in the hollow of my hand, if her fingers passed caressingly through my hair the while. I felt no longer mere admiration and desire: I was under the spell; I had met my destiny. When back again under my own roof, I still vaguely saw Fœdora in her own home, and had some indefinable share in her life; if she felt ill, I suffered too. The next day I used to say to her—

"'You were not well yesterday.'

"How often has she not stood before me, called by the power of ecstasy, in the silence of the night! Sometimes she would break in upon me like a ray of light, make me drop my pen, and put science and study to flight in grief and alarm, as she compelled my admiration by the alluring pose I had seen but a short time before. Sometimes I went to seek her in the spirit world, and would bow down to her as to a hope, entreating her to let me hear the silvery sounds of her voice, and I would wake at length in tears.

"Once, when she had promised to go to the theatre with me, she took it suddenly into her head to refuse to go out, and begged me to leave her alone. I was in such despair over the perversity which cost me a day's work, and (if I must confess it) my last shilling as well, that I went alone where she was to have been, desiring to see the play she had wished to see. I had scarcely seated myself when an electric shock went through me. A voice told me, 'She is here!' I looked round, and saw the Countess hidden in the shadow at the back of her box in the first tier. My look did not waver; my eyes saw her at once with incredible clearness; my soul hovered about her life like an insect above its flower. How had my senses received this warning? There is something in these inward tremors that shallow people find astonishing, but the phenomena of our inner consciousness are produced as simply as those of external vision; so I was not surprised, but much vexed. My studies of our mental faculties, so little understood, helped me at any rate to find in my own excitement some living proofs of my theories. There was something exceedingly odd in this combination of lover and man of science, of downright idolatry of a woman with the love of knowledge. The causes of the lover's despair were highly interesting to the man of science; and the exultant lover, on the other hand, put science far away from him in his joy. Fœdora saw me, and grew grave: I annoyed her. I went to her box during the first interval, and, finding her alone, I stayed there. Although we had not spoken of love, I foresaw an explanation. I had not told her my secret, still there was a kind of understanding between us. She used to tell me her plans for amusement, and on the previous evening had asked with friendly eagerness if I meant to call next day. After any witticism of hers, she would give me an inquiring glance, as if she had sought to please me alone by it. She would soothe me if I was vexed: and if she pouted, I had in some sort a right to ask an explanation. Before she would pardon any blunder, she would keep me a suppliant for long. All these things that we so relished were so many lovers' quarrels. What arch grace she threw into it all! and what happiness it was to me!

"But now we stood before each other as strangers, with the close relation between us both suspended. The Countess was glacial: a presentiment of trouble filled me.

"'Will you come home with me?' she said; when the play was over.

"There had been a sudden change in the weather, and sleet was falling in showers as we went out. Fœdora's carriage was unable to reach the doorway of the theatre. At the sight of a well-dressed woman about to cross the street, a commissionaire held an umbrella above us, and stood waiting at the carriage-door for his tip. I would have given ten years of life just then for a couple of halfpence, but I had not a penny. All the man in me and all my vainest susceptibilities were wrung with an infernal pain. The words, 'I haven't a penny about me, my good fellow!' came from me in the hard voice of thwarted passion; and yet I was that man's brother in misfortunes, as I knew too well; and once I had so lightly paid away seven hundred thousand francs! The footman pushed the man aside, and the horses sprang forward! As we returned, Fœdora, in real or feigned abstraction, answered all my questions curtly and by monosyllables. I said no more ; it was a hateful moment. When we reached her house, we seated ourselves by the hearth, and when the servant had stirred the fire and left us alone, the Countess turned to me with an inexplicable expression, and spoke. Her manner was almost solemn.

" 'Since my return to France, more than one young man, tempted by my money, has made proposals to me which would have satisfied my pride. I have come across men, too, whose attachment was so deep and sincere that they might have married me even if they had found me the penniless girl I used to be. Besides these, Monsieur de Valentin, you must know that new titles and newly-acquired wealth have been also offered to me, and that I have never received again any of those who were so ill-advised as to mention love to me. If my regard for you was but slight, I would not give you this warning, which is dictated by friendship rather than by pride. A woman lays herself open to a rebuff of some kind, if she imagines herself to be loved, and declines, before it is uttered, to listen to language which in its nature implies a compliment. I am well acquainted with the parts played by Arsinoe and Araminta, and with the sort of answer I might look for under such circumstances ; but I hope to-day that I shall not find myself mis-construed by a man of no ordinary character, because I have frankly spoken my mind.'

" She spoke with the cool self-possession of some attorney or solicitor explaining the nature of a contract or the conduct of a lawsuit to a client. There was not the least sign of feeling in the clear soft tones of her voice. Her steady face and dignified bearing seemed to me now full of diplomatic reserve and coldness. She had planned this scene, no doubt, and carefully chosen her words beforehand. Oh, my friend, there are women who take pleasure in piercing hearts, and deliberately plunge the dagger back again into the wound ; such women as these cannot but be worshipped, for such women either love or would fain be loved. A day comes when they make amends for all the pain they gave us; they repay us for the pangs, the keenness of which they recognize, in joys a hundredfold, even as God, they tell us, recompenses our good works. Does not their perversity spring from the strength of their feelings? But to be so tortured by a woman, who slaughters you with indifference ! was not the suffering intolerable ?

" Fœdora did not know it, but in that minute she trampled all my hopes beneath her feet ; she maimed my life and she blighted my future with the cool indifference and unconscious barbarity of an inquisitive child who plucks its wings from a butterfly.

" 'Later on,' resumed Fœdora, 'you will learn, I hope, the stability of the affection that I keep for my friends. You will always find that I have devotion and kindness for them. I would give my life to serve my friends ; but you could only despise me, if I allowed them to make love to me without return. That is enough. You are the only man to whom I have spoken such words as these last.'

" At first I could not speak, or master the tempest that arose within me; but I soon repressed my emotions in the depths of my soul, and began to smile.

" 'If I own that I love you,' I said, 'you will banish me at once ; if I plead guilty to indifference you will make me suffer for it. Women, magistrates, and priests never quite lay the gown aside. Silence is non-committal ; be pleased then, madame, to approve my silence. You must have feared, in some degree, to lose me, or I should not have received this friendly admonition ; and with that thought my pride ought to be satisfied. Let us banish all personal considerations. You are perhaps the only woman with whom I could discuss rationally a resolution so contrary to the laws of nature. Considered with regard to your species, you are a prodigy. Now let us investigate, in good faith, the causes of this psychological anomaly. Does there exist in you, as in many women, a certain pride in self, a love of your own loveliness, a refinement of egotism which makes you shudder at the idea of belonging to another; is it the thought of resigning your own will and submitting to a superiority, though only of convention, which displeases you? You would seem to me a thousand times the fairer for it. Can love formerly have brought you suffering? You probably set some value on your dainty figure and graceful appearance, and may perhaps wish to avoid the disfigurements of maternity. Is not this one of your strongest reasons for refusing a too importunate love? Some natural defect perhaps makes you insusceptible in spite of yourself? Do not be angry; my study, my inquiry is absolutely dispassionate. Some are born blind, and nature may easily have formed women who in like manner are blind, deaf, and dumb to love. You are really an interesting subject for medical investigation. You do not know your value. You feel perhaps a very legitimate distaste for mankind; in that I quite concur—to me they all seem ugly and detestable. And you are right,' I added, feeling my heart swell within me; ' how can you do otherwise than despise us? There is not a man living who is worthy of you.'

"I will not repeat all the biting words with which I ridiculed her. In vain; my bitterest sarcasms and keenest irony never made her wince nor elicited a sign of vexation. She heard me, with the customary smile upon her lips and in her eyes, the smile that she wore as a part of her clothing, and that never varied for friends, for mere acquaintances, or for strangers.

"'Isn't it very nice of me to allow you to dissect me like this?' she said at last, as I came to a temporary standstill, and looked at her in silence. 'You see,' she went on, laughing, 'that I have no foolish over-sensitiveness about my friendship. Many a woman would shut her door on you by way of punishing you for your impertinence.'

"'You could banish me without needing to give me the reasons for your harshness.' As I spoke I felt that I could kill her if she dismissed me.

"'You are mad,' she said, smiling still.

"'Did you never think,' I went on, 'of the effects of passionate love? A desperate man has often murdered his mistress.

"'It is better to die than to live in misery,' she said coolly. 'Such a man as that would run through his wife's money, desert her, and leave her at last in utter wretchedness.'

"This calm calculation dumbfounded me. The gulf between us was made plain; we could never understand each other.

"'Good-bye,' I said proudly.

"'Good-bye, till to-morrow,' she answered, with a little friendly bow.

"For a moment's space I hurled at her in a glance all the love I must forego; she stood there with that banal smile of hers, the detestable chill smile of a marble statue, with none of the warmth in it that it seemed to express. Can you form any idea, my friend, of the pain that overcame me on the way home through rain and snow, across a league of icy-sheeted quays, without a hope left? Oh, to think that she not only had not guessed my poverty, but believed me to be as wealthy as she was, and likewise borne as softly over the rough ways of life! What failure and deceit! It was no mere question of money now, but of the fate of all that lay within me.

"I went at haphazard, going over the words of our strange conversation with myself. I got so thoroughly lost in my reflections that I ended by doubts as to the actual value of words and ideas. But I loved her all the same; I loved this woman with the untouched heart that might surrender at any moment—a woman who daily disappointed the expectations of the previous evening, by appearing as a new mistress on the morrow.

"As I passed under the gateway of the Institute, a fevered thrill ran through me. I remembered that I was fasting, and that I had not a penny. To complete the measure of my misfortune, my hat was spoiled by the rain. How was I to appear in the drawing-room of a woman of fashion with an unpresentable hat! I had always cursed the inane and stupid custom that compels us to exhibit the lining of our hats, and to keep them always in our hands, but with anxious care I had so far kept mine in a precarious state of efficiency. It had been neither strikingly new, nor utterly shabby, neither nap-less nor over-glossy, and might have passed for the hat of a frugally given owner; but its artificially prolonged existence had now reached the final stage, it was crumpled, forlorn, and completely ruined, a downright rag, a fitting emblem of its master. My painfully preserved elegance must collapse for want of thirty *sous*.

"What unrecognized sacrifices I had made in the past three months for Fœdora! How often I had given the price of a week's sustenance to see her for a moment! To leave my work and go without food was the least of it! I must traverse the streets of Paris without getting splashed, run to escape showers, and reach her rooms at last, as neat and spruce as any of the coxcombs about her. For a poet and a distracted wooer the difficulties of this task were endless. My happiness, the course of my love, might be affected by a speck of mud upon my only white waistcoat! Oh, to miss the sight of her because I was wet through and bedraggled, and had not so much as five *sous* to give to a shoeblack for removing the least little spot of mud from my boot! The petty pangs of these nameless torments, which an irritable man finds so great, only strengthened my passion.

" The unfortunate must make sacrifices which they may not mention to women who lead refined and luxurious lives. Such women see things through a prism that gilds all men and their surroundings. Egoism leads them to take cheerful views, and fashion makes them cruel; they do not wish to reflect, lest they lose their happiness, and the absorbing nature of their pleasures absolves their indifference to the misfortunes of others. A penny never means millions to them; millions, on the contrary, seem a mere trifle. Perhaps love must plead his cause by great sacrifices, but a veil must be lightly drawn across them, they must go down into silence. So when wealthy men pour out their devotion, their fortunes, and their lives, they gain somewhat by these commonly entertained opinions, an additional lustre hangs about their lovers' follies; their silence is eloquent; there is a grace about the drawn veil; but my terrible distress bound me over to suffer fearfully ere I might speak of my love or of dying for her sake.

" Was it a sacrifice after all? Was I not richly rewarded by the joy I took in sacrificing everything to her? There was no ordinary event of my daily life to which the Countess had not given importance, had not overfilled with happiness. I had been hitherto careless of my clothes, now I respected my coat as if it had been a second self. I should not have hesitated between bodily harm and a tear in that garment. You must enter wholly into my circumstances to understand the stormy thoughts, the gathering frenzy, that shook me as I went, and which, perhaps, were increased by my walk. I gloated in an infernal fashion which I cannot describe over the absolute completeness of my wretchedness. I would have drawn from it an augury of my future, but there is no limit to the possibilities of misfortune. The door of my lodging-house stood ajar. A light streamed from the heart-shaped opening cut in the shutters. Pauline and her mother were sitting up for me and talking. I heard my name spoken and listened.

" ' Raphael is much nicer-looking than the student in number seven,' said Pauline; 'his fair hair is such a pretty color. Don't you think there is something in his voice, too, I don't know what it is, that gives you a sort of thrill? And, then, though he may be a little proud, he is very kind, and he has such fine manners; I am sure that all the ladies must be quite wild about him.'

" 'You might be fond of him yourself, to hear you talk,' was Madame Gaudin's comment.

" 'He is just as dear to me as a brother,' she laughingly replied. 'I should be finely ungrateful if I felt no friendship for him. Didn't he teach me music and drawing and grammar, and everything I know in fact? You don't much notice how I get on, dear mother; but I shall know enough, after a while, to give lessons myself, and then we can keep a servant.'

" I stole away softly, made some noise outside, and went into their room to take the lamp, that Pauline tried to light for me. The dear child had just poured soothing balm into my wounds. Her outspoken admiration had given me fresh courage. I so needed to believe in myself and to come by a just estimate of my advantages. This revival of hope in me perhaps colored my surroundings. Perhaps, also, I had never before really looked at the picture that so often met my eyes, of the two women in their room; it was a scene such as Flemish painters have reproduced so faithfully for us, that I admired it in its delightful reality. The mother, with the kind smile upon her lips, sat knitting stockings by the dying fire; Pauline was painting hand-screens, her brushes and paints, strewn over the tiny table, made bright spots of color for the eye to dwell on. When she had left her seat and stood lighting my lamp, one must have been under the yoke of a terrible passion, indeed, not to admire her faintly flushed transparent hands, the girlish charm of her attitude, the ideal grace of her head, as the lamplight fell full on her pale face. Night and silence added to the charms of this industrious vigil and peaceful interior. The light-heartedness that sustained such continuous toil could only spring from devout submission and the lofty feelings that it brings.

" There was an indescribable harmony between them and their possessions. The splendor of Fœdora's home did not satisfy; it called out all my worst instincts; something in this lowly poverty and unfeigned goodness revived me. It may have been that luxury abased me in my own eyes, while here my self-respect was restored to me, as I sought to extend the protection that a man is so eager to make felt, over these two women, who in the bare simplicity of the existence in their brown room seemed to live wholly in the feelings of their hearts. As I came up to Pauline, she looked at me in an almost motherly way; her hands shook a little as she held the lamp, so that the light fell on me, and cried—

"'Dieu! how pale you are! and you are wet through! My mother will try to wipe you dry. Monsieur Raphael,' she went on, after a little pause, ' you are so very fond of milk, and to-night we happen to have some cream. Here, will you not take some?'

" She pounced like a kitten, on a china bowl full of milk. She did it so quickly, and put it before me so prettily, that I hesitated.

" 'You are going to refuse me?' she said, and her tones changed.

" The pride in each felt for the other's pride. It was Pauline's poverty that seemed to humiliate her, and to re- proach me with want of consideration, and I melted at once, and accepted the cream that might have been meant for her morning's breakfast. The poor child tried not to show her joy, but her eyes sparkled.

" 'I needed it badly,' I said as I sat down. (An anxious look passed over her face.) ' Do you remember that pass- age, Pauline, where Bossuet tells how God gives more abun- dant reward for a cup of cold water than for a vic- tory?'

" ' Yes,' she said, her heart beating like some wild bird's in a child's hands.

" ' Well, as we shall part very soon, now,' I went on in an unsteady voice, ' you must let me show my gratitude to you and to your mother for all the care you have taken of me.'

" ' Oh, don't let us cast accounts,' she said, laughing. But her laughter covered an agitation that gave me pain. I went on without appearing to hear her words—

" ' My piano is one of Erard's best instruments ; and you must take it. Pray accept it without hesitation ; I really could not take it with me on the journey I am about to make.'

" Perhaps the melancholy tones in which I spoke enlightened the two women, for they seemed to understand, and eyed me with curiosity and alarm. Here was the affection that I had looked for in the glacial regions of the great world, true affection, unostentatious but tender, and possibly lasting.

" ' Don't take it to heart so,' the mother said ; ' stay on here. My husband is on his way towards us even now,' she went on. ' I looked into the Gospel of St. John this evening while Pauline hung our door-key in a Bible from her fingers. The key turned ; that means that Gaudin is in health and doing well. Pauline began again for you and for the young man in number seven—it turned for you, but not for him. We are all going to be rich. Gaudin will come back a millionaire. I dreamed once that I saw him in a ship full of serpents ; luckily the water was rough, and that means gold or precious stones from over-sea.'

" The silly, friendly words were like the crooning lullaby with which a mother soothes her sick child ; they in a manner calmed me. There was a pleasant heartiness in the worthy woman's looks and tones, which, if it could not remove trouble, at any rate soothed and quieted it, and deadened the pain. Pauline, keener-sighted than her mother, studied me uneasily ; her quick eyes seemed to read my life and my future. I thanked the mother and daughter by an inclination of the head, and turned away; I was afraid I should break down.

"I found myself alone under my roof, and laid myself down in my misery. My unhappy imagination suggested numberless baseless projects, and prescribed impossible resolutions. When a man is struggling in the wreck of his fortunes, he is not quite without resources, but I was engulfed. Ah, my dear fellow, we are too ready to blame the wretched. Let us be less harsh on the results of the most powerful of all social solvents. Where poverty is absolute there exist no such things as shame or crime, or virtue or intelligence. I knew not what to do; I was as defenceless as a maiden on her knees before a beast of prey. A penniless man who has no ties to bind him is master of himself at any rate, but a luckless wretch who is in love no longer belongs to himself, and may not take his own life. Love makes us almost sacred in our own eyes; it is the life of another that we revere within us then; and so begins for us the cruellest trouble of all—the misery with a hope in it, a hope for which we must even bear our torments. I thought I would go to Rastignac on the morrow to confide Fœdora's strange resolution to him, and with that I slept.

"'Ah, ha!' cried Rastignac, as he saw me enter his lodging at nine o'clock in the morning. 'I know what brings you here. Fœdora has dismissed you. Some kind souls, who were jealous of your ascendency over the Countess, gave out that you were going to be married. Heaven only knows what follies your rivals have equipped you with, and what slanders have been directed at you.'

"'That explains everything!' I exclaimed. I remembered all my presumptuous speeches, and gave the Countess credit for no little magnanimity. It pleased me to think that I was a miscreant who had not been punished nearly enough, and I saw nothing in her indulgence but the long-suffering charity of love.

" ' Not quite so fast,' urged the prudent Gascon ; 'Fœdora has all the sagacity natural to a profoundly selfish woman ; perhaps she may have taken your measure while you still coveted only her money and her splendor ; in spite of all your care, she could have read you through and through. She can dissemble far too well to let any dissimulation pass undetected. I fear,' he went on, ' that I have brought you into a bad way. In spite of her cleverness and her tact, she seems to me a domineering sort of person, like every woman who can only feel pleasure through her brain. Happiness for her lies entirely in a comfortable life and in social pleasures ; her sentiment is only assumed ; she will make you miserable ; you will be her head footman.'

" He spoke to the deaf. I broke in upon him, disclosing, with an affectation of light-heartedness, the state of my finances.

" ' Yesterday evening,' he rejoined, ' luck ran against me, and that carried off all my available cash. But for that trivial mishap, I would gladly have shared my purse with you. But let us go and breakfast at the restaurant ; perhaps there is good counsel in oysters.'

" He dressed, and had his tilbury brought round. We went to the Café de Paris like a couple of millionaires, armed with all the audacious impertinence of the speculator whose capital is imaginary. That devil of a Gascon quite disconcerted me by the coolness of his manners and his absolute self-possession. While we were taking coffee after an excellent and well-ordered repast, a young dandy entered, who did not escape Rastignac. He had been nodding here and there among the crowd to this or that young man, distinguished both by personal attractions and elegant attire, and now he said to me—

" ' Here's your man,' as he beckoned to this gentleman with a wonderful cravat, who seemed to be looking for a table that suited his ideas.

9

"'That rogue has been decorated for bringing out books that he doesn't understand a word of,' whispered Rastignac; 'he is a chemist, a historian, a novelist, and a political writer; he has gone halves, thirds, or quarters in the authorship of I don't know how many plays, and he is as ignorant as Dom Miguel's mule. He is not a man so much as a name, a label that the public is familiar with. So he would do well to avoid shops inscribed with the motto, "*Ici l'on peut écrire soi-même.*"* He is acute enough to deceive an entire congress of diplomatists. In a couple of words, he is a moral half-caste, not quite a fraud, nor entirely genuine. But, hush! he has succeeded already; nobody asks anything further, and every one calls him an illustrious man.'

"'Well, my esteemed and excellent friend, and how may your intelligence be?' So Rastignac addressed the stranger as he sat down at a neighboring table.

"'Neither well nor ill; I am overwhelmed with work. I have all the necessary materials for some very curious historical memoirs in my hands, and I cannot find any one to whom I can ascribe them. It worries me, for I shall have to be quick about it. Memoirs are falling out of fashion.'

"'What are the memoirs—contemporaneous, ancient, or memoirs of the court, or what?'

"'They relate to the Necklace affair.'

"'Now, isn't that a coincidence?' said Rastignac, turning to me and laughing. He looked again to the literary speculator, and said, indicating me—

"'This is M. de Valentin, one of my friends, whom I must introduce to you as one of our future literary celebrities. He had formerly an aunt, a marquise, much in favor once at court, and for about two years he has been writing a Royalist history of the Revolution.'

"Then, bending over this singular man of business, he went on—

* "Here one may compose himself."

" ' He is a man of talent, and a simpleton that will do your memoirs for you, in his aunt's name, for a hundred crowns a volume.'

" ' It's a bargain,' said the other, adjusting his cravat. ' Waiter, my oysters.'

" ' Yes, but you must give me twenty-five louis as commission, and you will pay him in advance for each volume,' said Rastignac.

" ' No, no. He shall only have fifty crowns on account, and then I shall be sure of having my manuscript punctually.'

" Rastignac repeated this business conversation to me in low tones; and then, without giving me any voice in the matter, he replied—

" ' We agree to your proposal. When can we call upon you to arrange the affair?'

" ' Oh, well! Come and dine here to-morrow at seven o'clock.'

" We rose. Rastignac flung some money to the waiter, put the bill in his pocket, and we went out. I was quite stupefied by the flippancy and ease with which he had sold my venerable aunt, la Marquise de Montbauron.

" ' I would sooner take ship for the Brazils, and give the Indians lessons in algebra, though I don't know a word of it, than tarnish my family name.'

" Rastignac burst out laughing.

" ' How dense you are! Take the fifty crowns in the first instance, and write the memoirs. When you have finished them, you will decline to publish them in your aunt's name, imbecile! Madame de Montbauron, with her hooped petticoat, her rank and beauty, rouge and slippers, and her death upon the scaffold, is worth a great deal more than six hundred francs. And then, if the trade will not give your aunt her due, some old adventurer, or some shady countess or other, will be found to put her name to the memoirs.'

" ' Oh,' I groaned; ' why did I quit the blameless life in

my garret? This world has aspects that are very vilely dis-
honorable.'

"'Yes,' said Rastignac, "that is all very poetical, but this
is a matter of business. What a child you are! Now, listen
to me. As to your work, the public will decide upon it; and
as for my literary middle-man, hasn't he devoted eight years
of his life to obtaining a footing in the book-trade, and paid
heavily for his experience? You divide the money and the
labor of the book with him very unequally, but isn't yours the
better part? Twenty-five louis means as much to you as a
thousand francs does to him. Come, you can write historical
memoirs, a work of art such as never was, since Diderot once
wrote six sermons for a hundred crowns?'

"'After all,' I said, in agitation, 'I cannot choose but do
it. So, my dear friend, my thanks are due to you. I shall
be quite rich with twenty-five louis.'

"'Richer than you think,' he laughed. 'If I have my com-
mission from Finot in this matter, it goes to you, can't you
see? Now let us go to the Bois de Boulogne,' he said; 'we
shall see your Countess there, and I will show you the pretty
little widow that I am to marry—a charming woman, an
Alsacienne, rather plump. She reads Kant, Schiller, Jean
Paul, and a host of lachrymose books. She has a mania for
continually asking my opinion, and I have to look as if I
entered into all this German sensibility, and to know a pack
of ballads—drugs, all of them, that my doctor absolutely
prohibits. As yet I have not been able to wean her from her
literary enthusiasms; she sheds torrents of tears as she reads
Goethe, and I have to weep a little myself to please her, for
she has an income of fifty thousand livres, my dear boy, and
the prettiest little hand and foot in the world. Oh, if she
would only say my angel and grumbler instead of my flute
and my fumbler, she would be perfection!'

"We saw the Countess, radiant amid the splendors of her
equipage. The coquette bowed very graciously to us both,

and the smile she gave me seemed to me to be divine and full of love. I was very happy; I fancied myself beloved; I had money, a wealth of love in my heart, and my troubles were over. I was light-hearted, blithe, and content. I found my friend's lady-love charming. Earth and air and heaven—all nature—seemed to reflect Fœdora's smile for me.

"As we returned through the Champs-Elyseés, we paid a visit to Rastignac's hatter and tailor. Thanks to the 'Necklace,' my insignificant peace-footing was to end, and I made formidable preparations for a campaign. Henceforward I need not shrink from a contest with the spruce and fashionable young men who made Fœdora's circle. I went home, locked myself in, and stood by my dormer window, outwardly calm enough, but in reality I bade a last good-bye to the roofs without. I began to live in the future, rehearsed my life drama, and discounted love and its happiness. Ah, how stormy life can grow to be within the four walls of a garret! The soul within us is like a fairy; she turns straw into diamonds for us; and for us, at a touch of her wand, enchanted palaces arise, as flowers in the meadows spring up towards the sun.

"Towards noon, next day, Pauline knocked gently at my door, and brought me—who could guess it?—a note from Fœdora. The Countess asked me to take her to the Luxembourg, and to go thence to see with her the Museum and Jardin des Plantes.

"'The man is waiting for an answer,' said Pauline, after quietly waiting for a moment.

"I hastily scrawled my acknowledgments, and Pauline took the note. I changed my dress. When my toilette was ended, and I looked at myself with some complaisance, an icy shiver ran through me as I thought—

"'Will Fœdora walk or drive? Will it rain or shine?—No matter, though,' I said to myself; 'whichever it is, can one ever reckon with feminine caprice! She will have no

money about her, and will want to give a dozen francs to some
little Savoyard because his rags are picturesque.'

"I had not a brass farthing, and should have no money till
the evening came. How dearly a poet pays for the intellec-
tual prowess that method and toil have brought him, at such
crises of our youth! Innumerable painfully vivid thoughts
pierced me like barbs. I looked out of my window; the
weather was very unsettled. If things fell out badly, I might
easily have a cab for the day; but would not the fear lie on
me every moment that I might not meet Finot in the evening?
I felt too weak to endure such fears in the midst of my felicity.
Though I felt sure that I should find nothing, I began a grand
search through my room; I looked for imaginary coins in the
recesses of 'my mattress; I hunted about everywhere—I even
shook out my old boots. A nervous fever seized me; I
looked with wild eyes at the furniture when I had ransacked
it all. Will you understand, I wonder, the excitement that
possessed me when, plunged deep in the listlessness of de-
spair, I opened my writing-table drawer, and found a fair and
splendid ten-franc piece that shone like a rising star, new and
sparkling, and slily hiding in a cranny between two boards?
I did not try to account for its previous reserve and the cruelty
of which it had been guilty in thus lying hidden; I kissed it
for a friend faithful in adversity, and hailed it with a cry that
found an echo, and made me turn sharply, to find Pauline
with a face grown white.

"'I thought,' she faltered, 'that you had hurt yourself!
The man who brought the letter——' (she broke off as if
something smothered her voice). 'But mother has paid him,'
she added, and flitted away like a wayward, capricious child.
Poor little one! I wanted her to share my happiness. I
seemed to have all the happiness in the world within me just
then; and I would fain have returned to the unhappy, all that
I felt as if I had stolen from them.

"The intuitive perception of adversity is sound for the

most part ; the Countess had sent away her carriage. One
of those freaks that pretty women can scarcely explain to
themselves had determined her to go on foot, by way of the
boulevards, to the Jardin des Plantes.

"'It will rain,' I told her, and it pleased her to contra-
dict me.

"As it fell out, the weather was fine while we went through
the Luxembourg ; when we came out, some drops fell from a
great cloud, whose progress I had watched uneasily, and we
took a cab. At the Museum I was about to dismiss the vehi-
cle, and Fœdora (what agonies !) asked me not to do so. But
it was like a dream in broad daylight for me, to chat with
her, to wander in the Jardin des Plantes, to stray down the
shady alleys, to feel her hand upon my arm ; the secret trans-
ports repressed in me were reduced, no doubt, to a fixed and
foolish smile upon my lips ; there was something unreal about
it all. Yet in all her movements, however alluring, whether we
stood or whether we walked, there was nothing either tender
or lover-like. When I tried to share in a measure the action
of movement prompted by her life, I became aware of a
check, or of something strange in her that I cannot explain,
of an inner activity concealed in her nature. There is no
suavity about the movements of women who have no soul
in them. Our wills were opposed, and we did not keep step
together. Words are wanting to describe this outward dis-
sonance between two beings ; we are not accustomed to read
a thought in a movement. We instinctively feel this phe-
nomenon of our nature, but it cannot be expressed.

"I did not dissect my sensations during those violent
seizures of passion," Raphael went on, after a moment of
silence, as if he were replying to an objection raised by him-
self. "I did not analyze my pleasures nor count my heart-
beats then, as a miser scrutinizes and weighs his gold-pieces.
No ; experience sheds its melancholy light over the events of
the past to-day, and memory brings these pictures back, as

the sea-waves in fair weather cast up fragment after fragment of the débris of a wrecked vessel upon the strand.

"'It is in your power to render me a rather important service,' said the Countess, looking at me in an embarrassed way. 'After confiding to you my aversion for lovers, I feel myself more at liberty to entreat your good offices in the name of friendship. Will there not be very much more merit in obliging me to-day?' she asked, laughing.

"I looked at her in anguish. Her manner was coaxing, but in no wise affectionate; she felt nothing for me; she seemed to be playing a part, and I thought her a consummate actress. Then all at once my hopes awoke once more, at a single look and word. Yet if reviving love expressed itself in my eyes, she bore its light without any change in the clearness of her own; they seemed, like a tiger's eyes, to have a sheet of metal behind them. I used to hate her in such moments.

"'The influence of the Duc de Navarreins would be very useful to me, with an all-powerful person in Russia,' she went on, persuasion in every modulation of her voice, 'whose intervention I need in order to have justice done me in a matter that concerns both my fortune and my position in the world, that is to say, the recognition of my marriage by the Emperor. Is not the Duc de Navarreins a cousin of yours? A letter from him would settle everything.

"'I am yours,' I answered; 'command me.'

"'You are very nice,' she said, pressing my hand. 'Come and have dinner with me, and I will tell you everything, as if you were my confessor.'

"So this discreet, suspicious woman, who had never been heard to speak a word about her affairs to any one, was going to consult me.

"'Oh, how dear to me is this silence that you have imposed on me!' I cried, 'but I would rather have had some sharper ordeal still.' And she smiled upon the intoxication in my eyes ; she did not reject my admiration in any way ; surely she loved me !

" Fortunately, my purse held just enough to satisfy the cabman. The day spent in her house, alone with her, was delicious ; it was the first time that I had seen her in this way. Hitherto we had always been kept apart by the presence of others, and by her formal politeness and reserved manners, even during her magnificent dinners ; but now it was as if I lived beneath her own roof—I had her all to myself, so to speak. My wandering fancy broke down barriers, arranged the events of life to my liking, and steeped me in happiness and love. I seemed to myself her husband, I liked to watch her busied with little details ; it was a pleasure to me even to see her take off her bonnet and shawl. She left me alone for a while, and came back, charming, with her hair newly arranged ; and this dainty change of toilette had been made for me !

" During the dinner she lavished attention upon me, and put charm without end into those numberless trifles to all seeming, that make up half of our existence nevertheless. As we sat together before a crackling fire, on silken cushions, surrounded by the most desirable creations of Oriental luxury ; as I saw this woman whose famous beauty made every heart beat, so close to me ; an unapproachable woman who was talking and bringing all her powers of coquetry to bear upon me ; then my blissful pleasure rose almost to the point of suffering. To my vexation, I recollected the important business to be concluded ; I determined to go to keep the appointment made for me for this evening.

" ' So soon ? ' she said, seeing me take my hat.

" She loved me, then ! or I thought so at least, from the bland tones in which those two words were uttered. I would then have bartered a couple of years of life for every hour she chose to grant me, and so prolong my ecstasy. My happiness was increased by the extent of the money I sacrificed. It was midnight before she dismissed me.   But on the morrow, for all that, my heroism cost me a good many remorseful pangs; I was afraid the affair of the memoirs, now of such importance for me, might have fallen through, and rushed off to Rastignac.   We found the nominal author of my future labors just getting up.

"Finot read over a brief agreement to me, in which nothing whatever was said about my aunt, and when it had been signed he paid me down fifty crowns, and the three of us breakfasted together.   I had only thirty francs left over, when I had paid for my new hat, for sixty tickets at thirty sous each, and settled my debts ; but for some days to come the difficulties of living were removed.   If I had but listened to Rastignac, I might have had abundance by frankly adopting the ' English system.'   He really wanted to establish my credit by setting me to raise loans, on the theory that borrowing is the basis of credit.   To hear him talk, the future was the largest and most secure kind of capital in the world.   My future luck was hypothecated for the benefit of my creditors, and he gave my custom to his tailor, an artist, and a young man's tailor, who was to leave me in peace until I married.

"The monastic life of study that I had led for three years past ended on this day.   I frequented Fœdora's house very diligently, and tried to outshine the heroes or the swaggerers to be found in her circle.   When I believed that I had left poverty forever · behind me, I regained my freedom of mind, humiliated my rivals, and was looked upon as a very attractive, dazzling, and irresistible sort of man.   But acute folks used to say with regard to me, 'A fellow as clever as that will keep all his enthusiasms in his brain,' and charitably extolled my faculties at the expense of my feelings.   'Isn't he lucky not to be in love !' they exclaimed.   'If he were could he be so light-hearted and animated !'   Yet in Fœdora's presence I was as dull as love could make me.   When I was alone with

her I had not a word to say, or if I did speak I renounced
love; and I affected gaiety but ill, like a courtier who has a
a bitter mortification to hide. I tried in every way to make
myself indispensable in her life, and necessary to her vanity
and to her comfort; I was a plaything at her pleasure, a slave
always at her side. And when I had frittered away the day
in this way, I went back to my work at night, securing merely
two or three hours' sleep in the early morning.

"But I had not, like Rastignac, the 'English system' at
my finger-ends, and I very soon saw myself without a penny.
I fell at once into that precarious way of life which industri-
ously hides cold and miserable depths beneath an elusive sur-
face of luxury; I was a coxcomb without conquests, a penni-
less fop, a nameless gallant. The old sufferings were renewed,
but less sharply; no doubt I was growing used to the painful
crises. Very often my sole diet consisted of the scanty pro-
vision of cakes and tea that is offered in drawing-rooms, or
one of the Countess' great dinners must sustain me for two
whole days. I used all my time, and exerted every effort and
all my powers of observation, to penetrate the imperturbable
character of Fœdora. Alternate hope and despair had swayed
my opinions; for me she was sometimes the tenderest, some-
times the most unfeeling of women. But these transitions
from joy to sadness became unendurable; I sought to end the
horrible conflict within me by extinguishing love. By the
light of warning gleams my soul sometimes recognized the
gulfs that lay between us. The Countess confirmed all my fears;
I had never yet detected any tear in her eyes; an affecting
scene in a play left her smiling and unmoved. All her instincts
were selfish; she could not divine another's joy or sorrow.
She had made a fool of me, in fact.

"I had rejoiced over a sacrifice to make for her, and almost
humiliated myself in seeking out my kinsman, the Duc de
Navarreins, a selfish man who was ashamed of my poverty,
and had injured me too deeply not to hate me. He received

me with the polite coldness that makes every word and gesture
seem an insult; he looked so ill at ease that I pitied him.   I
blushed for this pettiness amid grandeur, and penuriousness
surrounded by luxury.   He began to talk to me of his heavy
losses in the three per cents., and then I told him the object
of my visit.   The change in his manners, hitherto glacial,
which now gradually became affectionate, disgusted me.

"Well, he called upon the Countess, and completely eclipsed
me with her.

"On him Fœdora exercised spells and witcheries unheard
of; she drew him into her power, and arranged her whole
mysterious business with him; I was left out, I heard not a
word of it; she had made a tool of me!   She did not seem
to be aware of my existence while my cousin was present;
she received me less cordially perhaps than when I was first
presented to her.   One evening she chose to mortify me before
the Duke by a look, a gesture, that it is useless to try to ex-
press in words.   I went away with tears in my eyes, planning
terrible and outrageous schemes of vengeance without end.

"I often used to go with her to the theatre.   Love utterly
absorbed me as I sat beside her; as I looked at her I used to
give myself up to the pleasure of listening to the music, put-
ting all my soul into the double joy of love and of hearing
every emotion of my heart translated into musical cadences.
It was my passion that filled the air and the stage, that was
triumphant everywhere, but with my mistress.   Then I would
take Fœdora's hand.   I used to scan her features and her
eyes, imploring of them some indication that one blended
feeling possessed us both, seeking for the sudden harmony
awakened by the power of music, which makes our souls vibrate
in unison; but her hand was passive, her eyes said nothing.

"When the fire that burned in me glowed too fiercely from
the face I turned upon her, she met it with that studied smile
of hers, the conventional expression that sits on the lips of
every portrait in every exhibition.   She was not listening to

the music. The divine pages of Rossini, Cimarosa, or Zingarelli called up no emotion, gave no voice to any poetry in her life; her soul was a desert.

" Fœdora presented herself as a drama before a drama. Her lorgnette traveled restlessly over the boxes; she was restless too beneath the apparent calm; fashion tyrannized over her; her box, her bonnet, her carriage, her own personality absorbed her entirely. My merciless knowledge thoroughly tore away all my illusions. If good breeding consists in self-forgetfulness and consideration for others, in constantly showing gentleness in voice and bearing, in pleasing others, and in making them content in themselves, all traces of her plebeian origin were not yet obliterated in Fœdora, in spite of her cleverness. Her self-forgetfulness was a sham, her manners were not innate but painfully acquired, her politeness was rather subservient. And yet for those she singled out, her honeyed words expressed natural kindness, her pretentious exaggeration was exalted enthusiasm. I alone had scrutinized her grimacings, and stripped away the thin rind that sufficed to conceal her real nature from the world; her trickery no longer deceived me; I had sounded the depths of that feline nature. I blushed for her when some donkey or other flattered and complimented her. And yet I loved her through it all! I hoped that her snows would melt with the warmth of a poet's love. If I could only have made her heart capable of a woman's tenderness, if I could have made her feel all the greatness that lies in devotion, then I should have seen her perfected, she would have been an angel. I loved her as a man, a lover, and an artist; if it had been necessary not to love her so that I might win her, some cool-headed coxcomb, some self-possessed calculator would perhaps have had the advantage over me. She was so vain and sophisticated, that the language of vanity would appeal to her; she would have allowed herself to be taken in the toils of an intrigue; a hard, cold nature would have gained a complete ascendency over her. Keen grief had pierced me to my very soul, as she unconsciously revealed her absolute love of self. I seemed to see her as she one day would be, alone in the world, with no one to whom she could stretch her hand, with no friendly eyes for her own to meet and rest upon. I was bold enough to set this before her one evening; I painted in vivid colors her lonely, sad, deserted old age. Her comment on this prospect of so terrible a revenge of thwarted nature was horrible.

"'I shall always have money,'' she said; 'and with money we can always inspire such sentiments as are necessary for our comfort in those about us.'

" I went away confounded by the arguments of luxury, by the reasoning of this woman, of the world in which she lived; and blamed myself for my infatuated idolatry. I myself had not loved Pauline because she was poor; and had not the wealthy Fœdora a right to repulse Raphael? Conscience is our unerring judge until we finally stifle it. A specious voice said within me, ' Fœdora is neither attracted to nor repulses any one ; she has her liberty, but once upon a time she sold herself to the Russian count, her husband or her lover, for gold. But temptation is certain to enter into her life. Wait till that moment comes ! ' She lived remote from humanity, in a sphere apart, in a hell or a heaven of her own ; she was neither frail nor virtuous. This feminine enigma in embroideries and cashmeres had brought into play every emotion of the human heart in me—pride, ambition, love, curiosity.

" There was a craze just then for praising a play at a little Boulevard theatre, prompted perhaps by a wish to appear original that besets us all, or due to some freak of fashion. The Countess showed some signs of a wish to see the floured face of the actor who had so delighted several people of taste, and I obtained the honor of taking her to a first representation of some wretched farce or other. A box scarcely cost five francs, but I had not a brass farthing. I was but halfway through the volume of memoirs; I dared not beg for assistance of Finot, and Rastignac, my providence, was away. These constant perplexities were the bane of my life.

" We had once come out of the theatre when it was raining heavily ; Fœdora had called a cab for me before I could escape from her show of concern ; she would not admit any of my excuses—my liking for wet weather, and my wish to go to the gaming-table. She did not read my poverty in my embarrassed attitude, nor in my forced jests. My eyes would redden, but she did not understand a look. A young man's life is at the mercy of the strangest whims ! At every revolution of the wheels during the journey, thoughts that burned stirred in my heart. I tried to pull up a plank from the bottom of the vehicle, hoping to slip through the hole into the street; but finding insuperable obstacles I burst into a fit of laughter, and then sat stupefied in calm dejection, like a man in the pillory. When I reached my lodging, Pauline broke in through my first stammering words with—

" ' If you haven't any money——? '

" Ah, the music of Rossini was as nothing compared with those words. But to return to the performance at the Funambules.

" I thought of pawning the circlet of gold round my mother's portrait in order to escort the Countess. Although the pawnbroker loomed in my thoughts as one of the doors of a convinct's prison, I would rather myself have carried my bed thither than have begged for alms. There is something so painful in the expression of a man who asks money of you ! There are loans that mulct us of our self-respect, just as some rebuffs from a friend's lips sweep away our last illusion.

" Pauline was working ; her mother had gone to bed. I flung a stealthy glance over the bed ; the curtains were drawn back a little ; Madame Gaudin was in a deep sleep, I thought, when I saw her quiet, sallow profile outlined against the pillow.

"'You are in trouble?' Pauline said, dipping her brush into the coloring.

"'It is in your power to do me a great service, my dear child,' I answered.

"The gladness in her eyes frightened me.

"'Is it possible that she loves me?' I thought. 'Pauline,' I began. I went and sat near to her, so as to study her. My tones had been so searching that she read my thought; her eyes fell, and I scrutinized her face. It was so pure and frank that I fancied I could see as clearly into her heart as into my own.

"'Do you love me?' I asked.

"'A little,—passionately—not a bit,' she cried.

"Then she did not love me. Her jesting tones, and a little gleeful movement that escaped her, expressed nothing beyond a girlish, blithe goodwill. I told her about my distress and the predicament in which I found myself, and asked her to help me.

"'You do not wish to go to the pawnbroker's yourself, M. Raphael,' she answered, 'and yet you would send me!'

"I blushed in confusion at the child's reasoning. She took my hand in hers as if she wanted to compensate for this home-truth by her light touch upon it.

"'Oh, I would willingly go,' she said, 'but it is not necessary. I found two five-franc pieces at the back of the piano, that had slipped without your knowledge between the frame and the keyboard, and I laid them on your table.'

"'You will soon be coming into some money, M. Raphael,' said the kind mother, showing her face between the curtains, 'and I can easily lend you a few crowns meanwhile.'

"'Oh, Pauline!' I cried, as I pressed her hand, 'how I wish that I were rich!'

"'Bah! why should you?' she said petulantly. Her hand shook in mine with the throbbing of her pulse; she snatched it away, and looked at both of mine.

"' You will marry a rich wife,' she said, ' but she will give you a great deal of trouble. Ah, Dieu! she will be your death,—I am sure of it.'

" In her exclamation there was something like belief in her mother's absurd superstitions.

"' You are very credulous, Pauline!'

"' The woman whom you will love is going to kill you—there is no doubt of it,' she said, looking at me with alarm.

" She took up her brush again and dipped it in the color; her great agitation was evident; she looked at me no longer. I was ready to give credence just then to superstitious fancies; no man is utterly wretched so long as he is superstitious; a belief of that kind is often in reality a hope.

" I found that those two magnificent five-franc pieces were lying, in fact, upon my table when I reached my room. During the first confused thoughts of early slumber, I tried to audi⁺ my accounts so as to explain this unhoped-for windfall; but I lost myself in useless calculations, and slept. Just as I was leaving my room to engage a box the next morning, Pauline came to see me.

"' Perhaps your ten francs is not enough,' said the amiable, kind-hearted girl; ' my mother told me to offer you this money. Take it, please, take it!'

" She laid three crowns upon the table, and tried to escape, but I would not let her go. Admiration dried the tears that sprang to my eyes.

"' You are an angel, Pauline,' I said. ' It is not the loan that touches me so much as the delicacy with which it is offered. I used to wish for a rich wife, a fashionable woman of rank; and now, alas! I would rather possess millions, and find some girl, as poor as you are, with a generous nature like your own; and I would renounce a fatal passion which will kill me. Perhaps what you told me will come true.'

"' That is enough,' she said, and fled away; the fresh trills of her bird-like voice rang up the staircase.'

10

"'She is very happy in not yet knowing love,' I said to myself, thinking of the torments I had endured for many months past.

"Pauline's fifteen francs were invaluable to me. Fœdora, thinking of the stifling odor of the crowded place where we were to spend several hours, was sorry that she had not brought a bouquet; I went in search of flowers for her, as I had laid already my life and my fate at her feet. With a pleasure in which compunction mingled, I gave her a bouquet. I learned from its price the extravagance of superficial gallantry in the world. But very soon she complained of the heavy scent of a Mexican jessamine. The interior of the theatre, the bare bench on which she was to sit, filled her with intolerable disgust; she upbraided me for bringing her there. Although she sat beside me, she wished to go, and she went. I had spent sleepless nights, and squandered two months of my life for her, and I could not please her. Never had that tormenting spirit been more unfeeling or more fascinating.

"I sat beside her in the cramped back seat of the vehicle; all the way I could feel her breath on me and the contact of her perfumed glove; I saw distinctly all her exceeding beauty; I inhaled a vague scent of orris-root; so wholly a woman she was, with no touch of womanhood. Just then a sudden gleam of light lit up the depths of this mysterious life for me. I thought all at once of a book just published by a poet, a genuine conception of the artist, in the shape of the statue of Polycletus.

"I seemed to see that monstrous creation, at one time an officer, breaking in a spirited horse; at another, a girl, who gives herself up to her toilette and breaks her lovers' hearts; or, again, a false lover driving a timid and gentle maid to despair. Unable to analyze Fœdora by any other process, I told her this fanciful story; but no hint of her resemblance to this poetry of the impossible crossed her—it simply diverted her; she was like a child over a story from the 'Arabian Nights.'

"'Fœdora must be shielded by some talisman,' I thought to myself as I went back, 'or she could not resist the love of a man of my age, the infectious fever of that splendid malady of the soul. Is Fœdora, like Lady Delacour, a prey to a cancer? Her life is certainly an unnatural one.'

"I shuddered at the thought. Then I decided on a plan, at once the wildest and the most rational that lover ever dreamed of. I would study this woman from a physical point of view, as I had already studied her intellectually, and to this end I made up my mind to spend a night in her room without her knowledge. This project preyed upon me as a thirst for revenge gnaws at the heart of a Corsican monk. This is how I carried it out. On the days when Fœdora received, her rooms were far too crowded for the hall-porter to keep the balance even between goers and comers; I could remain in the house, I felt sure, without causing a scandal in it, and I waited the Countess' coming soirée with impatience. As I dressed I put a little English penknife into my waistcoat pocket, instead of a poniard. That literary implement, if found upon me, could awaken no suspicion, but I knew not whither my romantic resolution might lead, and I wished to be prepared.

"As soon as the rooms began to fill, I entered the bedroom and examined the arrangements. The inner and outer shutters were closed; this was a good beginning; and as the waiting-maid might come to draw back the curtains that hung over the windows, I pulled them together. I was running great risks in venturing to manœuvre beforehand in this way, but I had accepted the situation, and had deliberately reckoned with its dangers.

"About midnight I hid myself in the embrasure of the window. I tried to scramble on to a ledge of the wainscoting, hanging on by the fastening of the shutters with my back against the wall, in such a position that my feet could not be visible. When I had carefully considered my points of support, and the space between me and the curtains, I had become sufficiently acquainted with all the difficulties of my position to stay in it without fear of detection if undisturbed by cramp, coughs, or sneezings. To avoid useless fatigue, I remained standing until the critical moment, when I must hang suspended like a spider in its web. The white-watered silk and muslin of the curtains spread before me in great pleats like organ-pipes. With my penknife I cut loop-holes in them through which I could see.

" I heard vague murmurs from the salons, the laughter and the louder tones of the speakers. The smothered commotion and vague uproar lessened by slow degrees. One man and another came for his hat from the Countess' chest of drawers, close to where I stood. I shivered, if the curtains were disturbed, at the thought of the mischances consequent on the confused and hasty investigations made by the men in a hurry to depart, who were rummaging everywhere. When I experienced no misfortunes of this kind, I argued well of my enterprise. An old wooer of Fœdora's came for the last hat; he thought himself quite alone, looked at the bed, and heaved a great sigh, accompanied by some inaudible exclamation, into which he threw sufficient energy. In the boudoir close by, the Countess, finding only some five or six intimate acquaintances about her, proposed tea. The scandals for which existing society has reserved the little faculty of belief that it retains, mingled with epigrams and trenchant witticisms, and the clatter of cups and spoons. Rastignac drew roars of laughter by his merciless sarcasms at the expense of my rivals.

" 'M. de Rastignac is a man with whom it is better not to quarrel,' said the Countess, laughing.

" 'I am quite of that opinion,' was his candid reply. 'I have always been right about my aversions—and my friendships as well,' he added. 'Perhaps my enemies are quite as useful to me as my friends. I have made a particular study of modern phraseology, and of the natural craft that is used in all attack or defence. Official eloquence is one of our perfect social products.

" 'One of your friends is not clever, so you speak of his integrity and his candor. Another's work is heavy ; you introduce it as a piece of conscientious labor ; and if the book is ill written, you extol the ideas it contains. Such an one is treacherous and fickle, slips through your fingers every moment ; bah ! he is attractive, bewitching, he is delightful ! Suppose they are enemies, you fling every one, dead or alive, in their teeth. You reverse your phraseology for their benefit, and you are as keen in detecting their faults as you were before adroit in bringing out the virtues of your friends. This way of using the mental lorgnette is the secret of conversation nowadays, and the whole art of the complete courtier. If you neglect it, you might as well go out as an unarmed knight-banneret to fight against men in armor. And I make use of it, and even abuse it at times. So we are respected— I, my friends, and, moreover, my sword is quite as sharp as my tongue.'

" One of Fœdora's most fervid worshippers, whose presumption was notorious, and who even made it contribute to his success, took up the glove thrown down so scornfully by Rastignac. He began an unmeasured eulogy of me, my performances, and my character. Rastignac had overlooked this method of detraction. His sarcastic encomiums misled the Countess, who sacrificed without mercy ; she betrayed my secrets, and derided my pretentions and my hopes, to divert her friends.

" 'There is a future before him,' said Rastignac. 'Some day he may be in a position to take a cruel revenge ; his talents are at least equal to his courage ; and I should consider those who attack him very rash, for he has a good memory——'

" ' And writes memoirs,' put in the Countess, who seemed to object to the deep silence that prevailed.

" ' Memoirs of a sham countess, madame,' replied Rastignac. ' Another sort of courage is needed to write that sort of thing.'

" ' I give him credit for plenty of courage,' she answered; ' he is faithful to me.'

" I was greatly tempted to show myself suddenly among the railers, like the shade of Banquo in Macbeth. I should have lost the Countess; but I had a friend. But love inspired me all at once with one of those treacherous and fallacious subtleties that it can use to soothe all our pangs.

" If Fœdora loved me, I thought, she would be sure to disguise her feelings by some mocking jest. How often the heart protests against a lie on the lips !

" Well, very soon my audacious rival, left alone with the Countess, rose to go.

" ' What ! already ? ' asked she in a coaxing voice that set my heart beating. ' Will you not give me a few more minutes ? Have you nothing more to say to me ? will you never sacrifice any of your pleasures for me ? '

" He went away.

" ' Ah ! ' she yawned; ' how very tiresome they all are ! '

" She pulled a cord energetically till the sound of a bell rang through the place; then, humming a few notes of " Pria che spunti," the Countess entered her room. No one had ever heard her sing; her muteness had called forth the wildest explanations. She had promised her first· lover, so it was said, who had been held captive by her talent, and whose jealousy over her stretched beyond his grave, that she would never allow others to experience a happiness that he wished to be his and his alone.

" I exerted every power of my soul to catch the sounds. Higher and higher rose the notes; Fœdora's life seemed to dilate within her; her throat poured forth all its richest tones;

something well-nigh divine entered into the melody. There was a bright purity and clearness of tone in the Countess' voice, a thrilling harmony which reached the heart and stirred its pulses. Musicians are seldom unemotional; a woman who could sing like that must know how to love indeed. Her beautiful voice made one more puzzle in a woman mysterious enough before. I beheld her then as plainly as I see you at this moment. She seemed to listen to herself, to experience a secret rapture of her own; she felt, as it were, an ecstacy like that of love.

"She stood before the hearth during the execution of the principal theme of the *rondo;* and when she ceased her face changed. She looked tired; her features seemed to alter. She had laid the mask aside; her part as an actress was over. Yet the faded look that came over her beautiful face, a result either of this performance or of the evening's fatigues, had its charms, too.

"'This is her real self,' I thought.

"She set her foot on a bronze bar of the fender as if to warm it, took off her gloves, and drew over her head the gold chain from which her bejeweled scent-bottle hung. It gave me a quite indescribable pleasure to watch the feline grace of every movement; the supple grace a cat displays as it adjusts its toilette in the sun. She looked at herself in the mirror and said aloud ill-humoredly—'I did not look well this evening; my complexion is going with alarming rapidity; perhaps I ought to keep earlier hours, and give up this life of dissipation. Does Justine mean to trifle with me?' She rang again; her maid hurried in. Where she had been I cannot tell; she came in by a secret staircase. I was anxious to make a study of her. I had lodged accusations, in my romantic imaginings, against this invisible waiting-woman, a tall, well-made brunette.

"'Did madame ring?' exclaimed the waiting-maid as she hurriedly entered the room.

"'Yes, twice,' answered Fœdora; 'are you really growing deaf nowadays?'

"'I was preparing madame's milk of almonds.'

"Justine knelt down before her, unlaced her sandals and drew them off, while her mistress lay carelessly back on her cushioned armchair beside the fire, yawned, and scratched her head. Every movement was perfectly natural; there was nothing whatever to indicate the secret sufferings or emotions with which I had credited her.

"'George must be in love!' she remarked. 'I shall dismiss him. He has drawn the curtains again to-night! What does he mean by it?'

"All the blood in my veins rushed to my heart at this observation, but no more was said about curtains.

"'Life is very empty,' the Countess went on. 'Ah! be careful not to scratch me as you did yesterday. Just look here, I still have the marks of your nails about me,' and she held out a little silken knee. She thrust her bare feet into velvet slippers bound with swan's-down, and unfastened her dress, while Justine prepared to comb her hair.'

"'You ought to marry, madame, and have children.'

"'Children!' she cried; 'it wants no more than that to finish me at once; and a husband! What man is there to whom I could——? Was my hair well arranged to-night?'

"'Not particularly.'

"'You are a fool!'

"'That way of crimping your hair too much is the least becoming way possible for you. Large, smooth curls suit you a great deal better.'

"'Really?'

"'Yes, really, madame; that wavy style only looks nice in fair hair.'

"'Marriage? never, never! Marriage is a commercial arrangement, for which I was never made.'

"What a disheartening scene for a lover! Here was a

lonely woman, without friends or kin, without the religion of love, without faith in any affection. Yet however slightly she might feel the need to pour out her heart, a craving that every human being feels, it could only be satisfied by gossiping with her maid, by trivial and indifferent talk.——I grieved for her.

" Justine unlaced her. I watched her carefully when she was at last unveiled. Her maidenly form, in its rose-tinged whiteness, was visible through her shift in the taper light, as dazzling as some silver statue behind its gauze covering. No, there was no defect that need shrink from the stolen glances of love. Alas, a fair form will overcome the stoutest resolutions !

" The maid lighted the taper in the alabaster sconce that hung before the bed, while her mistress sat thoughtful and silent before the fire. Justine went for a warming-pan, turned down the bed, and helped to lay her mistress in it ; then, after some further time spent in punctiliously rendering various services that showed how seriously Fœdora respected herself, her maid left her. The Countess turned to and fro several times, and sighed ; she was ill at ease ; faint, just perceptible sounds, like signs of impatience, escaped from her lips. She reached out a hand to the table, and took a flask from it, from which she shook four or five drops of some brown liquid into some milk before taking it ; again there followed some painful sighs, and the exclamation, ' *Mon Dieu !* '

" The cry, and the tone in which it was uttered, wrung my heart. By degrees she lay motionless. This frightened me ; but very soon I heard a sleeper's heavy, regular breathing. I drew the rustling silk curtains apart, left my post, went to the foot of the bed, and gazed at her with feelings that I cannot define. She was so enchanting as she lay like a child, with her arm above her head ; but the sweetness of the fair, quiet visage, surrounded by the lace, only irritated me. I had not been prepared for the torture to which I was compelled to submit.

"' *Mon Dieu!*' that scrap of a thought which I understood not, but must even take as my sole light, had suddenly modified my opinion of Fœdora. Trite or profoundly signicant, frivolous or of deep import, the words might be construed as expressive of either pleasure or pain, of physical or of mental suffering. Was it a prayer or a malediction, a forecast or a memory, a fear or a regret? A whole life lay in that utterance, a life of wealth or of penury; perhaps it contained a crime!

"The mystery that lurked beneath this fair semblance of womanhood grew afresh; there were so many ways of explaining Fœdora, that she became inexplicable. Some sort of language seemed to flow from between her lips. I put thoughts and feelings into the accidents of her breathing, .whether weak or regular, gentle or labored. I shared her dreams; I would fain have divined her secrets by reading them through her slumber. I hesitated among contradictory opinions and decisions without number. I could not deny my heart to the woman I saw before me, with the calm, pure beauty in her face. I resolved to make one more effort. If I told her the story of my life, my love, my sacrifices, might I not awaken pity in her or draw a tear from her who never wept?

"As I set all my hopes on this last experiment, the sounds in the streets showed that day was at hand. For a moment's space I pictured Fœdora waking to find herself in my arms. I could have stolen softly to her side and slipped them about her in a close embrace. Resolved to resist the cruel tyranny of this thought, I hurried into the salon, heedless of any sounds I might make; but luckily I came upon a secret door leading to a little staircase. As I had expected, the key was in the lock; I slammed the door, went boldly out into the court, and gained the street in three bounds, without looking round to see whether I was observed.

"A dramatist was to read a comedy at the Countess' house in two days' time; I went thither, intending to outstay the others, so as to make a rather singular request of her; I meant to ask her to keep the following evening for me alone, and to deny herself to other comers; but when I found myself alone with her my courage failed. Every tick of the clock alarmed me. It wanted only a quarter of an hour of midnight.

"'If I do not speak,' I thought to myself, 'I must smash my head against the corner of the mantelpiece.'

"'I gave myself three minutes' grace; the three minutes went by, and I did not smash my head upon the marble; my heart grew heavy, like a sponge with water.

"'You are exceedingly amusing,' said she.

"'Ah, madame, if you could but understand me!' I answered.

"'What is the matter with you?' she asked. 'You are turning pale.'

"'I am hesitating to ask a favor of you.'

"Her gesture revived my courage. I asked her to make the appointment with me.

"'Willingly,' she answered; 'but why will you not speak to me now?'

"'To be candid with you, I ought to explain the full scope of your promise: I want to spend this evening by your side, as if we were brother and sister. Have no fear; I am aware of your antipathies; you must have divined me sufficiently to feel sure that I should wish you to do nothing that could be displeasing to you; presumption, moreover, would not thus approach you. You have been a friend to me, you have shown me kindness and great indulgence; know, therefore, that to-morrow I must bid you farewell. Do not take back your word,' I exclaimed, seeing her about to speak, and I went away.

"At eight o'clock one evening towards the end of May, Fœdora and I were alone together in her gothic boudoir. I feared no longer; I was secure of happiness. The Countess should be mine, or I would seek a refuge in death. I had condemned my faint-hearted love, and a man who acknowledges his weakness is strong indeed.

"The Countess, in her blue cashmere gown, was reclining on a sofa, with her feet on a cushion. She wore an Oriental turban such as painters assign to early Hebrews; its strangeness added an indescribable coquettish grace to her attractions. A transitory charm seemed to have laid its spell on her face; it might have furnished the argument that at every instant we become new and unparalleled beings, without any resemblance to the *us* of the future or of the past. I had never yet seen her so radiant.

"'Do you know that you have piqued my curiosity?' she said, laughing.

"'I will not disappoint it,' I said quietly, as I seated myself near her and took the hand that she surrendered to me. 'You have a very beautiful voice!'

"'You have never heard me sing!' she exclaimed, starting involuntarily with surprise.

"'I will prove that it is quite otherwise, whenever it is necessary. Is your delightful singing still to remain a mystery? Have no fear, I do not wish to penetrate it.'

"We spent about an hour in familiar talk. While I adopted the attitude and manner of a man to whom Fœdora must refuse nothing, I showed her all a lover's deference. Acting in this way, I received a favor—I was allowed to kiss her hand. She daintily drew off the glove; and my whole soul was dissolved and poured forth in that kiss. I was steeped in the bliss of an illusion in which I tried to believe.

"Fœdora lent herself most unexpectedly to my caress and my flatteries. Do not accuse me of faint-heartedness; if I had gone a step beyond these fraternal compliments, the claws would have been out of the sheath and into me. We remained perfectly silent for nearly ten minutes. I was admiring her, investing her with the charms she had not. She was mine just then, and mine only,—this enchanting being was mine, as was permissible, in my imagination ; my longing wrapped her round and held her close ; in my soul I wedded her. The Countess was subdued and fascinated by my magnetic influence. Ever since I have regretted that this subjugation was not absolute ; but just then I yearned for her soul, her heart alone, and for nothing else. I longed for an ideal and perfect happiness, a fair illusion that cannot last for very long. At last I spoke, feeling that the last hours of my frenzy were at hand.

"'Hear me, madame. I love you, and you know it ; I have said so a hundred times ; you must have understood me. I would not take upon me the airs of a coxcomb, nor would I flatter you, nor urge myself upon you like a fool ; I would not owe your love to such arts as these ; so I have been misunderstood. What sufferings have I not endured for your sake ! For these, however, you were not to blame ; but in a few minutes you shall decide for yourself. There are two kinds of poverty, madame. One kind openly walks the street in rags, an unconscious imitator of Diogenes, on a scanty diet, reducing life to its simplest terms ; he is happier, maybe, than the rich ; he has fewer cares at any rate, and accepts such portions of the world as stronger spirits refuse. Then there is poverty in splendor, a Spanish pauper, concealing the life of a beggar by his title, his bravery, and his pride ; poverty that wears a white waistcoat and yellow kid gloves, a beggar with a carriage, whose whole career will be wrecked for lack of a half-penny. Poverty of the first kind belongs to the populace ; the second kind is that of blacklegs, of kings, and of men of talent. I am neither a man of the people, nor a king, nor a swindler ; possibly I have no talent either ; I am an exception. With the name I bear I must die sooner than beg. Set your mind at rest, madame,' I said ; 'to-day I have abundance, I possess sufficient of the clay for my needs ; ' for the hard look passed over her face which we wear whenever a well-dressed beggar takes us by surprise. ' Do you remember the day when you wished to go to the Gymnase without me, never believing that I should be there? ' I went on.

" She nodded.

" ' I had laid out my last five-franc piece that I might see you there. Do you recollect our walk in the Jardin des Plantes? The hire of your cab took everything I had.'

" I told her about my sacrifices, and described the life I led; heated not with wine, as I am to-day, but by the generous enthusiasm of my heart, my passion overflowed in burning words; I have forgotten how the feelings within me blazed forth; neither memory nor skill of mine could possibly reproduce it. It was no colorless chronicle of blighted affections; my love was strengthened by fair hopes; and such words came to me, by love's inspirātion, that each had power to set forth a whole life—like echoes of the cries of a soul in torment. In such tones the last prayers ascend from dying men on the battle-field. I stopped, for she was weeping. *Grand Dieu!* I had reaped an actor's reward, the success of a counterfeit passion displayed at the cost of five francs paid at the theatre door. I had drawn tears from her.

" ' If I had known—— ' she said.

" ' Do not finish the sentence,' I broke in. ' Even now I love you well enough to murder you—— '

" She reached for the bell-pull. I burst into a roar of laughter.

" ' Do not call any one,' I said. ' I shall leave you to finish your life in peace. It would be a blundering kind of hatred that would murder you! You need not fear violence of any kind; I have spent a whole night at the foot of your bed without—— '

" ' Monsieur—— ' she exclaimed, blushing; but after that first impulse of modesty that even the most hardened women must surely own, she flung a scornful glance at me, and said—

" 'You must have been very cold.'

" 'Do you think that I set such value on your beauty, madame,' I answered, guessing the thoughts that moved her. 'Your beautiful face is for me a promise of a soul yet more beautiful. Madame, those to whom a woman is merely a woman can always purchase odalisques fit for the seraglio, and achieve their happiness at a small cost. But I aspired to something higher; I wanted the life of close communion of heart and heart with you that have no heart. I know that now. If you were to belong to another, I could kill him. And yet, no; for you would love him, and his death might hurt you perhaps. What agony this is!' I cried.

" 'If it is any comfort to you,' she retorted cheerfully, 'I can assure you that I shall never belong to any one——'

" 'So you offer an affront to God Himself,' I interrupted; 'and you will be punished for it. Some day you will lie upon your sofa suffering unheard-of ills, unable to endure the light or the slightest sound, condemned to live as it were in the tomb. Then, when you seek the causes of those lingering and avenging torments, you will remember the woes that you distributed so lavishly upon your way. You have sown curses, and hatred will be your reward. We are the real judges, the executioners of a justice that reigns here below, which overrules the justice of man and the laws of God.'

" 'No doubt it is very culpable in me not to love you,' she said, laughing. 'Am I to blame? No. I do not love you; you are a man, that is sufficient. I am happy by myself; why should I give up my way of living, a selfish way, if you will, for the caprices of a master? Marriage is a sacrament by virtue of which each imparts nothing but vexations to the other. Children, moreover, worry me. Did I not faithfully warn you about my nature? Why are you not satisfied to have my friendship? I wish I could make you amends for all the troubles I have caused you, through not guessing the value of your poor five-franc pieces. I appreciate the extent of your sacrifices; but your devotion and delicate tact can be repaid by love alone, and I care so little for you, that this scene has a disagreeable effect upon me.'

"'I am fully aware of my absurdity,' I said, unable to restrain my tears. 'Pardon me,' I went on, 'it was a delight to hear those cruel words you have just uttered, so well I love you. O, if I could testify my love with every drop of blood in me!'

"'Men always repeat these classical formulas to us, more or less effectively,' she answered, still smiling. 'But it appears very difficult to die at our feet, for I see corpses of that kind about me everywhere. It is twelve o'clock. Allow me to go to bed.'

"'And in two hours' time you will cry to yourself, *Ah, mon Dieu!*'

"'Like the day before yesterday! Yes,' she said, 'I was thinking of my stockbroker; I had forgotten to tell him to convert my five per cent. stock into the threes, and the three per cents. had fallen during the day.'

"I looked at her and my eyes glittered with anger. Sometimes a crime may be a whole romance; I understood that just then. She was so accustomed, no doubt, to the most impassioned declarations of this kind, that my words and my tears were forgotten already.

"'Would you marry a peer of France?' I demanded abruptly.

"'If he were a duke I might.'

"I seized my hat and made her a bow.

"'Permit me to accompany you to the door,' she said, cutting irony in her tones, in the poise of her head, and in her gesture.

"'Madame——'

"'Monsieur?'

"'I shall never see you again.'

"'I hope not,' and she insolently inclined her head.

"'You wish to be a duchess?' I cried, excited by a sort of madness that her insolence roused in me. 'You are wild for honors and titles? Well, only let me love you; bid my pen write and my voice speak for you alone; be the inmost soul of my life, my guiding star! Then only accept me for your husband as a minister, a peer of France, a duke. I will make of myself whatever you would have me be!'

"'You made good use of the time you spent with the advocate,' she said, smiling. 'There is a fervency about your pleadings.'

"'The present is yours,' I cried, 'but the future is mine! I only lose a woman; you are losing a name and a family. Time is big with my revenge; time will spoil your beauty, and yours will be a solitary death; and enduring glory waits for me!'

"'Thanks for your peroration!' she said, repressing a yawn; the wish that she might never see me again was expressed in her whole bearing.

"That remark silenced me. I flung at her a glance full of hatred, and hurried away.

"Fœdora must be forgotten; I must cure myself of my infatuation, and betake myself once more to my lonely studies, or die. So I set myself tremendous tasks; I determined to complete my labors. For fifteen days I never left my garret, spending whole nights in pallid thought. I worked with difficulty, and by fits and starts, despite my courage and the stimulation of despair. The muse had fled. I could not exorcise the brilliant mocking image of Fœdora. Something morbid brooded over every thought, a vague longing as dreadful as remorse. I imitated the anchorites of the Thebaid. If I did not pray as they did, I lived a life in the desert like theirs, hewing out my ideas as they were wont to hew their rocks. I could at need have girdled my waist with spikes, that physical suffering might quell mental anguish.

"One evening Pauline found her way into my room.

11

" ' You are killing yourself,' she said, imploringly; ' you should go out and see your friends——'

" ' Pauline, you were a true prophet ; Fœdora is killing me, I want to die.   My life is intolerable.''

" ' Is there only one woman in the world ?' she asked smiling.   ' Why make yourself so miserable in so short a life?'

" I looked at Pauline in bewilderment.   She left me before I noticed her departure ; the sound of her words had reached me, but not their sense.   Very soon I had to take my memoirs in manuscript to my literary contractor.   I was so absorbed by my passion, that I could not remember how I had managed to live without money; I only knew that the four hundred and fifty francs due to me would pay my debts.   So I went to receive my salary, and met Rastignac, who thought me changed and thinner.

" ' What hospital have you been discharged from ? ' he asked.

" ' That woman is killing me,' I answered ; ' I can neither despise her nor forget her.'

" ' You had much better kill her, then perhaps you would think no more of her,' he said, laughing.

" ' I have often thought of it,' I replied ; ' but though sometimes the thought of a crime revives my spirits, of violence and murder, either or both, I am really incapable of carrying out the design.   The Countess is an admirable monster who would crave for pardon, and not every man, you know, is an Othello.'

" ' She is like every woman who is beyond our reach,' Rastignac interrupted.

" ' I am mad,' I cried ; ' I can feel the madness raging at times in my brain.   My ideas are like shadows ; they flit before me, and I cannot grasp them.   Death would be preferable to this life, and I have carefully considered the best way of putting an end to the struggle.   I am not thinking of the living Fœdora in the Faubourg Saint Honoré, but of my

Fœdora here,' and I tapped my forehead.   'What do you say
to opium ?'

    " ' Pshaw ! horrid agonies,' said Rastignac.

    " ' Or charcoal fumes ? '

    " ' A low dodge.'

    " ' Or the Seine ? '

    " ' The drag-nets, and the morgue too, are filthy.'

    " ' A pistol-shot ? '

    " ' And if you miscalculate, you disfigure yourself for life.
Listen to me,' he went on, 'like all young men, I have pon-
dered over suicide.   Which of us hasn't killed himself two or
three times before he is thirty?   I find there is no better
course than to use existence as a means of pleasure.   Go in
for thorough dissipation, and your passion or you will perish
in it.   Intemperance, my dear fellow, commands all forms of
death.   Does she not wield the thunderbolt of apoplexy?
Apoplexy is a pistol-shot that does not miscalculate.   Orgies
are lavish in all physical pleasures ; is not that the small
change for opium ?   And the riot that makes us drink to
excess bears a challenge to mortal combat with wine.   That
butt of Malmsey of the Duke of Clarence's must have had a
pleasanter flavor than Seine mud.   When we sink gloriously
under the table, is not that a periodical death by drowning
on a small scale ?   If we are picked up by the police and
stretched out on those chilly benches of theirs at the police-
station, do we not enjoy all the pleasures of the morgue ?   For
though we are not blue and green, muddy and swollen corpses,
on the other hand we have the consciousness of the climax.

    " ' Ah,' he went on, ' this protracted suicide has nothing in
common with a bankrupt grocer's demise.   Tradespeople
have brought the river into disrepute ; they fling themselves
in to soften their creditors' hearts.   In your place I should
endeavor to die gracefully ; and if you wish to invent a novel
way of doing it, by struggling with life after this manner, I
will be your second.   I am disappointed and sick of every-

thing.   The Alsacienne, whom it was proposed that I should
marry, had six toes on her left foot ; I cannot possibly live
with a woman who has six toes !   It would get about to a
certainty, and then I should be ridiculous.   Her income was
only eighteen thousand francs ; her fortune diminished in
quantity as her toes increased.   The devil take it ; if we
begin an outrageous sort of life, we may come on some bit of
luck, perhaps ! '

" Rastignac's eloquence carried me away.   The attrac-
tions of the plan shone too temptingly, hopes were kindled,
the poetical aspects of the matter appealed to a poet.

" ' How about money ? ' I said.

" ' Haven't you four hundred and fifty francs ? '

" ' Yes, but debts to my landlady and the tailor——'

" ' You would pay your tailor ?   You will never be any-
thing whatever, not so much as a minister.'

" ' But can one do with twenty louis ? '

" ' Go to the gaming-table.'

" I shuddered.

" ' You are going to launch out into what I call systematic
dissipation,' said he, noticing my scruples, ' and yet you are
afraid of a green table-cloth.'

" ' Listen to me,' I answered.   ' I promised my father never
to set foot in a gaming-house.   Not only is that a sacred
promise, but I still feel an unconquerable disgust whenever I
pass a gambling-hell ; take the money and go without me.
While our fortune is at stake, I will set my own affairs straight,
and then I will go to your lodgings and wait for you."

" That was the way I went to perdition.   A young man
has only to come across a woman who will not love him,
or a woman who loves him too well, and his whole life
becomes a chaos.   Prosperity swallows up our energy just
as adversity obscures our virtues.   Back once more in my
Hôtel de Saint-Quentin, I gazed about me a long while in
the garret where I had led my scholar's temperate life, a life

which would perhaps have been a long and honorable one, and that I ought not to have quitted for the fevered existence which had urged me to the brink of a precipice. Pauline surprised me in this dejected attitude.

"'Why, what is the matter with you?' she asked.

"I rose and quietly counted out the money owing to her mother, and added to it sufficient to pay for six months' rent in advance. She watched me in some alarm.

"'I am going to leave you, dear Pauline.'

"'I knew it!' she exclaimed.

"'Listen, my child. I have not given up the idea of coming back. Keep my room for me for six months. If I do not return by the fifteenth of November, you will come into possession of my things. This sealed packet of manuscript is the fair copy of my great work on ' The Will,'' I went on, pointing to a package. Will you deposit it in the King's Library? And you may do as you wish with everything that is left here.'

"Her look weighed heavily on my heart; Pauline was an embodiment of conscience there before me.

"'I shall have no more lessons,' she said, pointing to the piano.'

"I did not answer that.

"'Will you write to me?'

"'Good-bye, Pauline.'

"I gently drew her towards me, and set a kiss on that innocent fair brow of hers, like snow that has not yet touched the earth—a father's or a brother's kiss. She fled. I would not see Madame Gaudin, hung my key in its wonted place, and departed. I was almost at the end of the Rue de Cluny when I heard a woman's light footstep behind me.

"'I have embroidered this purse for you,'' Pauline said; ' will you refuse even that?'

"By the light of the street lamp I thought I saw tears in Pauline's eyes, and I groaned. Moved perhaps by a common impulse, we parted in haste like people who fear the contagion of the plague.

" As I waited with dignified calmness for Rastignac's return, his room seemed a grotesque interpretation of the sort of life I was about to enter upon. The clock on the chimney-piece was surmounted by a Venus resting on her tortoise; a half-smoked cigar lay in her arms. Costly furniture of various kinds—love-tokens, very likely—was scattered about. Old shoes lay on a luxurious sofa. The comfortable armchair into which I had thrown myself bore as many scars as a veteran; the arms were gashed, the back was overlaid with a thick, stale deposit of pomade and hair-oil from the heads of all his visitors. Splendor and squalor were oddly mingled, on the walls, the bed, and everywhere else. You might have thought of a Neapolitan palace and the groups of beggars about it. It was the room of a gambler or a good-for-nothing, where the luxury exists merely for one individual, who leads the life of the senses and does not trouble himself over inconsistencies.

" There was a certain imaginative element about the picture it presented. Life was suddenly revealed there in its rags and spangles as the incomplete thing it really is, of course, but so vividly and picturesquely; it was like a den where a brigand has heaped up all the plunder in which he delights. Some pages were missing from a copy of Byron's poems; they had gone to light a fire of a few sticks for this young person, who played for stakes of a thousand francs, and had not a faggot; who kept a tilbury, and had not a whole shirt to his back. Any day a countess or an actress or a run of luck at écarté might set him up with an outfit worthy of a king. A candle had been stuck into the green bronze sheath of a vestaholder; a woman's portrait lay yonder, torn out of its carved gold setting. How was it possible that a young man, whose nature craved excitement, could renounce a life so attractive by reason of its contradictions; a life that afforded all the delights of war in the midst of peace? I was growing drowsy when Rastignac kicked the door open and shouted—

" ' Victory ! Now we can take our time about dying.'

" He held out his hat filled with gold to me, and put it down on the table ; then we pranced round it like a pair of cannibals about to eat a victim ; we stamped, and danced, and yelled, and sang ; we gave each other blows fit to kill an elephant, at sight of all the pleasures of the world contained in that hat.

" ' Twenty-seven thousand francs,' said Rastignac, adding a few bank-notes to the pile of gold. ' That would be enough for other folk to live upon ; will it be sufficient for us to die on ? Yes ! we will breathe our last in a bath of gold— hurrah !' and we capered afresh.

" We divided the windfall. We began with double-napoleons, and came down to the smaller coins, one by one. ' This for you, this for me,' we kept on saying, distilling our joy drop by drop.

" ' We won't go to sleep,' cried Rastignac. ' Joseph ! some punch ! '

" He threw gold to his faithful attendant.

" ' There is your share,'' he said, ' go and bury yourself, if you can.'

" Next day I went to Lesage and chose my furniture, took the rooms that you know in the Rue Taitbout, and left the decoration to one of the best upholsterers. I bought horses. I plunged into a vortex of pleasures, at once hollow and real. I went in for play, gaining and losing enormous sums, but only at friends' houses and in ball-rooms ; never in gaming-houses, for which I still retained the holy horror of my early days. Without meaning it, I made some friends, either through quarrels or owing to the easy confidence established among those who are going to the bad together ; nothing, possibly, makes us cling to one another so tightly as our evil propensities.

"I made several ventures in literature, which were flatteringly received. Great men who followed the profession of letters, having nothing to fear from me, belauded me, not so much on account of my merits as to cast a slur on those of their rivals.

"I became a 'free-liver,' to make use of the picturesque expression appropriated by the language of excess. I made it a point of honor not to be long about dying, and that my zeal and prowess should eclipse those displayed by all others in the jolliest company. I was always spruce and carefully dressed. I had some reputation for cleverness. There was no sign about me of that fearful way of living which makes a man into a mere digesting apparatus, a funnel, a pampered beast.

"Very soon debauch rose before me in all the majesty of its horror, and I grasped all that it meant. Those prudent, steady-going characters who are laying down wine in bottles for their heirs, can barely conceive, it is true, of so wide a theory of life, nor appreciate its normal condition ; but when will you instil poetry into the provincial intellect? Opium and tea, with all their delights, are merely drugs to folk of that calibre.

"Is not the imperfect sybarite to be met with even in Paris itself, that intellectual metropolis? Unfit to endure the fatigues of pleasure, this sort of person, after a drinking bout, is very much like those worthy bourgeois who fall foul of music after hearing a new opera by Rossini. Does he not renounce these courses in the same frame of mind that leads an abstemious man to forswear Ruffec patés, because the first one, forsooth, gave him the indigestion ?

"Debauch is as surely an art as poetry, and is not for craven spirits. To penetrate its mysteries and appreciate its charms, conscientious application is required ; and as with every path of knowledge, the way is thorny and forbidding at the outset. The great pleasures of humanity are hedged about with formidable obstacles ; not its single enjoyments, but enjoyment as a system, a system which establishes seldom-experienced sensations and makes them habitual, which concentrates and multiplies them for us, creating a dramatic life within our life, and imperatively demanding a prompt and enormous expenditure of vitality. War, power, art, like debauch, are all forms of demoralization, equally remote from the faculties of humanity, equally profound, and all are alike difficult of access. But when man has once stormed the heights of these grand mysteries, does he not walk in another world? Are not generals, ministers, and artists carried, more or less, towards destruction by the need of violent distractions in an existence so remote from ordinary life as theirs?

"War, after all, is the excess of bloodshed, as the excess of self-interest produces politics. Excesses of every sort are brothers. These social enormities possess the attraction of the abyss; they draw us towards themselves as St. Helena beckoned Napoleon; we are fascinated, our heads swim, we wish to sound their depths, though we cannot account for the wish. Perhaps the thought of infinity dwells in these precipices, perhaps they contain some colossal flattery for the soul of man; for is he not, then, wholly absorbed in himself?

"The wearied artist needs a complete contrast to his paradise of imaginings and of studious hours; he either craves, like God, the seventh day of rest, or with Satan, the pleasures of hell; so that his senses may have free play in opposition to the employment of his faculties. Byron could never have taken for his relaxation to the independent gentleman's delights of boston and gossip, for he was a poet, and so must needs pit Greece against Mahmoud.

"In war, is not man an angel of extirpation, a sort of executioner on a gigantic scale? Must not the spell be strong indeed that makes us undergo such horrid sufferings so hostile to our weak frames, sufferings that encircle every strong passion with a hedge of thorns? The tobacco-smoker is seized with convulsions, and goes through a kind of agony consequent upon his excesses; but has he not borne a part in delightful festivals in realms unknown? Has Europe ever ceased from wars? She has never given herself time to wipe the stains from her feet that are steeped in blood to the ankle. Mankind at large is carried away by fits of intoxication, as nature has its accessions of love.

"For men in private life, for a vegetating Mirabeau dreaming of storms in a time of calm, excess comprises all things; it perpetually embraces the whole sum of life; it is something better still—it is a duel with an antagonist of unknown power, a monster, terrible at first sight, that must be seized by the horns, a labor that cannot be imagined.

"Suppose that nature has endowed you with a feeble stomach or one of limited capacity; you acquire a mastery over it and improve it; you learn to carry your liquor; you grow accustomed to being drunk; you pass whole nights without sleep; at last you acquire the constitution of a colonel of cuirassiers; and in this way you create yourself afresh, as if to fly in the face of Providence.

"A man transformed after this sort is like a neophyte who has at last become a veteran, has accustomed his mind to shot and shell and his legs to lengthy marches. When the monster's hold on him is still uncertain, and it is not yet known which will have the better of it, they roll over and over, alternately victor and vanquished, in a world where everything is wonderful, where every ache of the soul is laid to sleep, where only the shadows of ideas are revived.

"This furious struggle has already become a necessity for us. The prodigal has struck a bargain for all the enjoyments with which life teems abundantly, at the price of his own death, like the mythical persons in the legends who sold themselves to the devil for the power of doing evil. For them, instead of flowing quietly on its monotonous course in the depths of some counting-house or study, life is poured out in a boiling torrent.

"Excess is, in short, for the body what the mystic's ecstasy is for the soul. Intoxication steeps you in fantastic imaginings every whit as strange as those of ecstatics. You know hours as full of rapture as a young girl's dreams; you travel without fatigue; you chat pleasantly with your friends; words come to you with a whole life in each, and fresh pleasures without regrets; poems are set forth for you in a few brief phrases. The coarse animal satisfaction, in which science has tried to find a soul, is followed by the enchanted drowsiness that men sigh for under the burden of consciousness. Is it not because they all feel the need of absolute repose? Because excess is a sort of toll that genius pays to pain?

"Look at all great men; nature made them pleasure-loving or base, every one. Some mocking or jealous power corrupted them in either soul or body, so as to make all their powers futile, and their efforts of no avail.

"All men and all things appear before you in the guise you choose, in those hours when wine has sway. You are lord of all creation; you transform it at your pleasure. And throughout this unceasing delirium, play may pour, at your will, its molten lead into your veins.

"Some day you will fall into the monster's power. Then you will have, as I had, a frenzied awakening, with impotence sitting by your pillow. Are you an old soldier? Phthisis attacks you. A diplomatist? An aneurism hangs death in your heart by a thread. It will perhaps be consumption that will cry to me, 'Let us be going!' as to Raphael of Urbino, in old time, killed by an excess of love.

"In this way I have existed. I was launched into the world too early or too late. My energy would have been dangerous there, no doubt, if I had not squandered it in such ways as these. Was not the world rid of an Alexander, by the cup of Hercules, at the close of a drinking bout.

"There are some, the sport of destiny, who must either have heaven or hell, the hospice of St. Bernard or riotous excess.   Only just now I lacked the heart to moralize about those two," and he pointed to Euphrasia and Aquilina. " They are types of my own personal history, images of my life !   I could scarcely reproach them ; they stood before me like judges.

"In the midst of this drama that I was enacting, and while my distracting disorder was at its height, two crises supervened ; each brought me keen and abundant pangs.   The first came a few days after I had flung myself, like Sardanapalus, on my pyre.   I met Fœdora under the peristyle of the Bouffons.   We both were waiting for our carriages.

" 'Ah ! so you are living yet.'

" That was the meaning of her smile, and probably of the spiteful words she murmured into the ear of her *cicisbeo*, telling him my history, no doubt, rating mine as a common love affair.   She was deceived, yet she was applauding her perspicacity.   Oh, that I should be dying for her, must still adore her, always see her through my potations, see her still when I was overcome with wine, or in the arms of courtesans ; and know that I was a target for her scornful jests ?   Oh, that I should be unable to tear the love of her out of my breast and to fling it at her feet !

" Well, I quickly exhausted my funds, but owing to those three years of discipline I enjoyed the most robust health, and on the day that I found myself without a penny I felt remarkably well.   In order to carry on the process of dying, I signed bills at short dates, and the day came when they must be met.   Painful excitements ! but how they quicken the pulses of youth !   I was not prematurely aged ; I was young yet, and full of vigor and life.

" At my first debt all my virtues came to life; slowly and despairingly they seemed to pace towards me ; but I could compound with them—they were like aged aunts that begin with a scolding and end by bestowing tears and money upon you.

" Imagination was less yielding ; I saw my name bandied

about through every city in Europe. 'One's name is oneself,' says Eusèbe Salverte. After these excursions I returned to the room I had never quitted, like a doppel-ganger in a German tale, and came to myself with a start.

"I used to see with indifference a banker's messenger going on his errands through the streets of Paris, like a commercial Nemesis, wearing his master's livery—a gray coat and a silver badge; but now I hated the species in advance. One of them came one morning to ask me to meet eleven bills that I had scrawled my name upon. My signature was worth three thousand francs! Taking me altogether, I myself was not worth that amount. Sheriff's deputies rose up before me, turning their callous faces upon my despair, as the hangman regards the criminal to whom he says, 'It has just struck half-past three.' I was in the power of their clerks; they could scribble my name, drag it through the mire, and jeer at it. I was a defaulter. Has a debtor any right to himself? Could not other men call me to account for my way of living? Why had I eaten puddings *à la chipolata?* Why had I iced my wine? Why had I slept, or walked, or thought, or amused myself when I had not paid them?

"At any moment, in the middle of a poem, during some train of thought, or while I was gaily breakfasting in the pleasant company of my friends, I might look to see a gentleman enter in a coat of chestnut-brown, with a shabby hat in his hand. This gentleman's appearance would signify my debt. The bill I had drawn; the spectre would compel me to leave the table to speak to him, blight my spirits, despoil me of my cheerfulness, of my mistress, of all I possessed, down to my very bedstead.

"Remorse itself is more easily endured. Remorse does not drive us into the street nor into the prison of Sainte-Pélagie; it does not force us into the detestable sink of vice. Remorse only brings us to the scaffold, where the executioner invests us with a certain dignity; as we pay the extreme penalty, everybody believes in our innocence ; but people will not credit a penniless prodigal with a single virtue.

"My debts had other incarnations. There is the kind that goes about on two feet, in a green-cloth coat, and blue spectacles, carrying umbrellas of various hues ; you come face to face with him at the corner of some street, in the midst of your mirth. These have the detestable prerogative of saying, 'M. de Valentin owes me something and does not pay. I have a hold on him. He had better not show me any offensive airs !' You must bow to your creditors, and, moreover, bow politely. 'When are you going to pay me ?' say they. And you must lie, and beg money of another man, and cringe to a fool seated on his strong box, and receive sour looks in return from these horse-leeches ; a blow would be less hateful ; you must put up with their crass ignorance and calculating morality. A debt is a feat of the imaginative that they cannot appreciate. A borrower is often carried away and overmastered by generous impulses ; nothing great, nothing magnanimous can move or dominate those who live for money, and recognize nothing but money. I myself held money in abhorrence.

"Or a bill may undergo a final transformation into some meritorious old man with a family dependent upon him. My creditor may be a living picture for Greuze, a paralytic with his children round him, a soldier's widow, holding out beseeching hands to me. Terrible creditors are those with whom we are forced to sympathize, and when their claims are satisfied we owe them a further debt of assistance.

"The night before the bills fell due, I lay down with the false calm of those who sleep before their approaching execution, or with a duel in prospect, rocked as they are by delusive hopes. But when I woke, when I was cool and collected, when I found myself imprisoned in a banker's portfolio, and floundering in statements covered with red ink—then my debts sprang up everywhere, like grasshoppers, before my eyes.

There were my debts, my clock, my armchairs; my debts were inlaid in the very furniture which I liked best to use. These gentle inanimate slaves were to fall a prey to the harpies of the Châtelet, were to be carried off by the broker's men, and brutally thrown on the market. Ah, my property was a part of myself!

"The sound of the door-bell rang through my heart; while it seemed to strike at me, where kings should be struck at—in the head. Mine was a martyrdom, without heaven for its reward. For a magnanimous nature, debt is a hell, and a hell, moreover, with sheriff's officers and brokers in it. An undischarged debt is something mean and sordid; it is a beginning of knavery; it is something worse, it is a lie; it prepares the way for crime, and brings together the planks for the scaffold. My bills were protested. Three days afterwards I met them, and this is how it happened.

"A speculator came, offering to buy the island in the Loire belonging to me, where my mother lay buried. I closed with him. When I went to his solicitor to sign the deeds, I felt a cavern-like chill in the dark office that made me shudder; it was the same cold dampness that had lain hold upon me at the brink of my father's grave. I looked upon this as an evil omen. I seemed to see the shade of my mother, and to hear her voice. What power was it that made my own name ring vaguely in my ears, in spite of the clamor of bells?

"The money paid down for my island, when all my debts were discharged, left me in possession of two thousand francs. I could now have returned to a scholar's tranquil life, it is true; I could have gone back to my garret after having gained an experience of life, with my head filled with the results of extensive observation, and with a certain sort of reputation attaching to me. But Fœdora's hold upon her victim was not relaxed. We often met. I compelled her admirers to sound my name in her ears, by dint of astonishing them with my cleverness and success, with my horses and equipages. It all found her impassive and uninterested; so did an ugly phrase of Rastignac's, ' He is killing himself for you.'

"I charged the world at large with my revenge, but I was not happy. While I was fathoming the miry depths of life, I only recognized the more keenly at all times the happiness of reciprocal affection; it was a shadow that I followed through all that befell me in my extravagance, and in my wildest moments. It was my misfortune to be deceived in my fairest beliefs, to be punished by ingratitude for benefiting others, and to receive uncounted pleasures as the reward of my errors—a sinister doctrine, but a true one for the prodigal!

"The contagious leprosy of Fœdora's vanity had taken hold of me at last. I probed my soul, and found it cankered and rotten. I bore the marks of the devil's claw upon my forehead. It was impossible to me thenceforward to do without the incessant agitation of a life fraught with danger at every moment, or to dispense with the execrable refinements of luxury. If I had possessed millions, I should still have gambled, reveled, and, racketed about. I wished never to be alone with myself, and I must have false friends and courtesans, wine and good cheer to distract me. The ties that attach a man to family life had been permanently broken for me. I had become a galley-slave of pleasure, and must accomplish my destiny of suicide. During the last days of my prosperity, I spent every night in the most incredible excesses; but every morning death cast me back upon life again. I would have taken a conflagration with as little concern as any man with a life annuity. However, I at last found myself alone with a twenty-franc piece; I bethought me then of Rastignac's luck——

"Eh, eh!——" Raphael exclaimed, interrupting himself, as he remembered the talisman and drew it from his pocket. Perhaps he was wearied by the long day's strain, and had no more strength left wherewith to pilot his head through the seas of wine and punch; or perhaps, exasperated by this symbol of his own existence, the torrent of his own eloquence gradually overwhelmed him. Raphael became excited and elated and like one completely deprived of reason.

"The devil take death!" he shouted, brandishing the skin; "I mean to live! I am rich, I have every virtue; nothing will withstand me. Who would not be generous, when everything is in his power? Aha! aha! I wished for two hundred thousand livres a year, and I shall have them. Bow down before me, all of you, wallowing on the carpets like swine in the mire! You all belong to me—a precious property truly! I am rich! I could buy you all, even the deputy snoring over there. Scum of society, give me your benediction! I am the Pope."

Raphael's vociferations had been hitherto drowned by a thorough-bass of snores, but now they became suddenly audible. Most of the sleepers started up with a cry, saw the cause of the disturbance on his feet, tottering uncertainly, and cursed him in concert for a drunken brawler.

"Silence!" shouted Raphael. "Back to your kennels, you dogs! Emile, I have riches, I will give you Havana cigars!"

"I am listening," the poet replied. "Death or Fœdora! On with you! That silky Fœdora deceived you. Women are all daughters of Eve. There is nothing dramatic about that rigmarole of yours."

"Ah, but you were sleeping, slyboots."

"No—'Death or Fœdora!'—I have it!"

"Wake up!" Raphael shouted, beating Emile with the piece of shagreen as if he meant to draw electric fluid out of it.

"Thunder!" said Emile, springing up and flinging his arms round Raphael; "my friend, remember the sort of women you are with."

"I am a millionaire!"

"If you are not a millionaire, you are most certainly drunk."

12

"Drunk with power. I can kill you! Silence! I am Nero! I am Nebuchadnezzar!"

"But, Raphael, we are in queer company, and you ought to keep quiet for the sake of your own dignity."

"My life has been silent too long. I mean to have my revenge now on the world at large. I will not amuse myself by squandering paltry five-franc pieces; I will reproduce and sum up my epoch by absorbing human lives, human minds, and human souls. There are the treasures of pestilence—that is no paltry kind of wealth, is it? I will wrestle with fevers—yellow, blue, or green—with whole armies, with gibbets. I can possess Fœdora. Yet no, I do not want Fœdora; she is a disease; I am dying of Fœdora. I want to forget Fœdora!"

"If you keep on calling out like this, I shall take you into the dining-room."

"Do you see this skin? It is Solomon's will. Solomon belongs to me—a little varlet of a king! Arabia is mine, Arabia Petræa to boot; and the universe, and you too, if I choose. If I choose—ah! be careful. I can buy up all your journalist's shop; you shall be my valet. You shall be my valet, you shall manage my newspaper. Valet! *valet*, that is to say, free from aches and pains, because he has no brains."

At the word, Emile carried Raphael off into the dining-room.

"All right," he remarked; "yes, my friend, I am your valet. But you are about to be editor-in-chief of a newspaper; so be quiet, and behave properly, for my sake. Have you no regard for me?"

"Regard for you! You shall have Havana cigars, with this bit of shagreen; always with this skin, this supreme bit of shagreen. It is a cure for corns, an efficacious remedy. Do you suffer? I will remove them."

"Never have I known you so senseless——"

"Senseless, my friend? Not at all. This skin contracts

whenever I form a wish—'tis a paradox. There is a Brahmin underneath it ! The Brahmin must be a droll fellow, for our desires, look you, are bound to expand——"

" Yes, yes——"

" I tell you——"

" Yes, yes, very true, I am quite of your opinion—our desires expand——"

" The skin, I tell you."

" Yes."

" You don't believe me. I know you, my friend ; you are as full of lies as a new-made king."

" How can you expect me to follow your drunken maunderings?"

" I will bet you I can prove it. Let us measure it——"

" Goodness ! he will never get off to sleep," exclaimed Emile, as he watched Raphael rummaging busily in the dining-room.

Thanks to the peculiar clearness with which external objects are sometimes projected on an inebriated brain, in sharp contrast to its own obscure imaginings, Valentin found an inkstand and a table-napkin, with the quickness of a monkey, repeating all the time—

" Let us measure it ! Let us measure it ! "

" All right," said Emile ; " let us measure it."

The two friends spread out the table-napkin and laid the Wild Ass' Skin upon it. As Emile's hand appeared to be steadier than Raphael's, he drew a line with pen and ink round the talisman, while his friend said—

" I wished for an income of two hundred thousand livres, didn't I ? Well, when that comes, you will observe a mighty diminution of my shagreen."

" Yes—now go to sleep. Shall I make you comfortable on that sofa ? Now then, are you all right ? "

" Yes, my nursling of the press. You shall amuse me ; you shall drive the flies away from me. The friend of adversity should be the friend of prosperity. So I will give you some Havan—na—cig——"

" Come, now, sleep. Sleep off your gold, you millionaire!"

"You! sleep off your paragraphs! Good-night! Say good-night to Nebuchadnezzar! —love!—wine!—France!— glory and tr—treas——"

Very soon the snorings of the two friends were added to the music with which the rooms resounded—an ineffectual concert! The lights went out one by one, their crystal sconces cracking in the final flare. Night threw dark shadows over this prolonged revelry, in which Raphael's narrative had been a second orgy of speech, of words without ideas, of ideas for which words had often been lacking.

Towards noon, next day, the fair Aquilina bestirred her-self. She yawned wearily. She had slept with her head upon a painted velvet footstool, and her cheeks were mottled over by contact with the surface. Her movements awoke Euphrasia, who suddenly sprang up with a hoarse cry; her pretty face, that had been so fresh and fair in the evening, was sallow now and pallid; she looked like a candidate for the hospital. The rest awoke also by degrees, with portentous groanings, to feel themselves over in every stiffened limb, and to experience the infinite varieties of weariness that weighed upon them.

A servant came in to throw back the shutters and open the windows. There they all stood, brought back to conscious-ness by the warm rays of sunlight that shone upon the sleepers' heads. Their movements during slumber had disordered the elaborately arranged hair and toilettes of the women. They presented a ghastly spectacle in the bright daylight. Their hair fell ungracefully about them; their eyes, lately so bril-liant, were heavy and dim; the expression of their faces was entirely changed. The sickly hues, which daylight brings out so strongly, were frightful. An olive tint had crept over the lymphatic faces, so fair and soft when in repose; the dainty red lips were grown pale and dry, and bore tokens of the degradation of excess. Each disowned his mistress of the night before; the women looked wan and discolored, like flowers trampled under foot by a passing procession.

The men who scorned them looked even more horrible. Those human faces would have made you shudder. The hollow eyes with the dark circles round them seemed to see nothing; they were dull with wine and stupefied with heavy slumbers that had been exhausting rather than refreshing. There was an indescribable, ferocious and stolid bestiality about the haggard faces, where bare physical appetite appeared shorn of all the poetical illusion with which the intellect invests it. Even these fearless champions, accustomed to measure themselves with excess, were struck with horror at this awakening of vice, stripped of its disguises, at being confronted thus with sin, the skeleton in rags, lifeless and hollow, bereft of the sophistries of the intellect and the enchantments of luxury. Artists and courtesans scrutinized in silence and with haggard glances the surrounding disorder, the rooms where everything had been laid waste at the havoc wrought by heated passions.

Demoniac laughter broke out when Taillefer, catching the smothered murmurs of his guests, tried to greet them with a grin. His darkly flushed, perspiring countenance loomed upon this pandemonium, like the image of a crime that knows no remorse (see "L'Auberge rouge"). The picture was complete. A picture of foul life in the midst of luxury, a hideous mixture of the pomp and squalor of humanity; an awakening after the frenzy of debauch has crushed and squeezed all the fruits of life in her strong hands, till nothing but unsightly refuse is left to her, and lies in which she believes no longer. You might have thought of death gloating over a family stricken with the plague.

The sweet scents and dazzling lights, the mirth and the excitement were all no more; disgust with its nauseous sensa-

tions and searching philosophy was there instead. The sun
shone in like truth, the pure outer air was like virtue ; in con-
trast with the heated atmosphere, heavy with the fumes of the
previous night of revelry.

Accustomed as they were to their life, many of the girls
thought of other days and other wakings ; pure and innocent
days when they looked out and saw the roses and honeysuckle
about the casement, and the fresh country-side without enrap-
tured by the glad music of the skylark ; while earth lay
in mists, lighted by the dawn, and all the glittering radiance
of dew. Others imagined the family breakfast, the father
and children round the table, the innocent laughter, the un-
speakable charm that pervaded it all, the simple hearts and
their meal as simple.

An artist mused upon his quiet studio, on his statue in its
severe beauty, and the graceful model who was waiting for
him. A young man recollected a lawsuit on which the fortunes
of a family hung, and an important transaction that needed
his presence. The scholar regretted his study and the noble
work that called for him. Nearly everybody was sorry for
himself. Emile appeared just then as smiling, blooming, and
fresh as the smartest assistant in a fashionable shop.

" You are all as ugly as bailiffs. You won't be fit for any-
thing to-day, so this day is lost, and I vote for breakfast."

At this Taillefer went out to give some orders. The women
went languidly up to the mirrors to set their toilettes in order.
Each one shook herself. The wilder sort lectured the steadier
ones. The courtesans made fun of those who looked unable
to continue the boisterous festivity ; but these wan forms
revived at once, stood in groups, and talked and smiled. Some
servants quickly and adroitly set the furniture and everything
else in its place, and a magnificent breakfast was gotten ready.

The guests hurried to the dining-room. Everything there
bore indelible marks of yesterday's excess, it is true, but there
were at any rate some traces of ordinary, rational existence,

such traces as may be found in a sick man's dying struggles. And so the revelry was laid away and buried, like carnival of a Shrove Tuesday by masks, wearied out with dancing, drunk with drunkenness, and quite ready to be persuaded of the pleasures of lassitude, lest they be forced to admit their own exhaustion.

As soon as these bold spirits surrounded the capitalist's breakfast table, Cardot appeared. He had left the rest to make a night of it after the dinner, and finished the evening after his own fashion in the retirement of domestic life. Just now a sweet smile wandered over his features. He seemed to have a presentiment that there would be some inheritance to sample and divide, involving inventories and engrossing; an inheritance rich in fees and deeds to draw up, and something as juicy as the trembling fillet of beef in which their host had just plunged his knife.

"Oh, ho! we are to have breakfast in the presence of a notary," cried Cursy.

"You have come here just at the right time," said the banker, indicating the breakfast; "you can jot down the numbers, and initial off all the dishes."

"There is no will to make here, but contracts of marriage there may be, perhaps," said the scholar, who had made a satisfactory arrangement on this occasion for the first time in twelve months.

"Oh! Oh!"

"Ah! Ah!"

"One moment," cried Cardot, fairly deafened by a chorus of wretched jokes. "I came here on serious business. I am bringing six millions for one of you. (Dead silence.) "Monsieur," he went on, turning to Raphael, who at that moment was unceremoniously wiping his eyes on a corner of the table-napkin, "was not your mother a Mlle. O'Flaharty?"

"Yes," said Raphael, mechanically enough; "Barbara Marie."

" Have you your certificate of birth about you," Cardot went on, "and Mme. de Valentin's as well?"

" I believe so."

" Very well, then, monsieur; you are the sole heir of Major O'Flaharty, who died in August, 1828, at Calcutta."

" An *incalcuttable* fortune," said the critic.

" The Major having bequeathed several amounts to public institutions in his will, the French government sent in a claim for the remainder to the East India Company," the notary continued. " The estate is clear and ready to be transferred at this moment. I had been looking in vain for the heirs and assigns of Mlle. Barbara Marie O'Flaharty for a fortnight past, when yesterday at dinner——"

Just then Raphael suddenly staggered to his feet; he looked like a man who has just received a blow. Acclamation took the form of silence, for stifled envy had been the first feeling in every breast, and all eyes devoured him like flames. Then a murmur rose, and grew like the voice of a discontented audience, or the first mutterings of a riot, as everybody made some comment on this news of great wealth brought by the notary.

This abrupt subservience of fate brought Raphael thoroughly to his senses. He immediately spread out the table-napkin with which he had lately taken the measure of the piece of shagreen. He heeded nothing as he laid the talisman upon it, and shuddered involuntarily at the sight of a slight difference between the present size of the skin and the outline traced upon the linen.

" Why, what is the matter with him?" Taillefer cried. " He comes by his fortune very cheaply."

" Support him," said Bixiou to Emile. " The joy will kill him."

A ghastly white hue overspread every line of the wan features of the heir-at-law. His face was drawn, every outline grew haggard; the hollows in his livid countenance grew deeper, and his eyes were fixed and staring. He was facing death.

The opulent banker, surrounded by faded women, and faces with satiety written on them, the enjoyment that had reached the pitch of agony, was a living illustration of his own life.

Raphael looked thrice at the talisman, which lay passively within the merciless outlines on the table-napkin; he tried not to believe it, but his incredulity vanished utterly before the light of an inner presentiment. The whole world was his; he could have all things, but the will to possess them was utterly extinct. Like a traveler in the midst of the desert, with but a little water left to quench his thirst, he must measure his life by the draughts he took of it. He saw what every desire of his must cost him in the days of his life. He believed in the powers of the Wild Ass' Skin at last; he listened to every breath he drew; he felt ill already; he asked himself:

"Am I not consumptive? Did not my mother die of a lung complaint?"

"Aha, Raphael! what fun you will have! What will you give me?" asked Aquilina.

"Here's to the death of his uncle, Major O'Flaharty! There's a man for you!"

"He will be a peer of France."

"Pooh! what is a peer of France since July?" said the amateur critic.

"Are you going to take a box at the Bouffons?"

"You are going to treat us all, I hope?" put in Bixiou.

"A man of his sort will be sure to do things in style," said Emile.

The hurrah set up by the jovial assembly rang in Valentin's ears, but he could not grasp the sense of a single word. Vague thoughts crossed him of the Breton peasant's life of mechanical labor, without a wish of any kind; he pictured him burdened with a family, tilling the soil, living on buckwheat meal, drinking cider out of a pitcher, believing in the Virgin and the King, taking the sacrament at Easter, dancing of a Sunday on the green sward, and understanding never a word of the rector's sermon. The actual scene that lay before him, the gilded furniture, the courtesans, the feast itself, and the surrounding splendors, seemed to catch him by the throat and made him cough.

"Do you wish for some asparagus?" the banker cried.

"*I wish for nothing!*" thundered Raphael.

"Bravo!" Taillefer exclaimed; "you understand your position; a fortune confers the privilege of being impertinent. You are one of us. Gentlemen, let us drink to the might of gold! M. Valentin here, six times a millionaire, has become a power. He is a king, like all the rich; everything is at his disposal, everything lies under his feet. From this time forth the axiom that 'all Frenchmen are alike in the eyes of the law,' is for him a fib at the head of the Constitutional Charter. He is not going to obey the law—the law is going to obey him. There are neither scaffolds nor executioners for millionaires."

"Yes, there are," said Raphael; "they are their own executioners."

"Here is another victim of prejudices," cried the banker.

"Let us drink!" Raphael said, putting the talisman into his pocket.

"What are you doing?" said Emile, checking his movement. "Gentlemen," he added, addressing the company, who were rather taken aback by Raphael's behavior, "you must know that our friend Valentin here—what am I saying? —I mean my Lord Marquis de Valentin—is in possession of a secret for obtaining wealth. His wishes are fulfilled as soon as he knows them. He will make us all rich together, or he is a flunkey, and devoid of all decent feeling."

"Oh, Raphael dear, I should like a set of pearl ornaments!" Euphrasia exclaimed.

"If he has any gratitude in him, he will give me a couple of carriages with fast steppers," said Aquilina.

"Wish for a hundred thousand a year for me!"

"India shawls!"

"Pay my debts!"

"Send an apoplexy to my uncle, the old stick!"

"Ten thousand a year in the funds, and I'll cry quits with you, Raphael!"

"Deeds of gift and no mistake," was the notary's comment.

"He ought, at least, to rid me of the gout!"

"Lower the funds!" shouted the banker.

These phrases flew about like the last discharge of rockets at the end of a display of fireworks; and were uttered, perhaps more in earnest than in jest.

"My good friend," Emile said solemnly, "I shall be quite satisfied with an income of two hundred thousand livres. Please to set about it at once."

"Do you not know the cost, Emile?" asked Raphael.

"A nice excuse!" the poet cried; "ought we not to sacrifice ourselves for our friends?"

"I have almost a mind to wish that you were all dead," Valentin made answer, with a dark, inscrutable look at his boon companions.

"Dying people are frightfully cruel," said Emile, laughing. "You are rich now," he went on gravely; "very well, I will give you two months at most before you grow vilely selfish. You are so dense already that you cannot understand a joke. You have only to go a little further to believe in your Wild Ass' Skin.

Raphael kept silent, fearing the banter of the company; but he drank immoderately, trying to drown in intoxication the recollection of his fatal power.

THE AGONY.

IN the early days of December an old man of some seventy years of age pursued his way along the Rue de Varenne, in spite of the falling rain. He peered up at the door of each house, trying to discover the address of the Marquis Raphael de Valentin, in a simple, childlike fashion, and with the abstracted look peculiar to philosophers. His face plainly showed traces of a struggle between a heavy mortification and an authoritative nature; his long gray hair hung in disorder about a face like a piece of parchment, shriveling in the fire. If a painter had come upon this curious character, he would, no doubt, have transferred him .to his sketch-book on his return, a thin, bony figure, clad in black, and have inscibed beneath it : "Classical poet in search of a rhyme." When he had identified the number that had been given to him, this re-incarnation of Rollin knocked meekly at the door of a splendid mansion.

"Is Monsieur Raphael in ?" the worthy man inquired of the Swiss in livery.

"My Lord the Marquis sees nobody," said the servant, swallowing a huge morsel that he had just dipped in a large bowl of coffee.

"There is his carriage," said the elderly stranger, pointing to a fine equipage that stood under the wooden canopy that sheltered the steps before the house, in place of a striped linen awning. "He is going out ; I will wait for him."

"Then you might wait here till to-morrow morning, old boy," said the Swiss. "A carriage is always waiting for monsieur. Please go away. If I were to let any stranger

come into the house without orders, I should lose an income
of six hundred francs.''

A tall old man, in a costume not unlike that of a subordi-
nate in the civil service, came out of the vestibule and hurried
part of the way down the steps, while he made a survey of the
astonished elderly applicant for admission.

'' What is more, here is M. Jonathan,'' the Swiss remarked ;
'' speak to him.''

Fellow-feeling of some kind, or curiosity, brought the two
old men together in a central space in the great entrance
court. A few blades of grass were growing in the crevices of
the pavement; a terrible silence reigned in that great house.
The sight of Jonathan's face would have made you long to
understand the mystery that brooded over it, and that was
announced by the smallest trifles about the melancholy place.

When Raphel inherited his uncle's vast estate, his first care
had been to seek out the old and devoted servitor of whose
affection he knew that he was secure. Jonathan had wept
tears of joy at the sight of his young master, of whom he
thought he had taken a final farewell ; and when the Marquis
exalted him to the high office of steward, his happiness could
not be surpassed. So old Jonathan became an intermediary
power between Raphael and the world at large. He was the
absolute disposer of his master's fortune, the blind instrument
of an unknown will, and a sixth sense, as it were, by which
the emotions of life were communicated to Raphael.

'' I should like to speak with M. Raphael, sir,'' said the
elderly person to Jonathan, as he climbed up the steps some
way, into a shelter from the rain.

'' To speak with my lord the Marquis ? '' the steward cried.
'' He scarcely speaks even to me, his foster-father !''

'' But I am likewise his foster-father,'' said the old man.
'' If your wife was his foster-mother, I fed him myself with
the milk of the Muses. He is my nursling, my child, *carus
àlumnus !* I formed his mind, cultivated his understanding,

developed his genius, and, I venture to say it, to my own
honor and glory. Is he not one of the most remarkable men
of our epoch? He was one of my pupils in two lower forms,
and in rhetoric. I am his professor.''

" Ah, sir, then you are M. Porriquet?''

" Exactly, sir, but——''

" Hush! hush!'' Jonathan called to two underlings, whose
voices broke the monastic silence that shrouded the house.

" But is the Marquis ill, sir?'' the professor continued.

" My dear sir,'' Jonathan replied, " heaven only knows
what is the matter with my master. You see, there are not a
couple of houses like ours anywhere in Paris. Do you under-
stand? Not two houses. Faith, that there are not. My
lord the Marquis had this hotel purchased for him; it form-
erly belonged to a duke and a peer of France; then he spent
three hundred thousand francs over furnishing it. That's a
good deal, you know, three hundred thousand francs! But
every room in the house is a perfect wonder. ' Good,' said
I to myself when I saw this magnificence; ' it is just like it
used to be in the time of my lord, his late grandfather; and
the young Marquis is going to entertain all Paris and the
Court!' Nothing of the kind! My lord refused to see any
one whatever. 'Tis a funny life that he leads, M. Porriquet,
you understand. An *inconciliable* life. He rises every day at
the same time. I am the only person, you see, that may
enter his room. I open the shutters at seven o'clock, summer
or winter. It is all arranged very oddly. As I come in I
say to him—

" ' You must get up and dress, my lord Marquis.'

" Then he rises and dresses hinself. I have to give him
his dressing-gown, and it is always after the same pattern,
and of the same material. I am obliged to replace it when it
can be used no longer, simply to save him the trouble of ask-
ing for a new one. A queer fancy! As a matter of fact, he
has a thousand francs to spend every day, and he does as he

pleases, the dear child. And besides, I am so fond of him that if he gave me a box on the ear on one side, I should hold out the other to him! The most difficult things he will tell me to do, and yet I do them, you know! He gives me such a lot of trifles to attend to, that I am well set to work! He reads the newspapers, doesn't he? Well, my instructions are to put them always in the same place, on the same table. I always go at the same hour and shave him myself; and don't I tremble! The cook would forfeit the annuity of a thousand crowns that he is to come into after my lord's death, if breakfast is not served *inconciliably* at ten o'clock precisely. The menus are drawn up for the whole year round, day after day. My lord the Marquis has not a thing to wish for. He has strawberries whenever there are any, and he has the earliest mackerel to be had in Paris. The programme is printed every morning. He knows his dinner by rote. In the next place, he dresses himself at the same hour, in the same clothes, the same linen, that I always put on the same chair, you understand? I have to see that he always has the same cloth; and if it should happen that his coat came to grief (a mere supposition), I should have to replace it by another without saying a word about it to him. If it is fine, I go in and say to my master—

"'You ought to go out, sir.'

"He says Yes, or No. If he has a notion that he will go out, he doesn't wait for his horses; they are always ready harnessed; the coachman stops there *inconciliably*, whip in hand, just as you see him out there. In the evening, after dinner, my master goes one day to the opera, the other to the Ital——no, he hasn't yet gone to the Italiens, though, for I could not find a box for him until yesterday. Then he comes in at eleven o'clock precisely, to go to bed. At any time in the day when he has nothing to do, he reads—he is always reading, you see—it is a notion he has. My instructions are to read the *Journal de la Librairie* before he sees it, and to

buy new books, so that he finds them on his chimney-piece on
the very day that they are published. I have orders to go
into his room every hour or so, to look after the fire and
everything else, and to see that he wants nothing. He gave
me a little book, sir, to learn off by heart, with all my duties
written in it—a regular catechism! In summer I have to
keep a cool and even temperature with blocks of ice, and at
all seasons to put fresh flowers all about. He is rich! He
has a thousand francs to spend every day; he can indulge his
fancies! And he hadn't even necessaries for so long, poor
child! He doesn't annoy anybody; he is as good as gold;
he never opens his mouth, for instance; the house and garden
are absolutely silent. In short, my master has not a single
wish left; everything comes in the twinkling of an eye, if he
raises his hand, and *instanter*. Quite right, too. If servants
are not looked after, everything falls into confusion. You
would never believe the lengths he goes about things. His
rooms are all—what do you call it!—er—er—*en suite*. Very
well; just suppose, now, that he opens his room door or the
door of his study; presto! all the other doors fly open them-
selves by a patent contrivance; and then he can go from one
end of the house to the other and not find a single door shut;
which is all very nice and pleasant and convenient for us great
folk! But, on my word, it costs us a lot of money! And,
after all, M. Porriquet, he said to me at last—

"'Jonathan, you will look after me as if I were a baby in
long clothes.' Yes, sir, 'long clothes!' those were his very
words. 'You will think of all my requirements for me.' I
am the master, so to speak, and he is the servant, you under-
stand? The reason of it? Ah, my word, that is just what
nobody on earth knows but he himself and God Almighty.
It is quite *inconciliable!*"

"He is writing a poem!" exclaimed the old professor.

"You think he is writing a poem, sir? It is a very absorbing
affair, then! But, you know, I don't think he is. He often

tells me that he wants to live like a *vergetation;* he wants to *vergetate.* Only yesterday he was looking at a tulip while he was dressing, and he said to me—

" ' There is my own life—I am *vergetating,* my poor Jonathan.' Now, some of them insist that that is monomania. It is *inconciliable!* "

" All this makes it very clear to me, Jonathan," the professor answered, with a magisterial solemnity that greatly impressed the old servant, " that your master is absorbed in a great work. He is deep in vast meditations, and has no wish to be distracted by the petty preoccupations of ordinary life. A man of genius forgets everything among his intellectual labors. One day the famous Newton——"

" Newton?—oh, ah! I don't know the name," said Jonathan.

" Newton, a great geometrician," Porriquet went on, " once sat for twenty-four hours leaning his elbow on the table; when he emerged from his musings, he was a day out in his reckoning, just as if he had been sleeping. I will go to see him, dear lad; I may perhaps be of some use to him."

" Not for a moment ! " Jonathan cried. " Not though you were King of France—I mean the real one. You could not go in unless you forced the doors open and walked over my body. But I will go and tell him you are here, M. Porriquet, and I will put it to him like this, ' Ought he to come up ? ' And he will say Yes or No. I never say, ' Do you wish ? ' or ' Will you ? ' or ' Do you want ? ' Those words are scratched out of the dictionary. He let out at me once with a ' Do you want to kill me ? ' he was so very angry."

Jonathan left the old schoolmaster in the vestibule, signing to him to come no further, and soon returned with a favorable answer. He led the old gentleman through one magnificent room after another, where every door stood open. At last Porriquet beheld his pupil at some distance seated beside the fire.

13

Raphael was reading the paper. He sat in an arm-chair, wrapped in a dressing-gown with some large pattern on it. The intense melancholy that preyed upon him could be discerned in his languid posture and feeble frame; it was depicted on his brow and white face; he looked like some plant bleached by darkness. There was a kind of effeminate grace about him; the fancies peculiar to wealthy invalids were also noticeable. His hands were soft and white, like a pretty woman's; he wore his fair hair, now grown scanty, curled about his temples with a refinement of vanity.

The Greek cap that he wore was pulled to one side by the weight of its tassel; too heavy for the light material of which it was made. He had let the paper-knife fall at his feet, a malachite blade with gold mounting, which he had used to cut the leaves of a book. The amber mouth-piece of a magnificent India hookah lay on his knee; the enameled coils lay like a serpent in the room, but he had forgotten to draw out its fresh perfume. And yet there was a complete contradiction between the general feebleness of his young frame and the blue eyes, where all his vitality seemed to dwell; an extraordinary intelligence seemed to look out from them and to grasp everything at once.

That expression was painful to see. Some would have read despair in it, and others some inner conflict terrible as remorse. It was the inscrutable glance of helplessness that must perforce consign its desires to the depth of its own heart; or of a miser enjoying in imagination all the pleasures that his money could procure for him, while he declines to lessen his hoard; the look of a bound Prometheus, of the fallen Napoleon of 1815, when he learned at the Elysée the strategical blunder that his enemies had made, and asked for twenty-four hours of command in vain; or rather it was the same look that Raphael had turned upon the Seine, or upon his last piece of gold at the gaming table only a few months ago.

He was submitting his intelligence and his will to the homely common-sense of an old peasant whom fifty years of domestic service had scarcely civilized. He had given up all the rights of life in order to live; he had despoiled his soul of all the romance that lies in a wish; and almost rejoiced at thus becoming a sort of automaton. The better to struggle with the cruel power that he had challenged, he had followed Origen's example, and had maimed and chastened his imagination.

The day after he had seen the dimunition of the Wild Ass' Skin, at his sudden accession of wealth, he happened to be at his notary's house. A well-known physician had told them quite seriously, at dessert, how a Swiss attacked by consumption had cured himself. The man had never spoken a word for ten years, and had compelled himself to draw six breaths only, every minute, in the close atmosphere of a cow-house, adhering all the time to a regimen of exceedingly light diet. "I will be like that man," thought Raphael to himself. He wanted life at any price, and so he led the life of a machine in the midst of all the luxury around him.

The old professor confronted this youthful corpse and shuddered; there seemed something unnatural about the meagre, enfeebled frame. In the Marquis, with his eager eyes and careworn forehead, he could hardly recognize the fresh-cheeked and rosy pupil with the active limbs, whom he remembered. If the worthy classicist, sage critic, and general preserver of the traditions of correct taste had read Byron, he would have thought that he had come on a Manfred when he looked to find Childe Harold.

"Good-day, Père Porriquet," said Raphael, pressing the old schoolmaster's frozen fingers in his own hot damp ones; "how are you?"

"I am very well," replied the other, alarmed by the touch of that feverish hand. "But how about you?"

"Oh, I am hoping to keep myself in health."

"You are engaged on some great work, no doubt?"

"No," Raphael answered. "*Exegi monumentum*, Père Por-

riquet; I have contributed an important page to science, and
have now bidden her farewell forever. I scarcely know where
my manuscript is."

"The style is no doubt correct?" queried the schoolmaster.
"You, I hope, would never have adopted the barbarous lan-
guage of the new school, which fancies it has worked such
wonders by discovering Ronsard!"

"My work treats of physiology pure and simple."

"Oh, then, there is no more to be said," the schoolmaster
answered. "Grammar must yield to the exigencies of dis-
covery. Nevertheless, young man, a lucid and harmonious
style—the diction of Massillon, of M. de Buffon, of the great
Racine—a classical style, in short, can never spoil anything—
But, my friend," the schoolmaster interrupted himself, "I
was forgetting the object of my visit, which concerns my own
interests."

Too late Raphael recalled to mind the verbose eloquence
and elegant circumlocutions which in a long professorial career
had grown habitual to his old tutor, and almost regretted that
he had admitted him; but just as he was about to wish to see
him safely outside, he promptly suppressed his secret desire
with a stealthy glance at the Wild Ass' Skin. It hung there
before him, fastened down upon some white material, sur-
rounded by a red line accurately traced about its prophetic
outlines. Since that fatal carouse, Raphael had stifled every
least whim, and had lived so as not to cause the slightest
movement in the terrible talisman. The Wild Ass' Skin was
like a tiger with which he must live without exciting its fero-
city. He bore patiently, therefore, with the old schoolmaster's
prolixity.

Porriquet spent an hour in telling him about the persecu-
tions directed against him ever since the Revolution of July.
The worthy man, having a liking for strong governments, had
expressed the patriotic wish that grocers should be left to
their counters, statesmen to the management of public busi-

ness, advocates to the Palais de Justice, and the peers of France to the Luxembourg; but one of the popularity-seeking ministers of the Citizen King had ousted him from his chair, on an accusation of Charlism, and the old man now found himself without pension or post, and with no bread to eat. As he played the part of guardian angel to a poor nephew, for whose schooling at Saint Sulpice he was paying, he came less on his own account than for his adopted child's sake, to entreat his former pupil's interest with the new minister. He did not ask to be reinstated, but only for a position at the head of some provincial school.

Raphael had fallen a victim to unconquerable drowsiness by the time that the worthy man's monotonous voice ceased to sound in his ears. Civility had compelled him to look at the pale and unmoving eyes of the deliberate and tedious old narrator, till he himself had reached stupefaction, magnetized in an inexplicable way by the power of inertia.

"Well, my dear Père Porriquet," he said, not very certain what the question was to which he was replying, "but I can do nothing for you, nothing at all. *I wish very heartily* that you may succeed——"

All at once, without seeing the change wrought on the old man's sallow and wrinkled brow by these conventional phrases, full of indifference and selfishness, Raphael sprang to his feet like a startled roebuck. He saw a thin white line between the black piece of hide and the red tracing about it, and gave a cry so fearful that the poor professor was frightened by it.

"Old fool! Go!" he cried. "You will be appointed as headmaster. Couldn't you have asked me for an annuity of a thousand crowns rather than a murderous wish? Your visit would have cost me nothing. There are a hundred thousand situations to be had in France, but I have only one life. A man's life is worth more than all the situations in the world. —Jonathan!"

Jonathan appeared.

"This is your doing, double-distilled idiot! What made you suggest that I should see M. Porriquet?" and he pointed to the old man, who was petrified with fright. "Did I put myself into your hands for you to tear me in pieces? You have just shortened my life by ten years! Another blunder of this kind, and you will lay me where I have laid my father. Would I not far rather have possessed the beautiful Fœdora? And I have obliged that old hulk instead—that rag of humanity! I had money enough for him. And, moreover, if all the Porriquets in the world were dying of hunger, what is that to me?"

Raphael's face was white with anger; a slight froth marked his trembling lips; there was a savage gleam in his eyes. The two elders shook with terror in his presence like two children at the sight of a snake. The young man fell back in his armchair, a kind of reaction took place in him, the tears flowed fast from his angry eyes.

"Oh, my life!" he cried, "that fair life of mine. Never to know a kindly thought again, to love no more; nothing is left to me!"

He turned to the professor and went on in a gentle voice—"The harm is done, my old friend. Your services have been well repaid; and my misfortune has at any rate contributed to the welfare of a good and worthy man."

His tones betrayed so much feeling that the almost unintelligible words drew tears from the two old men, such tears as are shed over some pathetic song in a foreign tongue.

"He is epileptic," muttered Porriquet.

"I understand your kind intentions, my friend," Raphael answered gently. "You would make excuses for me. Ill-health cannot be helped, but ingratitude is a grievous fault. Leave me now," he added. "To-morrow, or the next day, or possibly to-night, you will receive your appointment; resistance has triumphed over motion. Farewell."

The old schoolmaster went away, full of keen apprehension

as to Valentin's sanity. A thrill of horror ran through him ; there had been something supernatural, he thought, in the scene he had passed through. He could hardly believe his own impressions, and questioned them like one awakened from a painful dream.

"Now attend to me, Jonathan," said the young man to his old servant. "Try to understand the charge confided to you."

"Yes, my Lord Marquis."

"I am as a man outlawed from humanity."

"Yes, my Lord Marquis."

"All the pleasures of life disport themselves round my bed of death, and dance about me like fair women ; but if I beckon to them I must die. Death always confronts me. You must be the barrier between the world and me."

"Yes, my Lord Marquis," said the old servant, wiping the drops of perspiration from his wrinkled forehead. "But if you don't wish to see pretty women how will you manage at the Italiens this evening? An English family is returning to London, and I have taken their box for the rest of the season, and it is in a splendid position—superb ; in the first row."

Raphael, deep in his own musings, paid no attention to him.

Do you see that splendid equipage, a brougham painted a dark brown color, but with the arms of an ancient and noble family shining from the panels? As it rolls past, all the shop-girls admire it, and look longingly at the yellow satin lining, the rugs from la Savonnerie, the daintiness and freshness of every detail, the silken cushions and tightly-fitting glass windows. Two liveried footmen are mounted behind this aristocratic carriage ; and within, a head lies back among the silken cushions, the feverish face and hollow eyes of Raphael, melancholy and sad. Emblem of the doom of wealth ! He flies across Paris like a rocket, and reaches the peristyle of the Théâtre Favart. The passers-by make way for him ; the two footmen help him to alight, an envious crowd looking on the while.

"What has that fellow done to be so rich?" asks a poor law-student, who cannot listen to the magical music of Rossini for lack of a five-franc piece.

Raphael walked slowly along the gangway; he expected no enjoyment from these pleasures he had once coveted so eagerly. In the interval before the second act of *Semiramide* he walked up and down in the lobby, and along the corridors, leaving his box, which he had not yet entered, to look after itself. The instinct of property was dead within him already. Like all invalids, he thought of nothing but his own sufferings. He was leaning against the chimney-piece in the green-room. A group had gathered about it of dandies, young and old, of ministers and ex-ministers, of peers without peerages, and peerages without peers, for so the Revolution of July had ordered matters. Among a host of adventurers and journalists, in fact, Raphael beheld a strange, unearthly figure a few paces away among the crowd. He went towards this grotesque object to see it better, half-closing his eyes with exceeding superciliousness.

"What a wonderful bit of painting!" he said to himself. The stranger's hair and eyebrows and a Mazarin tuft on the chin had been dyed black, but the result was a spurious, glossy, purple tint that varied its hues according to the light; the hair had been too white, no doubt, to take the preparation. Anxiety and cunning were depicted in the narrow, insignificant face, with its wrinkles incrusted by thick layers of red and white paint. This red enamel, lacking on some portions of his face, strongly brought out his natural feebleness and livid hues. It was impossible not to smile at this visage with the protuberant forehead and pointed chin, a face not unlike those grotesque wooden figures that German herdsmen carve in their spare moments.

An attentive observer looking from Raphael to this elderly

Adonis would have remarked a young man's eyes set in a mask of age, in the case of the marquis, and in the other case the dim eyes of age peering forth from behind a mask of youth. Valentin tried to recollect when and where he had seen this little old man before. He was thin, fastidiously cravatted, booted and spurred like one-and-twenty ; he crossed his arms and clinked his spurs as if he possessed all the wanton energy of youth. He seemed to move about without constraint or difficulty. He had carefully buttoned up his fashionable coat, which disguised his powerful, elderly frame, and gave him the appearance of an antiquated coxcomb who still follows the fashions.

For Raphael this animated puppet possessed all the interest of an apparition. He gazed at it as if it had been some smoke-begrimed Rembrandt, recently restored and newly framed. This idea found him a clue to the truth among his confused recollections ; he recognized the dealer in antiquities, the man to whom he owed his calamities !

A noiseless laugh broke just then from the fantastical personage, straightening the line of his lips that stretched across a row of artificial teeth. That laugh brought out, for Raphael's heated fancy, a strong resemblance between the man before him and the type of head that painters have assigned to Goethe's Mephistopheles. A crowd of superstitious thoughts entered Raphael's sceptical mind ; he was convinced of the powers of the devil and of all the sorcerer's enchantments embodied in mediæval tradition, and since worked up by poets. Shrinking in horror from the destiny of Faust, he prayed for the protection of Heaven with all the ardent faith of a dying man in God and the Virgin. A clear, bright radiance seemed to give him a glimpse of the heaven of Michel Angelo or of Raphael of Urbino : a venerable white-bearded man, a beautiful woman seated in an aureole of the clouds and winged cherub heads. Now he had grasped and received the meaning of those imaginative, almost human creations ;

they seemed to explain what had happened to him, to leave him yet one hope.

But when the greenroom of the Italiens returned upon his sight, he beheld not the Virgin, but a very handsome young person. The execrable Euphrasia, in all the splendor of her toilette, with its orient pearls, had come thither, impatient for her ardent, elderly admirer. She was insolently exhibiting herself with her defiant face and glittering eyes to an envious crowd of stockbrokers, a visible testimony to the inexhaustible wealth that the old dealer permitted her to squander.

Raphael recollected the mocking wish with which he had accepted the old man's luckless gift, and tasted all the sweets of revenge when he beheld the spectacle of sublime wisdom fallen to such a depth as this, wisdom for which such humiliation had seemed a thing impossible. The centenarian greeted Euphrasia with a ghastly smile, receiving her honeyed words in reply. He offered her his emaciated arm, and went twice or thrice round the greenroom with her; the envious glances and compliments with which the crowd received his mistress delighted him; he did not see the scornful smiles, nor hear the caustic comments to which he gave rise.

"In what cemetery did this young ghoul unearth that corpse of hers?" asked the dandy of the romantic faction.

"Euphrasia began to smile. The speaker was a slender, fair-haired youth, with bright blue eyes, and a moustache. His short dress coat, hat tilted over one ear, and sharp tongue, all denoted the species.

"How many old men," said Raphael to himself, " bring an upright, virtuous, and hard-working life to a close in folly! His feet are cold already, and he is making love."

"Well, sir," exclaimed Valentin, stopping the merchant's progress, while he stared hard at Euphrasia, " have you quite forgotten the stringent maxims of your philosophy?"

"Ah, I am as happy now as a young man," said the other, in a cracked voice. "I used to look at existence from a

wrong standpoint. One hour of love has a whole life in it."
The playgoers heard the bell ring, and left the greenroom
to take their places again. Raphael and the old merchant sepa-
rated. As he entered his box, the Marquis saw Fœdora sitting
exactly opposite to him on the other side of the theatre. The
Countess had probably only just come, for she was just flinging
off her scarf to leave her throat uncovered, and was occupied
with going through all the indescribable manœuvres of a
coquette arranging herself. All eyes were turned upon her.
A young peer of France had come with her; she asked him
for the lorgnette which she had given him to carry. Raphael
knew the despotism to which his successor had resigned him-
self, in her gestures, and in the way she treated her companion.
He was also under the spell no doubt, another dupe beating
with all the might of a real affection against the woman's cold
calculations, enduring all the tortures from which Valentin
had luckily freed himself.

Fœdora's face lighted up with indescribable joy. After
directing her lorgnette upon every box in turn, to make a rapid
survey of all the dresses, she was conscious that by her toilette
and her beauty she had eclipsed the loveliest and best-dressed
women in Paris. She laughed to show her white teeth; her
head with its wreath of flowers was never still, in her quest
of admiration. Her glances went from one box to another,
as she diverted herself with the awkward way in which a
Russian princess wore her bonnet, or over the utter failure of
a bonnet with which a banker's daughter had disfigured her-
self.

All at once she met Raphael's steady gaze and turned pale,
aghast at the intolerable contempt in her rejected lover's eyes.
Not one of her exiled suitors had failed to own her power over
them; Valentin alone was proof against her attractions. A
power that can be defied with impunity is drawing to its end.
This axiom is as deeply engraved on the heart of woman as
in the minds of kings. In Raphael, therefore, Fœdora saw

the deathblow of her influence and her ability to please.   An epigram of his, made at the opera the day before, was already known in the salons of Paris.   The biting edge of that terrible speech had already given the Countess an incurable wound. We know how to cauterize a wound, but we know of no treatment as yet for the stab of a phrase.   As every other woman in the house looked by turns at her and at the Marquis, Fœdora would have consigned them all to the dungeons of some Bastille ; for in spite of her capacity for dissimulation, her discomfiture was discerned by her rivals.   Her unfailing consolation had slipped from her at last.   The delicious thought, "I am the most beautiful," the thought that all times had soothed every mortification, had turned into a lie.

At the opening of the second act a woman took up her position not very far from Raphael, in a box that had been empty hitherto.   A murmur of admiration went up from the whole house.   In that 'sea of human faces there was a movement of every living wave ; all eyes were turned upon the stranger lady.   The applause of young and old were so prolonged, that when the orchestra began, the musicians turned to the audience to request silence, and then they themselves joined in the plaudits and swelled the confusion.   Excited talk began in every box, every woman equipped herself with an opera glass, elderly men grew young again, and polished the glasses of their lorgnettes with their gloves.   The enthusiasm subsided by degrees, the stage echoed with the voices of the singers, and order reigned as before.   The aristocratic section, ashamed of having yielded to a spontaneous feeling, again assumed their wonted politely frigid manner.   The well-to-do dislike to be astonished at anything ; at the first sight of a beautiful thing it becomes their duty to discover the defect in it which absolves them from admiring it—the feeling of all ordinary minds.   Yet a few still remained motionless and heedless of the music, artlessly absorbed in the delight of watching Raphael's neighbor.

Valentin noticed Taillefer's mean, obnoxious countenance by Aquilina's side in a lower box, and received an approving smirk from him. Then he saw Emile, who seemed to say from where he stood in the orchestra, "Just look at that lovely creature there, close beside you!" Lastly, he saw Rastignac, with Mme. de Nucingen and her daughter, twisting his gloves like a man in despair, because he was tethered to his place, and could not leave it to go any nearer to the unknown fair divinity.

Raphael's life depended upon a covenant that he had made with himself, and had hitherto kept sacred. He would give no special heed to any woman whatever; and the better to guard against temptation, he used a cunningly contrived opera-glass which destroyed the harmony of the fairest features by hideous distortions. He had not recovered from the terror that had seized on him in the morning when, at a mere expression of civility, the Wild Ass' Skin had contracted so abruptly. So Raphael was determined not to turn his face in the direction of his neighbor. He sat imperturbable as a duchess, with his back against the corner of the box, thereby shutting out half of his neighbor's view of the stage, appearing to disregard her, and even to be unaware that a pretty woman sat there just behind him.

His neighbor copied Valentin's position exactly! she leaned her elbow on the edge of her box and turned her face in three-quarter profile upon the singers on the stage, as if she were sitting to a painter. These two people looked like two estranged lovers still sulking, still turning their backs upon each other, who will go into each other's arms at the first tender word.

Now and again his neighbor's ostrich feathers or her hair came in contact with Raphael's head, giving him a pleasurable thrill, against which he sternly fought. In a little while he felt the touch of the soft frill of lace that went round her dress; he could hear the gracious sounds of the folds of her dress itself, light rustling noises full of enchantment; he could even feel her movements as she breathed, with the gentle stir thus imparted to her form and to her draperies, it seemed to Raphael that all her being was suddenly communicated to him in an electric spark. The lace and tulle that caressed him imparted the delicious warmth of her bare, white shoulders. By a freak in the ordering of things, these two creatures, kept apart by social conventions, with the abysses of death between them, breathed together and perhaps thought of one another. Finally, the subtle perfume of aloes completed the work of Raphael's intoxication. Opposition heated his imagination, and his fancy, become the wilder for the limits imposed upon it, sketched a woman for him in outlines of fire. He turned abruptly, the stranger made a similar movement, startled no doubt at being brought in contact with a stranger; and they remained face to face, each with the same thought.

"Pauline!"

"M. Raphael!"

Each surveyed the other, both of them petrified with astonishment. Raphael noticed Pauline's daintily simple costume. A woman's experienced eyes would have discerned and admired the outlines beneath the modest gauze folds of her bodice and the lily whiteness of her throat. And then her more than mortal clearness of soul, her maidenly modesty, her graceful bearing, all were unchanged. Her sleeve was quivering with agitation, for the beating of her heart was shaking her whole frame.

"Come to the Hôtel de Saint-Quentin to-morrow for your papers," she said. "I will be there at noon. Be punctual."

She rose hastily and disappeared. Raphael thought of following Pauline, feared to compromise her, and stayed. He looked at Fœdora; she seemed to him positively ugly. Unable to understand a single phrase of the music, and feeling stifled in the theatre, he went out, and returned home.

"Jonathan," he said to the old servant, as soon as he lay in bed, "give me half a drop of laudanum on a piece of sugar, and don't wake me to-morrow till twenty minutes to twelve."

"I want Pauline to love me," he cried next morning, looking at the talisman the while in unspeakable anguish.

The skin did not move in the least; it seemed to have lost its power to shrink; doubtless it could not fulfil a wish fulfilled already.

"Ah!" exclaimed Raphael, feeling as if a mantle of lead had fallen away, which he had worn ever since the day when the talisman had been given to him; "so you are playing me false, you are not obeying me, the pact is broken! I am free; I shall live. Then was it all a wretched joke?" But he did not dare to believe in his own thought as he uttered it.

He dressed himself as simply as had formerly been his wont, and set out on foot for his old lodging, trying to go back in fancy to the happy days when he abandoned himself without peril to vehement desires, the days when he had not yet condemned all human enjoyment. As he walked he beheld Pauline—not the Pauline of the Hôtel Saint-Quentin, but the Pauline of last evening. Here was the accomplished mistress he had so often dreamed of, the intelligent young girl with the loving nature and artistic temperament, who understood poets, who understood poetry, and lived in luxurious surroundings. Here, in short, was Fœdora, gifted with a great soul; or Pauline become a countess, and twice a millionaire, as Fœdora had been. When he reached the worn threshold, and stood upon the broken step at the door, where in other days he had so many desperate thoughts, an old woman came out of the room within and spoke to him.

"You are M. Raphael de Valentin, are you not?"

"Yes, good mother," he replied.

"You know your old room then," she replied; "you are expected up there."

" Does Mme. Gaudin still own the house ? " Raphael asked.

" Oh no, sir.   Mme. Gaudin is a baroness now.   She lives in a fine house of her own on the other side of the river.   Her husband has come back.   My goodness, he brought back thousands and thousands,   They say she could buy up all the Quartier Saint-Jacques if she liked.   She gave me her basement room for nothing, and the remainder of her lease. Ah, she's a kind woman all the same; she is no more proud to-day than she was yesterday."

Raphael hurried up the staircase to his garret ; as he reached the last few steps he heard the sounds of a piano. Pauline was there, simply dressed in a cotton gown, but the way that it was made, like the gloves, hat, and shawl that she had thrown down carelessly upon the bed, revealed a change of fortune.

" Ah, there you are ! " cried Pauline, turning her head, and rising with unconcealed delight.

Raphael went to sit beside her, flushed, confused, and happy ; he looked at her in silence.

" Why did you leave us then ? " she asked, dropping her eyes as the flush deepened on his face.   " What became of you ? "

" Ah, I have been very miserable, Pauline ; I am very miserable still."

" Alas ! " she said, filled with pitying tenderness.   " I guessed your fate yesterday when I saw you so well dressed, and apparently so wealthy ; but in reality ?   Eh, M. Raphael, is it as it always used to be with you ? "

Valentin could not restrain the tears that sprang to his eyes.

" Pauline," he exclaimed, " I ——"

He went no further, love sparkled in his eyes, and his emotion overflowed his face.

" Oh, he loves me ! he loves me ! " cried Pauline.

Raphael felt himself unable to say one word ; he bent his

PAULINE DREW HER HANDS AWAY, LAID THEM ON
RAPHAEL'S SHOULDERS, AND DREW HIM
TOWARDS HER.

PAULINE DREW HER HANDS AWAY, LAID THEM ON
RAPHAEL'S SHOULDERS, AND DREW HIM
TOWARDS HER.

head. The young girl took his hand at this; she pressed it as she said, half-sobbing and half-laughing—

"Rich, rich, happy and rich! Your Pauline is rich. But I? Oh, I ought to be very poor to-day. I have said, times without number, that I would give all the wealth upon this earth for those words, 'He loves me!' O my Raphael! I have millions. You like luxury, you will be glad; but you must love me and my heart besides, for there is so much love for you in my heart. You don't know! My father has come back. I am a wealthy heiress. Both he and my mother leave me completely free to decide my own fate. I am free—do you understand!"

Seized with a kind of frenzy, Raphael grasped Pauline's hands and kissed them eagerly and vehemently, with an almost convulsive caress. Pauline drew her hands away, laid them on Raphael's shoulders, and drew him towards her. They understood one another—in that close embrace, in the unalloyed and sacred fervor of that one kiss without an afterthought—the first kiss by which two souls take possession of each other.

"Ah, I will not leave you any more," said Pauline, falling back in her chair. "I do not know how I come to be so bold!" she added, blushing.

"Bold, my Pauline! Do not fear it. It is love, love true and deep and everlasting like my own, is it not?"

"Speak!" she cried. "Go on speaking, so long your lips have been dumb for me."

"Then you have loved me all along?"

"Loved you? *Mon Dieu!* How often I have wept here, setting your room straight, and grieving for your poverty and my own. I would have sold myself to the evil one to spare you one vexation! You are *my* Raphael to-day, really my own Raphael, with that handsome head of yours, and your heart is mine too; yes, that above all, your heart—O wealth inexhaustible! Well, where was I?" she went on after a

14

pause. "Oh yes! We have three, four, or five millions, I believe. If I were poor, I should perhaps desire to bear your name, to be acknowledged as your wife; but as it is, I would give up the whole world for you, I would be your servant still, now and always. Why, Raphael, if I give you my fortune, my heart, myself to-day, I do no more than I did that day when I put a certain five-franc piece in the drawer there," and she pointed to the table. "Oh, how your exultation hurt me then!"

"Oh, why are you rich?" Raphael cried; "why is there no vanity in you? I can do nothing for you."

He wrung his hands in despair and happiness and love.

"When you are the Marquise de Valentin, I know that the title and the fortune for thee, heavenly soul, will not be worth——"

"One hair of your head," she cried.

"I have millions too. But what is wealth to either of us now? There is my life—ah, that I can offer, take it."

"Your love, Raphael, your love is all the world to me. Are your thoughts of me? I am the happiest of the happy!"

"Can any one overhear us?" asked Raphael.

"Nobody," she replied, with a mischievous gesture.

"Come, then!" cried Valentin, holding out his arms.

She sprang upon his knees and clasped her arms about his neck.

"Kiss me!" she cried, "after all the pain you have given me; to blot out the memory of the grief that your joys have caused me; and for the sake of the nights that I spent in painting hand-screens——"

"Those hand-screens of yours?"

"Now that we are rich, my darling, I can tell you all about it. Poor boy! how easy it is to delude a clever man! Could you have had white waistcoats and clean shirts twice a week for three francs every month to the laundress? Why, you used to drink twice as much milk as your money would have paid for. I deceived you all round—over firing, oil, and even money. O Raphael mine, don't have me for your wife, I am far too cunning!" she said laughingly.

"How did you manage it?"

"I used to work till two o'clock in the morning; I gave my mother half the money made by my screens, and the other half went to you."

They looked at one another for a moment, both bewildered by love and gladness.

"Some day we shall have to pay for this happiness by some terrible sorrow," cried Raphael.

"Perhaps you are married!" cried Pauline. "Oh, I will not give you up to another woman."

"I am free, my beloved."

"Free?" she repeated. "Free, and mine?"

She slipped down upon her knees, clasped her hands, and looked at Raphael in an enthusiasm of devotion.

"I am afraid I shall go mad. How handsome you are!" she went on, passing her fingers through her lover's fair hair. "How stupid your Countess Fœdora is! How pleased I was yesterday with the homage they all paid to me! *She* has never been applauded. Dear, when I felt your arm against my back, I heard a vague voice within me that cried, 'He is there!' and I turned round and saw you. I fled, for I longed so to throw my arms about you before them all."

"How happy you are—you can speak!" Raphael exclaimed. "My heart is overwhelmed; I would weep, but I cannot. Do not draw your hand away. I could stay here looking at you like this for the rest of my life, I think; happy and content."

"O my love, say that once more!"

"Ah, what are words?" answered Valentin, letting a hot tear fall on Pauline's hands. "Some time I will try to tell you of my love; just now I can only feel it."

"You," she said, " with your lofty soul and your great

genius, with that heart of yours, that I know so well; are you really mine, as I am yours?"

"For ever and ever, my sweet creature," said Raphael in an uncertain voice. "You shall be my wife, my protecting angel. My griefs have always been dispelled by your presence, and my courage revived; that angelic smile now on your lips has purified me, so to speak. A new life seems about to begin for me. The cruel past and my wretched follies are hardly more to me than evil dreams. At your side I breathe an atmosphere of happiness, and I am pure. Be with me always," he added, pressing her solemnly to his beating heart.

"Death may come when it will," said Pauline in ecstasy; "I have lived!"

Happy he who shall divine their joy, for he must have experienced it.

"I wish that no one might enter this dear garret again, my Raphael," said Pauline, after two hours of silence.

"We must have the door walled up, put bars across the windows, and buy the house," the Marquis answered.

"Yes, we will," she said. Then a moment later she added: "Our search for your manuscripts has been a little lost sight of," and they both laughed like children.

"Pshaw! I don't care a jot for the whole circle of the sciences," Raphael answered.

'Ah, sir, and how about glory?"

"I glory in you alone."

"You used to be very miserable as you made these little scratches and scrawls," she said, turning the papers over.

"My Pauline——"

"Oh, yes, I am your Pauline—and what then?"

"Where are you living now?"

"In the Rue Saint Lazare. And you?"

"In the Rue de Varenne."

"What a long way apart we shall be until——" She

stopped, and looked at her lover with a mischievous and coquettish expression.

"But at the most we need only be separated for a fort-night," Raphael answered.

"Really! we are to be married in a fortnight?" and she jumped for joy like a child.

"I am an unnatural daughter?" she went on. "I give no more thought to my father or my mother, or to anything in the world. Poor love, you don't know that my father is very ill? He returned from the Indies in very bad health. He nearly died at Havre, where we went to find him. Good heavens!" she cried, looking at her watch; "it is three o'clock already! I ought to be back again when he wakes at four. I am mistress of the house at home; my mother does everything that I wish, and my father worships me; but I will not abuse their kindness; that would be wrong. My poor father! He would have me go to the Italiens yesterday. You will come to see him to-morrow, will you not?"

"Will Madame la Marquise de Valentin honor me by tak-ing my arm?"

"I am going to take the key of this room away with me," she said. "Isn't our treasure-house a palace?"

"One more kiss, Pauline."

"A thousand, *Mon Dieu!*" she said, looking at Raphael. "Will it always be like this? I feel as if I were dreaming."

They went slowly down the stairs together, step for step, with arms closely linked, trembling both of them beneath their load of joy. Each pressing close to the other's side, like a pair of doves, they reached the Place de la Sorbonne, where Pauline's carriage was waiting.

"I want to go home with you," she said. "I want to see your own room and your study, and sit at the table where you work. It will be like old times," she said, blushing.

She spoke to the servant. "Joseph, before returning home I am going to the Rue de Varenne. It is a quarter-past three

now, and I must be back again by four o'clock. George must
hurry the horses."   And so in a few moments the lovers came
to Valentin's abode.

"How glad I am to have seen all this for myself!" Pauline
cried, creasing the silken bed-curtains in Raphael's room be-
tween her fingers. "As I go to sleep, I shall be here in
thought. I shall imagine your dear head on the pillow there.
Raphael, tell me, did no one advise you about the furniture
of your hôtel?"

"No one whatever."

"Really? It was not a woman who——"

"Pauline!"

"Oh, I know I am fearfully jealous. You have good taste.
I will have a bed like yours to-morrow."

Quite beside himself with happiness, Raphael caught Pauline
in his arms.

"Oh, my father!" she said; "my father——"

"I will take you back to him," cried Valentin, "for I want
to be away from you as little as possible."

"How loving you are! I did not venture to suggest it——"

"Are you not my life?"

It would be tedious to set down accurately the charm-
ing prattle of the lovers, for tones and looks and gestures
that cannot be rendered alone gave it significance. Valentin
went back with Pauline to her own door, and returned
with as much happiness in his heart as mortal man can
know.

When he was seated in his armchair beside the fire, think-
ing over the sudden and complete way in which his wishes had
been fulfilled, a cold shiver went through him, as if the blade
of a dagger had been plunged into his breast—he thought
of the Wild Ass' Skin, and saw that it had shrunk a little. He
uttered the most tremendous French oaths, without any of the
Jesuitical reservations made by the Abbess of Andouillettes,
leaned his head against the back of the chair, and sat motion-

less, fixing his unseeing eyes upon the bracket of the curtain pole.

"Good God!" he cried; every wish! Every desire of mine! Poor Pauline——"

He took a pair of compasses and measured the extent of existence that the morning had cost him.

"I have scarcely enough for two months!" he said.

A cold sweat broke out over him; moved by an ungovernable spasm of rage, he seized the Wild Ass' Skin, exclaiming—

"I am a perfect fool!"

He rushed out of the house and across the garden, and flung the talisman down a well.

"*Vogue la galère*," cried he. The devil take all this nonsense."

So Raphael gave himself up to the happiness of being beloved, and led with Pauline the life of heart and heart. Difficulties which it would be somewhat tedious to describe had delayed their marriage, which was to take place early in March. Each was sure of the other; their affection had been tried, and happiness had taught them how strong it was. Never has love made two souls, two natures, so absolutely one. The more they came to know each other, the more they loved. On either side there was the same hesitating delicacy, the same transports of joy such as angels know; there were no clouds in their heaven; the will of either was the other's law.

Wealthy as they both were, they had not a caprice which they could not gratify, and for that reason had no caprices. A refined taste, a feeling for beauty and poetry, was instinct in the soul of the bride; her lover's smile was more to her than all the pearls of Ormuz. She disdained feminine finery; a muslin dress and flowers formed her most elaborate toilette.

Pauline and Raphael shunned every one else, for solitude was abundantly beautiful to them. The idlers at the opera, or at the Italiens, saw this charming and unconventional pair evening after evening. Some gossip went the round of the salons at first, but the harmless lovers were soon forgotten in the course of events which took place in Paris; their marriage was announced at length to excuse them in the eyes of the prudish; and as it happened, their servants did not babble; so their bliss did not draw down upon them any very severe punishment.

One morning towards the end of February, at the time when the brightening days bring a belief in the nearness of the joys of spring, Pauline and Raphael were breakfasting together in a small conservatory, a kind of a drawing-room filled with flowers, on a level with the garden. The mild rays of the pale winter sunlight, breaking through the thicket of exotic plants, warmed the air somewhat. The vivid contrast made by the variety of foliage, the colors of the masses of flowing shrubs, the freaks of light and shadow, gladdened the eyes. While all the rest of Paris still sought warmth from its melancholy hearth, these two were laughing in a bower of camellias, lilacs, and blossoming heath. Their happy faces rose above lilies of the valley, narcissus blooms, and Bengal roses. A mat of plaited African grass, variegated like a carpet, lay beneath their feet in this luxurious conservatory. The walls, covered with a green linen material, bore no traces of damp. The surfaces of the rustic wooden furniture shone with cleanliness. A kitten, attracted by the odor of milk, had established itself upon the table; it allowed Pauline to bedabble it in coffee; she was playing merrily with it, taking away the cream that she had just allowed the kitten to sniff at, so as to exercise its patience, and to keep up the contest. She burst out laughing at every antic, and by the comical remarks she constantly made, she hindered Raphael from perusing the paper; he had dropped it a dozen times already. This morning picture seemed to overflow with inexpressible gladness, like everything that is natural and genuine.

Raphael, still pretending to read his paper, furtively watched Pauline with the cat—his Pauline, in the dressing-gown that hung carelessly about her; his Pauline, with her hair loose on her shoulders, with a tiny, white, blue-veined foot peeping out of a velvet slipper. It was pleasant to see her in this negligent dress; she was delightful as some fanciful picture by Westall; half-girl, half-woman, as she seemed to be, or perhaps more of a girl than a woman, there was no alloy in the happiness she enjoyed, and of love she knew as yet only its first ecstasy. When Raphael, absorbed in happy musing, had forgotten the existence of the newspaper, Pauline flew upon it, crumpled it up into a ball, and threw it out into the garden; the kitten sprang after the rotating object, which spun round and round, as politics are wont to do. This childish scene recalled Raphael to himself. He would have gone on reading, and felt for the sheet he no longer possessed. Joyous laughter rang out like the song of a bird, one peal leading to another.

"I am quite jealous of the paper," she said, as she wiped away the tears that her childlike merriment had brought into her eyes. "Now, is it not a heinous offence," she went on, as she became a woman all at once, "to read Russian proclamations in my presence, and to attend to the prosings of the Emperor Nicholas rather than to looks and words of love!"

"I was not reading, my dear angel; I was looking at you."

Just then the gravel walk outside the conservatory rang with the sound of the gardener's heavily nailed boots.

"I beg your pardon, my Lord Marquis—and yours, too, madame—if I am intruding, but I have brought you a curiosity the like of which I never set eyes on. Drawing a bucket of water just now, with due respect, I got out this strange salt-water plant. Here it is. It must be thoroughly used to water, anyhow, for it isn't saturated or even damp at all. It is as dry as a piece of wood, and has not swelled a bit. As my Lord Marquis certainly knows a great deal more

about things than I do, I thought I ought to bring it, and
that it would interest him."

Therewith the gardener showed Raphael the inexorable
piece of skin; there were barely six square inches of the skin
left.

"Thanks, Vanière," Raphael said. "The thing is very
curious."

"What is the matter with you, my angel; you are growing
quite white!" Pauline cried.

"You can go, Vanière."

"Your voice frightens me," the girl went on; it is so
strangely altered. What is it? How are you feeling? Where
is the pain? You are in pain!—Jonathan! here! call a
doctor!" she cried.

"Hush, my Pauline," Raphael answered, as he regained
composure. "Let us get up and go. Some flower here has
a scent that is too much for me. It is that verbena, perhaps."

Pauline flew upon the innocent plant, seized it by the stalk,
and flung it out into the garden; then with all the might of
the love between them, she clasped Raphael in a close em-
brace, and with languishing coquetry raised her red lips to his
for a kiss.

"Dear angel," she cried, "when I saw you turn so white
I understood that I could not live on without you; your life
is my life too. Lay your hand on my back, Raphael mine;
I feel a chill like death; the feeling of cold is there yet.
Your lips are burning. How is your hand?—Cold as ice,"
she added.

"Mad girl!" exclaimed Raphael.

"Why that tear? Let me drink it."

"O Pauline, Pauline, you love me far too much!"

"There is something very extraordinary going on in your
mind, Raphael! Do not dissimulate. I shall very soon find
out your secret. Give that to me," she went on, taking the
Wild Ass' Skin.

"You are my executioner!" the young man exclaimed, glancing in horror at the talisman.

"How changed your voice is!" cried Pauline, as she dropped the fatal symbol of destiny.

"Do you love me?" he asked.

"Do I love you? Is there any doubt?"

"Then leave me; go away!"

The poor child went.

"So!" cried Raphael, when he was alone. "In an enlightened age, when we have found out that diamonds are a crystallized form of charcoal, at a time when everything is made clear, when the police would hail a new Messiah before the magistrates, and submit his miracles to the Académie des Sciences—in an epoch when we no longer believe in anything but a notary's signature—that I, forsooth, should believe in a sort of *Mene, Tekel, Upharsin!* No, by heaven, I will not believe that the Supreme Being would take pleasure in torturing a harmless creature—Let us see the learned about it."

Between the Halle des Vins, with its extensive assembly of barrels, and the Salpétrière, that extensive seminary of drunkenness, lies a small pond, which Raphael soon reached. All sorts of ducks of rare varieties were there disporting themselves; their colored markings shone in the sun like the glass in cathedral windows. Every kind of duck in the world was represented, quacking, dabbling, and moving about—a kind of parliament of ducks assembled against its will, but luckily without either charter or political principles, living in complete immunity from sportsmen, under the eyes of any naturalist that chanced to see them.

"That is M. Lavrille," said one of the keepers to Raphael, who had asked for that high priest of zoölogy.

The Marquis saw a short man buried in profound reflections, caused by the appearance of a pair of ducks. The man of science was middle aged; he had a pleasant face, made pleasanter still by a kindly expression, but an absorption in scien-

tific ideas engrossed his whole person.   His peruke was
strangely turned up, by being constantly raised to scratch his
head ; so that a line of white hair was left plainly visible, a
witness to an enthusiasm for investigation, which, like every
other strong passion, so withdraws us from mundane consid-
erations, that we lose all consciousness of the " I " within us.
Raphael, the student and man of science, looked respectfully
at the naturalist, who devoted his nights to enlarging the
limits of human knowledge, and whose very errors reflected
glory upon France ; but a she-coxcomb would have laughed,
no doubt, at the break in continuity between the breeches and
striped waistcoat worn by the man of learning ; the interval,
moreover, was modestly filled by a shirt which had been con-
siderably creased, for he stooped and raised himself by turns,
as his zoölogical observations required.

After the first interchange of civilities, Raphael thought it
necessary to pay M. Lavrille a bland compliment upon his
ducks.

" Oh, we are well off for ducks," the naturalist replied.
" The genus, moreover, as you doubtless know, is the most
prolific in the order of palmipeds.   It begins with the swan
and ends with the *zin-zin* duck, comprising in all one hundred
and thirty-seven very distinct varieties, each having its own
name, habits, country, and character, and every one no more
like another than a white man is like a negro.   Really, sir,
when we dine off a duck, we have no notion for the most part
of the vast extent——"

" He interrupted himself as he saw a small pretty duck
come up to the surface of the pound.

" There you see the cravatted swan, a poor native of
Canada ; he has come a very long way to show us his brown
and gray plumage and his little black cravat !   Look, he is
preening himself.   That one is the famous eider duck that
provides the down, the eider-down under which our fine ladies
sleep ; isn't it pretty ?   Who wouldn't admire the little pink-

ish white breast and the green beak? I have just been a witness, sir,'' he went on, ''to a marriage that I had long despaired of bringing about; they have paired rather auspiciously, and I shall await the results very eagerly. This will be a hundred and thirty-eighth species, I flatter myself, to which, perhaps, my name will be given. That is the newly-mated pair,'' he said, pointing out two of the ducks; ''one of them is a laughing goose (*anas albifrons*), and the other the great whistling duck, Buffon's *anas ruffina*. I have hesitated a long while between the whistling duck, the duck with white eyebrows, and the shoveler duck (*anas clypeata*). Stay, that is the shoveler—that fat, brownish-black rascal, with the greenish neck and that coquettish iridescence on it. But the whistling duck was a crested one, sir, and you will understand that I deliberated no longer. We only lack the variegated black-capped duck now. These gentlemen here, unanimously claim that that variety of duck is only a repetition of the curve-beaked teal, but for my own part,''—and the gesture he made was worth seeing. He expressed at once the modesty and pride of a man of science; the pride full of obstinacy, and the modesty well tempered with assurance.

''I don't think it is,'' he added. '' You see, my dear sir, that we are not amusing ourselves here. I am engaged at this moment upon a monograph on the genus duck. But I am at your disposal.''

While they went towards a rather pleasant house in the Rue de Buffon, Raphael submitted the skin to M. Lavrille's inspection.

''I know the product,'' said the man of science, when he had turned his magnifying glass upon the talisman. '' It used to be used for covering boxes. The shagreen is very old. They prefer to use skate's skin nowadays for making sheaths. This, as you are doubtless aware, is the hide of the *raja sephen*, a Red Sea fish.''

'' But this, sir, since you are so exceedingly good——''

"This," the man of science interrupted, as he resumed, "this is quite another thing; between these two shagreens, sir, there is a difference just as wide as between sea and land, or fish and flesh. The fish's skin is harder, however, than the skin of the land animal. This," he said, as he indicated the talisman, "is, as you doubtless know, one of the most curious of zoölogical products."

"But to proceed——" said Raphael.

"This," replied the man of science, as he flung himself down into his armchair, "is an ass' skin, sir."

"Yes, I know," said the young man.

"A very rare variety of ass is found in Persia," the naturalist continued, "the onager of the ancients, *equus asinus*, the *koulan* of the Tartars; Pallas went out there to observe it, and has made it known to science, for as a matter of fact the animal for a long time was believed to be mythical. It is mentioned, as you know, in Holy Scripture; Moses forbade that it should be coupled with its own species, and the onager is yet more famous for the prostitutions of which it was the object, and which are often mentioned by the prophets of the Bible. Pallas, as you know doubtless, states in his *Act. Petropy.*, tome II., that these bizarre excesses are still devoutly believed in among the Persians and the Nogais as a sovereign remedy for lumbago and sciatic gout. We poor Parisians scarcely believe that. The Museum has no example of the onager.

"What a magnificent animal!" he continued. "It is full of mystery; its eyes are provided with a sort of burnished covering, to which the Orientals attribute the powers of fascination; it has a glossier and finer coat than our handsomest horses possess, striped with more or less tawny bands, very much like the zebra's hide. There is something pliant and silky about its hair, which is sleek to the touch. Its powers of sight vie in precision and accuracy with those of man; it is rather larger than our largest domestic donkeys, and is possessed of extraordinary courage. If it is surprised by any chance, it defends itself against the most dangerous wild beasts with remarkable success; the rapidity of its movements can only be compared with the flight of birds; an onager, sir, would run the best Arab or Persian horses to death. According to the father of the conscientious Doctor Niebuhr, whose recent loss we are deploring, as you doubtless know, the ordinary average pace of one of these wonderful creatures would be seven thousand geometric feet per hour. Our own degenerate race of donkeys can give no idea of the ass in his pride and independence. He is active and spirited in his demeanor; he is cunning and sagacious; there is grace about the outlines of his head; every movement is full of attractive charm. In the East he is the king of beasts. Turkish aud Persian superstition even credits him with a mysterious origin; and when stories of the prowess attributed to him are told in Thibet or in Tartary, the speakers mingle Solomon's name with that of this noble animal. A tame onager, in short, is worth an enormous amount; it is well-nigh impossible to catch them among the mountains, where they leap like roe-bucks, and seem as if they could fly like birds. Our myth of the winged horse, our Pegasus, had its origin doubtless in these countries, where the shepherds could see the onager springing from one rock to another. In Persia they breed asses for the saddle, a cross between a tamed onager and a she-ass, and they paint them red, following immemorial tradition. Perhaps it was this custom that gave rise to our own proverb, 'Surly as a red donkey.' At some period when natural history was much neglected in France, I think a traveler must have brought over one of these strange beasts that endures servitude with such impatience. Hence the adage. The skin that you have lain before me is the skin of an onager. Opinions differ as to the origin of the name. Some claim that *Chagri* is a Turkish word; others insist that *Chagri* must be the name of the place where this animal product underwent the chemical process of preparation so clearly described by Pallas, to which the peculiar graining that we admire is due ; Martellens has written to me saying that *Chăagri* is a river——"

"I thank you, sir, for the information that you have given me ; it would furnish an admirable footnote for some Dom Calmet or other, if such erudite hermits yet exist ; but I have had the honor of pointing out to you that this scrap was in the first instance quite as large as that map," said Raphael, indicating an open atlas to Lavrille ; "but it has shrunk visibly in three months' time——"

"Quite so," said the man of science. "I understand. The remains of any substance primarily organic are naturally subject to a process of decay. It is quite easy to understand, and its progress depends upon atmospherical conditions. Even metals contract and expand appreciably, for engineers have remarked somewhat considerable interstices between great blocks of stone originally clamped together with iron bars. The field of science is boundless, but human life is very short, so that we do not claim to be acquainted with all the phenomena of nature."

"Pardon the question that I am about to ask you, sir," Raphael began, half-embarassed, " but are you quite sure that this piece of skin is subject to the ordinary laws of zoölogy, and that it can be stretched ? "

"Certainly——oh, bother ! "—— muttered M. Lavrille, trying to stretch the talisman. "But if you, sir, will go to see Planchette," he added, "the celebrated professor of mechanics, he will certainly discover some method of acting upon this skin, of softening and expanding it."

"Ah, sir, you are the preserver of my life," and Raphael took leave of the learned naturalist and hurried off to Planchette, leaving the worthy Lavrille in his study, all among the bottles and dried plants that filled it up.

Quite unconsciously Raphael brought away with him from this visit, all of science that man can grasp, and terminology to wit. Lavrille, the worthy man, was very much like Sancho Panza giving to Don Quixote the history of the goats ; he was entertaining himself by making out a list of animals and ticking them off. Even now that his life was nearing its end, he was scarcely acquainted with a mere fraction of the countless numbers of the great tribes that God has scattered, for some unknown end, throughout the ocean of worlds.

Raphael was well pleased. " I shall keep my ass well in hand," cried he. Sterne had said before his day, " Let us take care of our ass, if we wish to live to old age." But it is such a fantastic brute !

Planchette was a tall, thin man, a poet of a surety, lost in one continual thought, and always employed in gazing into the bottomless abyss of motion. Commonplace minds accuse these lofty intellects of madness ; they form a misinterpreted race that lives apart in a wonderful carelessness of luxuries or other people's notions. They will spend whole days at a stretch, smoking a cigar that has gone out, and enter a drawing-room with the buttons on their garments not in every case formally wedded to the button-holes. Some day or other, after a long time spent in measuring space, or in accumulating Xs under Aa-Gg, they succeed in analyzing some natural law, and resolve it into its elemental principles, and all on a sudden the crowd gapes at a new machine ; or it is a handcart perhaps that overwhelms us with astonishment by the apt simplicity of its construction. The modest man of science smiles at his admirers, and remarks, " What is that invention of mine ? Nothing whatever. Man cannot create a force ; he can but direct it ; and science consists in learning from nature."

The mechanician was standing bolt upright, planted on both feet, like some victim dropped straight from the gibbet, when Raphael broke in upon him. He was intently watching an agate ball that rolled over a sun-dial, and awaited its final settlement. The worthy man had received neither pension nor

15

decoration ; he had not known how to make the right use of his
ability for calculation.   He was happy in his life spent on the
watch for a discovery ; he had no thought either of reputa-
tion, of the outer world, nor even of himself, and led the
life of science for the sake of science.

"It is inexplicable," he exclaimed.   "Ah, your servant,
sir," he went on, becoming aware of Raphael's existence.
"How is your mother?   You must go and see my wife."

"And I also could have lived thus," thought Raphael, as
he recalled the learned man from his meditations by asking
of him how to produce any effect on the talisman, which he
placed before him.

"Although my credulity must amuse you, sir," so the
Marquis ended, "I will conceal nothing from you.   That
skin seems to me to be endowed with an insuperable power
of resistance."

"People of fashion, sir, always treat science rather super-
ciliously," said Planchette.   "They all talk to us pretty
much as the incredulous did when he brought some ladies to
see Lalande just after an eclipse, and remarked, 'Be so good
as to begin it over again.'   What effect do you want to pro-
duce?   The object of the science of mechanics is either the
application or the neutralization of the laws of motion.   As
for motion pure and simple, I tell you humbly, that we cannot
possibly define it.   That disposed of, unvarying phenomena
have been observed which accompany the actions of solids
and fluids.   If we set up the conditions by which these phe-
nomena are brought to pass, we can transport bodies or com-
municate locomotive power to them at a predetermined rate
of speed.   We can project them, divide them up in a few or
an infinite number of pieces, accordingly as we break them or
grind them to powder ; we can twist bodies or make them
rotate, modify, compress, expand, or extend them.   The
whole science, sir, rests upon a single fact.

"You see this ball," he went on ; "here it lies upon this

slab. Now, it is over there. What name shall we give to what has taken place, so natural from a physical point of view, so amazing from a moral? Movement, locomotion, changing of place? What prodigious vanity lurks underneath the words. Does a name solve the difficulty? Yet it is the whole of our science for all that. Our machines either make direct use of this agency, this fact, or they convert it. This trifling phenomenon, applied to large masses, would send Paris flying. We can increase speed by an expenditure of force, and augment the force by an increase of speed. But what are speed and force? Our science is as powerless to tell us that as to create motion. Any movement whatever is an immense power, and man does not create power of any kind. Everything is movement, thought itself is a movement, upon movement nature is based. Death is a movement whose limitations are little known. If God is eternal, be sure that He moves perpetually; perhaps God is movement. That is why movement, like God, is inexplicable, unfathomable, unlimited, incomprehensible, intangible. Who has ever touched, comprehended, or measured movement? We feel its effects without seeing it; we can even deny them as we can deny the existence of a God. Where is it? Where is it not? Whence comes it? What is its source? What is its end? It surrounds us, it intrudes upon us, and yet escapes us. It is evident as a fact, obscure as an abstraction; it is at once effect and cause. It requires space, even as we, and what is space? Movement alone recalls it to us; without movement, space is but an empty meaningless word. Like space, like creation, like the infinite, movement is an insoluble problem which confounds human reason; man will never conceive it, whatever else he may be permitted to conceive.

"Between each point in space occupied in succession by that ball," continued the man of science, "there is an abyss confronting human reason, an abyss into which Pascal fell. In order to produce any effect upon an unknown substance, we ought first of all to study that substance; to know whether, in accordance with its nature, it will be broken by the force of a blow, or whether it will withstand it; if it breaks in pieces, and you have no wish to split it up, we shall not achieve the end proposed. If you want to compress it, a uniform impulse must be communicated to all the particles of the substance, so as to diminish the interval that separates them in an equal degree. If you wish to expand it, we should try to bring a uniform eccentric force to bear on every molecule; for unless we conform accurately to this law, we shall have breaches in continuity. The modes of motion, sir, are infinite, and no limit exists to combinations of movement. Upon what effect have you determined?"

"I want any kind of pressure that is strong enough to expand the skin indefinitely," began Raphael, quite out of patience.

"Substance is finite," the mathematician put in, "and therefore will not admit of indefinite expansion, but pressure will necessarily increase the extent of surface at the expense of the thickness, which will be diminished until the point is reached when the material gives out——"

"Bring about that result, sir," Raphael cried, "and you will have earned millions."

"Then I should rob you of your money," replied the other, phlegmatic as a Dutchman. "I am going to show you, in a word or two, that a machine can be made that is fit to crush Providence itself in pieces like a fly. It would reduce a man to the condition of a piece of wastepaper; a man—boots and spurs, hat and cravat, trinkets and gold and all——"

"What a fearful machine!"

"Instead of flinging their brats into the water, the Chinese ought to make them useful in this way," the man of science went on, without reflecting on the regard man has for his progeny.

Quite absorbed by his idea, Planchette took an empty flower-pot, with a hole in the bottom, and put it on the surface of the dial, then he went to look for a little clay in a corner of the garden. Raphael stood spellbound, like a child to whom his nurse is telling some wonderful story. Planchette put the clay down upon the slab, drew a pruning-knife from his pocket, cut two branches from an elder tree, and began to clear them of pith by blowing through them, as if Raphael had not been present.

"There are the rudiments of the apparatus," he said. Then he connected one of the wooden pipes with the bottom of the flower-pot by a clay joint, in such a way that the mouth of the elder stem was just under the hole of the flower-pot; you might have compared it to a big tobacco-pipe. He spread a bed of clay over the surface of the slab, in a shovel-shaped mass, set down the flower-pot at the wider end of it, and laid the pipe of elder stem along the portion which represented the handle of the shovel. Next he put a lump of clay at the end of the elder stem and therein planted the other pipe, in an upright position, forming a second elbow which connected it with the first horizontal pipe in such a manner that the air, or any given fluid in circulation, could flow through this improvised piece of mechanism from the mouth of the vertical tube, along the intermediate passages, and so into the large empty flower-pot.

"This apparatus, sir," he said to Raphael, with all the gravity of an academician pronouncing his initiatory discourse, "is one of the great Pascal's grandest claims upon our admiration."

"I don't understand."

The man of science smiled. He went up to a fruit-tree and took down a little phial in which the druggist had sent him some liquid for catching ants; he broke off the bottom and made a funnel of the top, carefully fitting it to the mouth of the vertical hollowed stem that he had set in the clay, and at the opposite end to the great reservoir, represented by the

flower-pot. Next, by means of a watering-pot, he poured
in sufficient water to rise to the same level in the large
vessel and in the tiny circular funnel at the end of the
elder stem.

Raphael was thinking of his piece of skin.

"Water is considered to-day, sir, to be an incompressible
body," said the mechanician ; "never lose sight of that
fundamental principle ; still it can be compressed, though
only so very slightly that we should regard its faculty for
contracting as a zero. You see the amount of surface pre-
sented by the water at the brim of the flower-pot ? "

" Yes, sir."

" Very good ; now suppose that that surface is a thousand
times larger than the orifice of the elder stem through which
I poured out the liquid. Here, I am taking the funnel
away——"

" Granted."

" Well, then, if by any method whatever I increase the volume
of that quantity of water by pouring in yet more through the
mouth of the little tube ; the water thus compelled to flow
downwards would rise in the reservoir, represented by the
flower-pot, until it reached the same level at either end."

" 'That is quite clear," cried Raphael.

" But there is this difference," the other went on. " Suppose
that the thin column of water poured into the little vertical
tube there exerts a force equal, say, to a pound weight, for
instance, its action will be punctually communicated to the
great body of the liquid, and will be transmitted to every
part of the surface represented by the water in the flower-pot,
so that at the surface there will be a thousand columns of
water, every one pressing upwards as if they were impelled by
a force equal to that which compels the liquid to descend in
the vertical tube ; and of necessity they reproduce here,"
said Planchette, indicating to Raphael the top of the flower-
pot, " the force introduced over there, a thousandfold, "and

the man of science pointed out to the Marquis the upright wooden pipe set in the clay.

"That is quite simple," said Raphael.

Planchette smiled again.

"In other words," he went on, with the mathematician's natural stubborn propensity for logic, "in order to resist the force of the incoming water, it would be necessary to exert, upon every part of the large surface, a force equal to that brought into action in the vertical column, but with this difference—if the column of liquid is a foot in height, the thousand little columns of the wide surface will only have a very slight elevating power.

"Now," said Planchette, as he gave a fillip to his bits of stick, "let us replace this funny little apparatus by steel tubes of suitable strength and dimensions; and if you cover the liquid surface of the reservoir with a strong sliding plate of metal, and if to this metal plate you oppose another, solid enough and strong enough to resist any test, if, furthermore, you give me the power of continually adding water to the volume of liquid contents by means of the little vertical tube, the object fixed between the two solid metal plates must of necessity yield to the tremendous crushing force which indefinitely compresses it. The method of continually pouring in water through a little tube, like the manner of communicating force through the volume of the liquid to a metal plate, is an absurdly primitive mechanical device. A brace of pistons and a few valves would do it all. Do you perceive, my dear sir," he said, taking Valentin by the arm, "there is scarcely a substance in existence that would not be compelled to dilate when fixed in between these two indefinitely resisting surfaces?"

"What! the author of the *Lettres provinciales* invented it?" Raphael exclaimed.

"He and no other, sir. The science of mechanics knows no simpler nor more beautiful contrivance. The opposite principle, the capacity of expansion possessed by water, has brought the steam-engine into being. But water will only expand up to a certain point, while its incompressibility, being a force in a manner negative, is, of necessity, infinite."

"If this skin is expanded," said Raphael, "I promise you to erect a colossal statue to Blaise Pascal; to found a prize of a hundred thousand francs to be offered every ten years for the solution of the grandest problem of mechanical science effected during the interval; to find dowries for all your cousins and second cousins, and finally to build an asylum on purpose for impoverished or insane mathematicians."

"That would be exceedingly useful," Planchette replied. "We will go to Spieghalter to-morrow, sir," he continued, with the serenity of a man living on a plane wholly intellectual. "That distinguished mechanic has just completed, after my own designs, an improved mechanical arrangement by which a child could get a thousand trusses of hay inside his cap."

"Then good-bye till to-morrow."

"Till to-morrow, sir."

"Talk of mechanics!" cried Raphael; "isn't it the greatest of the sciences? The other fellow with his onagers, classifications, ducks, and species, and his phials full of bottled monstrosities, is at best only fit for a billiard-marker in a saloon."

The next morning Raphael went off in great spirits to find Planchette, and together they set out for the Rue de la Santé —auspicious appellation! Arrived at Spieghalter's, the young man found himself in a vast foundry; his eyes lighted upon a multitude of glowing and roaring furnaces. There was a storm of sparks, a deluge of nails, an ocean of pistons, vices, levers, valves, girders, files, and nuts; a sea of melted metal, balks of timber and bar-steel. Iron filings filled your throat. There was iron in the atmosphere; the men were covered with it ; everything reeked of iron. The iron seemed to be a living organism ; it became a fluid, moved, and seemed to shape itself intelligently after every fashion, to obey the worker's every caprice. Through the uproar made by the bellows, the crescendo of the falling hammers, and the shrill sounds of the lathes that drew groans from the steel, Raphael passed into a large, clean, and airy place where he was able to inspect at his leisure the great press that Planchette had told him about. He admired the cast-iron beams, as one might call them, and the twin bars of steel coupled together with indestructible bolts.

"If you were to give seven rapid turns to that crank," said Spieghalter, pointing out a beam of polished steel, "you would make a steel bar spurt out in thousands of jets, that would get into your legs like needles."

" The deuce," exclaimed Raphael.

Planchette himself slipped the piece of skin between the metal plates of the all-powerful press ; and, brimful of the certainty of a scientific conviction, he worked the crank energetically.

"Lie flat, all of you; we are dead men!" thundered Spieghalter, as he himself fell prone on the floor.

A hideous shrieking sound rang through the workshops. The water in the machine had broken the chamber, and now spouted out in a jet of incalculable force ; luckily it went in the direction of an old furnace, which was overthrown, knocked to pieces, and twisted like a house that has been enveloped and carried away by a waterspout.

" Ha!" remarked Planchette serenely, " the piece of skin is as safe and sound as my eye. There was a flaw in your reservoir somewhere, or a crevice in the large tube——"

" No, no; I know my reservoir. The devil is in your contrivance, sir ; you can take it away," and the German pounced upon a smith's hammer, flung the skin down on an anvil, and, with all the strength that rage gives, dealt the talisman the most formidable blow that had ever resounded through his workshops.

" There is not so much as a mark on it ! " said Planchette, stroking the perverse bit of skin.

The workmen hurried in. The foreman took the skin and buried it in the glowing coal of a forge, while, in a semicircle round the fire, they all awaited the action of a huge pair of bellows. Raphael, Spieghalter, and Professor Planchette stood in the midst of the grimy, expectant crowd. Raphael, looking round on faces dusted over with iron filings, white eyes, greasy, blackened clothing, and hairy chests, could have fancied himself transported into the wild nocturnal world of German ballad poetry. After the skin had been in the fire for ten minutes, the foreman pulled it out with a pair of pincers.

" Hand it over to me," said Raphael.

The foreman held it out by way of a joke. The Marquis readily handled it ; it was cool and flexible between his fingers. An exclamation of alarm went up ; the workmen fled in terror. Valentin was left alone with Planchette in the empty workshop.

" There is certainly something infernal in the thing ! " cried Raphael, in desperation. " Is no human power able to give me one day more of existence ? "

" I made a mistake, sir," said the mathematician, with a penitent expression ; " we ought to have subjected that peculiar skin to the action of a rolling machine. Where could my eyes have been when I suggested the use of compression ? "

" It was I that asked for it," Raphael answered.

The mathematician heaved a sigh of relief, like a culprit acquitted by a dozen jurors. Still, the strange problem afforded by the skin interested him ; he meditated a moment, and then remarked—

" This unknown material ought to be treated chemically

by reagents. Let us call on Japhet—perhaps the chemist may have better luck than the mechanic."

Valentin thereupon urged his horse into a rapid trot, hoping to find the chemist, the celebrated Japhet, in his laboratory.

"Well, old friend," Planchette began, seeing Japhet in his armchair, examining a precipitate; "how goes chemistry?"

"Gone to sleep. Nothing new at all. The Académie, however, has recognized the existence of salicine, but salicine, asparagine, vanqueline, and digitaline are not really discoveries——"

"Since you cannot invent substances," said Raphael, "you are obliged to fall back on inventing names."

"Most emphatically true, young man."

"Here," said Planchette, addressing the chemist, "try to analyze this composition; if you can extract any element whatever from it, I christen it *diaboline* beforehand, for we have just smashed a hydraulic press in trying to compress it."

"Let's see! let's have a look at it!" cried the delighted chemist; "it may, perhaps, be a fresh element."

"It is simply a piece of the skin of an ass, sir," said Raphael.

"Sir!" said the illustrious chemist sternly.

"I am not joking," the Marquis answered, laying the piece of skin before him.

Baron Japhet applied the nervous fibres of his tongue to the skin; he had skill in thus detecting salts, acids, alkalis, and gases. After several experiments, he remarked—

"No taste whatever! Come, we will give it a little fluoric acid to drink."

Subjected to the influence of this ready solvent of animal tissue, the skin underwent no change whatsoever.

"It is not shagreen at all!" the chemist cried. "We will treat this unknown mystery as a mineral, and try its mettle by dropping it in a crucible where I have at this moment some red potash.''

Japhet went out, and returned almost immediately.

''Allow me to cut away a bit of this strange substance, sir,'' he said to Raphael; ''it is so extraordinary——''

''A bit!'' exclaimed Raphael; ''not so much as a hair's-breadth. You may try though,'' he added half-banteringly, half-sadly.

The chemist broke a razor in his desire to cut the skin; he tried to break it by a powerful electric shock; next he submitted it to the influence of a galvanic battery; but all the thunderbolts his science wotted of fell harmless on the dreadful talisman.

It was seven o'clock in the evening. Planchette, Japhet, and Raphael, unaware of the flight of time, were awaiting the outcome of a final experiment. The Wild Ass' Skin emerged triumphant from a formidable encounter in which it had been engaged with a considerable quantity of chloride of nitrogen.

''It is all over with me,'' Raphael wailed. ''It is the finger of God? I shall die!——'' and he left the two amazed scientific men.

''We must be very careful not to talk about this affair at the Académie; our colleagues there would laugh at us,'' Planchette remarked to the chemist, after a long pause, in which they looked at each other without daring to communicate their thoughts. The learned pair looked like two Christians who had issued from their tombs to find no God in the heavens. Science had been powerless; acids so much clear water; red potash had been discredited; the galvanic battery and electric shock had been a couple of playthings.

''A hydraulic press broken like a biscuit!'' commented Planchette.

''I believe in the devil,'' said the Baron Japhet, after a moment's silence.

''And I in God,'' replied Planchette.

Each spoke in character. The universe for a mechanician is a machine that requires an operator; for chemistry—that fiendish employment of decomposing all things—the world is a gas endowed with the power of movement.

"We cannot deny the fact," the chemist replied.

"Pshaw! those gentlemen the doctrinaires have invented a nebulous aphorism for our consolation—'Stupid as a fact.'"

"Your aphorism," said the chemist, "seems to me as a fact very stupid."

They began to laugh, and went off to dine like folk for whom a miracle is nothing more than a phenomenon.

Valentin reached his own house shivering with rage and consumed with anger. He had no more faith in anything. Conflicting thoughts shifted and surged to and fro in his brain, as is the case with every man brought face to face with an inconceivable fact. He had readily believed in some hidden flaw in Spieghalter's apparatus; he had not been surprised by the incompetence and failure of science and of fire; but the flexibility of the skin as he handled it, taken with its stubbornness when all the means of destruction that man possesses had been brought to bear upon it in vain—these things terrified him. The incontrovertible fact made him dizzy.

"I am mad," he muttered. "I have had no food since the morning, and yet I am neither hungry nor thirsty, and there is a fire in my breast that burns me."

He put back the skin in the frame where it had been enclosed but lately, drew a line in red ink about the actual configuration of the talisman, and seated himself in his armchair.

"Eight o'clock already!" he exclaimed. "To-day has gone like a dream."

He leaned his elbow on the arm of the chair, propped his head with his left hand, and so remained, lost in secret dark reflections and consuming thoughts that men condemned to die bear away with them.

"O Pauline!" he cried. "Poor child! there are gulfs

that love can never traverse, despite the strength of his wings."
Just then he very distinctly heard a smothered sigh, and
knew by one of the most tender privileges of passionate love
that it was Pauline's breathing.

"That is my death warrant," he said to himself. "If she
were there, I should wish to die in her arms."

A burst of gleeful and heavy laughter made him turn his
face towards the bed; he saw Pauline's face through the
transparent curtains, smiling like a child for gladness over a
successful piece of mischief. Her pretty hair fell over her
shoulders in countless curls; she looked like a Bengal rose
upon a pile of white roses.

"I cajoled Jonathan," said she. "Doesn't the bed be-
long to me, to me who am your wife? Don't scold me, dar-
ling; I only wanted to surprise you, to sleep beside you.
Forgive me for my freak."

She sprang out of bed like a kitten, showed herself gleaming
in her lawn raiment, and sat down on Raphael's knee.

"Love, what gulf were you talking about?" she said, with
an anxious expression apparent upon her face.

"Death."

"You hurt me," she answered. "There are some thoughts
upon which we, poor women that we are, cannot dwell; they
are death to us. Is it strength of love in us, or lack of cour-
age? I cannot tell. Death does not frighten me," she be-
gan again, laughingly. "To die with you, both together,
to-morrow morning, in one last embrace, would be joy. It
seems to me that even then I should have lived more than a
hundred years. What does the number of days matter if we
have spent a whole lifetime of peace and love in one night, in
one hour?"

"You are right; Heaven is speaking through that pretty
mouth of yours. Grant that I may kiss you, and let us die,"
said Raphael.

"Then let us die," she said, laughing.

Towards nine o'clock in the morning the daylight streamed through the chinks of the window shutters. Obscured somewhat by the muslin curtains, it yet sufficed to show clearly the rich colors of the carpet, the silks and furniture of the room, where the two lovers were lying asleep. The gilding sparkled here and there. A ray of sunlight fell and faded upon the soft down quilt that the freaks of love had thrown to the floor. The outlines of Pauline's dress, hanging from a cheval glass, appeared like a shadowy ghost. Her dainty shoes had been left at a distance from the bed. A nightingale came to perch upon the sill; its trills repeated over again, and the sounds of its wings suddenly shaken out for flight, awoke Raphael.

"For me to die," he said, following out a thought begun in his dream, "my organization, the mechanism of flesh and bone, that is quickened by the will in me, and makes of me an individual *man*, must display some perceptible disease. Doctors ought to understand the symptoms of any attack on vitality, and could tell me whether I am sick or sound."

He gazed at his sleeping wife. She had stretched her head out to him, expressing in this way even while she slept the anxious tenderness of love. Pauline seemed to look at him as she lay with her face turned towards him in an attitude as full of grace as a young child's, with her pretty, half-opened mouth held out towards him, as she drew her light, even breath. Her little pearly teeth seemed to heighten the redness of the fresh lips with the smile hovering over them. The red glow in her complexion was brighter, and its whiteness was, so to speak, whiter still just then than in the most impassioned moments of the waking day. In her unconstrained grace, as she lay, so full of believing trust, the adorable attractions of childhood were added to the enchantments of love.

Even the most unaffected women still obey certain social conventions, which restrain the free expansion of the soul within them during their waking hours ; but slumber seems to give them back the spontaneity of life which makes infancy lovely. Pauline blushed for nothing ; she was like one of those beloved and heavenly beings, in whom reason has not yet put motives into their actions and mystery into their glances. Her profile stood out in sharp relief against the fine cambric of the pillows ; there was a certain sprightliness about her loose hair in confusion, mingled with the deep lace ruffles ; but she was sleeping in happiness, her long lashes were tightly pressed against her cheeks, as if to secure her eyes from too strong a light, or to aid an effort of her soul to recollect and to hold fast a bliss that had been perfect but fleeting. Her tiny pink and white ear, framed by a lock of her hair and outlined by a wrapping of Mechlin lace, would have made an artist, a painter, an old man, wildly in love, and would perhaps have restored a madman to his senses.

Is it not an ineffable bliss to behold the woman that you love, sleeping, smiling in a peaceful dream beneath your protection, loving you even in dreams, even at the point where the individual seems to cease to exist, offering to you yet the mute lips that speak to you in slumber of the latest kiss ? Is it not indescribable happiness to see a trusting woman, half-clad, but wrapped round in her love as by a cloak—modesty in the midst of dishevelment—to see admiringly her scattered clothing, the silken stocking hastily put off to please you last evening, the unclasped girdle that implies a boundless faith in you. A whole romance lies there in that girdle ; the woman that it used to protect exists no longer ; she is yours, she has become *you ;* henceforward any betrayal of her is a blow dealt at yourself.

In this softened mood Raphael's eyes wandered over the room, now filled with memories and love, and where the very daylight seemed to take delightful hues. Then he turned his gaze at last upon the outlines of the woman's form, upon youth and purity, and love that even now had no thought that was not for him alone, above all things, and longed to live for ever. As his eyes fell upon Pauline, her own opened at once as if a ray of sunlight had lighted on them.

"Good morning," she said, smiling. "How handsome you are, bad man!"

The grace of love and youth, of silence and dawn, shone in their faces, making a divine picture, with the fleeting spell over it all that belongs only to the earliest days of passion, just as simplicity and artlessness are the peculiar possession of childhood. Alas! love's springtide joys, like our own youthful laughter, must even take flight, and live for us no longer save in memory; either for our despair, or to shed some soothing fragrance over us, according to the bent of our inmost thoughts.

"What made me wake you?" said Raphael. "It was so great a pleasure to watch you sleeping that it brought tears to my eyes."

"And to mine, too," she answered. "I cried in the night while I watched you sleeping, but not with happiness. Raphael, dear, pray listen to me. Your breathing is labored while you sleep, and something rattles in your chest that frightens me. You have a little dry cough when you are asleep, exactly like my father's, who is dying of phthisis. In those sounds from your lungs I recognized some of the peculiar symptoms of that complaint. Then you are feverish; I know you are, your hand was moist and burning—— Darling, you are young," she added with a shudder, "and you could still get over it if unfortunately—— But, no," she cried cheerfully, "there is no 'unfortunately,' the disease is contagious, so the doctors say."

She flung both arms about Raphael, drawing in his breath through one of those kisses in which the soul reaches its end.

"I do not wish to live to old age," she said. "Let us
16

both die young, and go to heaven while flowers fill our hands."

"We always make such designs as those when we are well and strong," Raphael replied, burying his hands in Pauline's hair. But even then a horrible fit of coughing came on, one of those deep ominous coughs that seem to come from the depths of the tomb, a cough that leaves the sufferer ghastly pale, trembling, and perspiring ; with aching sides and quivering nerves, with a feeling of weariness pervading the very marrow of the spine, and unspeakable languor in every vein. Raphael slowly laid himself down, pale, exhausted, and overcome, like a man who has spent all the strength in him over one final effort. Pauline's eyes, grown large with terror, were fixed upon him ; she lay quite motionless, pale, and silent.

"Let us commit no more follies, my angel," she said, trying not to let Raphael see the dreadful forebodings that disturbed her. She covered her face with her hands, for she saw death before her—the hideous skeleton. Raphael's face had grown as pale and livid as any skull unearthed from a churchyard to assist the studies of some scientific man. Pauline remembered the exclamation that had escaped from Valentin the previous evening, and to herself she said—

"Yes, there are gulfs that love can never cross, and therein love must bury itself."

On a March morning, some days after this wretched scene, Raphael found himself seated in an armchair, placed in the window in the full light of day. Four doctors stood round him, each in turn trying his pulse, feeling him over, and questioning him with apparent interest. The invalid sought to guess their thoughts, putting a construction on every movement they made, and on the slightest contraction of their brows. His last hope lay in this consultation. This court of appeal was about to pronounce its decision—life or death.

Valentin had summoned the oracles of modern medicine, so that he might have the last word of science. Thanks to his wealth and title, there stood before him three embodied theories ; human knowledge fluctuated round the three points. Three of the doctors brought among them the complete circle of medical philosophy ; they represented the points of conflict round which the battle raged, between spiritualism, analysis, and goodness knows what in the way of mocking eclecticism.

The fourth doctor was Horace Bianchon, a man of science with a future before him, the most distinguished man of the new school in medicine, a discreet and unassuming representative of a studious generation that is preparing to receive the inheritance of fifty years of experience treasured up by the École de Paris, a generation that perhaps will erect the monument for the building of which the centuries behind us have collected the different materials. As a personal friend of the Marquis and of Rastignac, he had been in attendance on the former for some days past, and was helping him to answer the inquiries of the three professors, occasionally insisting somewhat upon those symptoms which, in his opinion, pointed to pulmonary disease.

"You have been living at a great pace, leading a dissipated life, no doubt, and you have devoted yourself largely to intellectual work?" queried one of the three celebrated authorities, addressing Raphael. He was a square-headed man, with a large frame and energetic organization, which seemed to mark him as superior to his two rivals.

"I made up my mind to kill myself with debauchery, after spending three years over an extensive work, with which perhaps you may some day occupy yourselves," Raphael replied.

The great doctor shook his head, and so displayed his satisfaction. "I was sure of it," he seemed to say to himself. He was the illustrious Brisset, the successor of Cabanis and Bichat, head of the Organic School, a doctor popular with believers in material and positive science, who see in man a complete individual, subject solely to the laws of his own particular

organization ; and who consider that his normal condition
and abnormal states of disease can both be traced to obvious
causes.

After this reply, Brisset looked, without speaking, at a
middle-sized person, whose darkly flushed countenance and
glowing eyes seemed to belong to some antique satyr, and
who, leaning his back against the corner of the embrasure,
was studying Raphael, without saying a word.   Doctor Camé-
ristus, a man of creeds and enthusiasms, the head of the
"Vitalists," a romantic champion of the esoteric doctrines
of Van Helmont, discerned a lofty informing principle in
human life, a mysterious and inexplicable phenomenon which
mocks at the scalpel, deceives the surgeon, eludes the drugs
of the pharmacopœia, the formulæ of algebra, the demonstra-
tions of anatomy, and derides all our efforts ; a sort of invisi-
ble, intangible flame, which, obeying some divinely appointed
law, will often linger on in a body in our opinion devoted to
death, while it takes flight from an organization well fitted
for prolonged existence.

A bitter smile hovered upon the lips of the third doctor,
Maugredie, a man of acknowledged ability, but a Pyrrhonist
and a scoffer, with the scalpel for his one article of faith. He
would consider, as a concession to Brisset, that a man who, as
a matter of fact, was perfectly well was dead, and recognize
with Caméristus that a man might be living on after his ap-
parent demise.   He found something sensible in every theory,
and embraced none of them, claiming that the best of all
systems of medicine was to have none at all, and to stick to
the facts.   This Panurge of the Clinical Schools, the king of
observers, the great investigator, great sceptic, the man of
desperate expedients, was scrutinizing the Wild Ass' Skin.

"I should very much like to be a witness of the coinci-
dence of its retrenchment with your wish," he said to the
Marquis.

"Where is the use ?" cried Brisset.

"Where is the use?" echoed Caméristus.

"Ah, you are both of the same mind," replied Maugredie.

"The contraction is perfectly simple," Brisset went on.

"It is supernatural," remarked Caméristus.

"In short," Maugredie made answer, with affected solemnity, and handing the piece of skin to Raphael as he spoke, "the shriveling faculty of the skin is a fact inexplicable, and yet quite natural, which, ever since the world began, has been the despair of medicine and of pretty women.

All Valentin's observation could discover no trace of a feeling for his troubles in any of the three doctors. The three received every answer in silence, scanned him unconcernedly, and interrogated him unsympathetically. Politeness did not conceal their indifference; whether deliberation or certainty was the cause, their words at any rate came so seldom and so languidly, that at times Raphael thought that their attention was wandering. From time to time Brisset, the sole speaker, remarked, "Good! just so!" as Bianchon pointed out the existence of each desperate symptom. Caméristus seemed to be deep in meditation; Maugredie looked like a comic author, studying two queer characters with a view to reproducing them faithfully upon the stage. There was deep, unconcealed distress and grave compassion in Horace Bianchon's face. He had been a doctor for too short a time to be untouched by suffering and unmoved by a deathbed; he had not learned to keep back the sympathetic tears that obscure a man's clear vision and prevent him from seizing, like the general of an army, upon the auspicious moment for victory, in utter disregard of the groans of dying men.

After spending about half an hour over taking in some sort the measure of the patient and the complaint, much as a tailor measures a young man for a coat when he orders his wedding outfit, the authorities uttered several commonplaces, and even talked of politics. Then they decided to go into Raphael's study to exchange their ideas and frame their verdict.

"May I not be present during the discussion, gentlemen?" Valentin had asked them, but Brisset and Maugredie protested against this, and, in spite of their patient's entreaties, declined altogether to deliberate in his presence.

Raphael gave way before their custom, thinking that he could slip into a passage adjoining, whence he could easily overhear the medical conference in which the three professors were about to engage.

"Permit me, gentlemen," said Brisset, as they entered, "to give you my own opinion at once. I neither wish to force it upon you nor to have it discussed. In the first place, it is unbiased, concise, and based on an exact similarity that exists between one of my own patients and the subject that we have been called in to examine; and, moreover, I am expected at my hospital. The importance of the case that demands my presence there will excuse me for speaking the first word. The subject with which we are concerned has been exhausted in an equal degree by intellectual labors—what did he set about, Horace?" he asked of the young doctor.

"A 'Theory of the Will.'"

"The devil! but that's a big subject. He is exhausted, I say, by too much brain-work, by irregular courses, and by the repeated use of too powerful stimulants. Violent exertion of body and mind has demoralized the whole system. It is easy, gentlemen, to recognize in the symptoms of the face and body generally intense irritation of the stomach, an affection of the great sympathetic nerve, acute sensibility of the epigastric region, and contraction of the right and left hypochondriac. You have noticed, too, the large size and prominence of the liver. M. Bianchon has, besides, constantly watched the patient, and he tells us that indigestion is troublesome and difficult. Strictly speaking, there is no stomach left, and so the man has disappeared. The brain is atrophied because the man digests no longer. The progressive deterioration wrought in the epigastric region, the seat of vitality, has vitiated the whole system. Thence, by continued fevered vibrations, the disorder has reached the brain by means of the nervous plexus, hence the excessive irritation in that organ. There is monomania. The patient is burdened with a fixed idea. That piece of skin really contracts, to his way of thinking ; very likely it always has been as we have seen it ; but whether it contracts or no, that thing is for him just like the fly that some Grand Vizier or other had on his nose. If you put leeches at once on the epigastrium, and reduce the irritation in that part, which is the very seat of man's life, and if you diet the patient, the monomania will leave him. I will say no more to Dr. Bianchon ; he should be able to grasp the whole treatment as well as the details. There may be, perhaps, some complication of the disease—the bronchial tubes, possibly, may be also inflamed ; but, I believe, that treatment for the intestinal organs is very much more important and necessary, and more urgently required than for the lungs. Persistent study of abstract matters and certain violent passions have induced serious disorders in that vital mechanism. However, we are in time to set these conditions right. Nothing is too seriously affected. You will easily get your friend round again," he remarked to Bianchon.

"Our learned colleague is taking the effect for the cause," Caméristus replied. "Yes, the changes that he has observed so keenly certainly exist in the patient ; but it is not the stomach that, by degrees, has set up nervous action in the system, and so affected the brain, like a hole in a window-pane spreading cracks round about it. It took a blow of some kind to make a hole in the window ; who gave the blow? Do we know that ? Have we investigated the patient's case sufficiently ? Are we acquainted with all the events of his life ?

"The vital principle, gentlemen," he continued, "the Archeus of Van Helmont, is affected in his case—the very essence and centre of life is attacked. The divine spark, the transitory intelligence which holds the organism together, which is the source of the will, the inspiration of life, has ceased to regulate the daily phenomena of the mechanism and the functions of every organ ; thence arise all the complications which my learned colleague has so thoroughly appreciated. The epigastric region does not affect the brain, but the brain affects the epigastric region. No," he went on, vigorously slapping his chest, " no, I am not a stomach in the form of a man. No, everything does not lie there. I do not feel that I have the courage to say that if the epigastric region is in good order, everything else is in a like condition——

" We cannot trace," he went on more mildly, " to one physical cause the serious disturbances that supervene in this or that subject which has been dangerously attacked, nor submit them to a uniform treatment. No one man is like another. We have each peculiar organs, differently affected, diversely nourished, adapted to perform different functions, and to induce a condition necessary to the accomplishment of an order of things which is unknown to us. The sublime will has so wrought that a little portion of the great All is set within us to sustain the phenomena of living ; in every man it formulates itself distinctly, making each, to all appearance, a separate individual, yet in one point coexistent with the infinite cause. So we ought to make a separate study of each subject, discover all about it, find out in what its life consists, and wherein its power lies. From the softness of a wet sponge to the hardness of pumice-stone there are infinite fine degrees of difference. Man is just like that. Between the sponge-like organizations of the lymphatic and the vigorous iron muscles of such men as are destined for a long life, what a margin for errors for the single inflexible system of a lowering treatment to commit ; a system that reduces the capacities of the human frame, which you always conclude have been over-excited. Let us look for the origin of the disease in the mental and not in the physical viscera. A doctor is an inspired being, endowed by God with a special gift—the power to read the secrets of vitality; just as the prophet has received the eyes that foresee the future, the poet his faculty of evoking nature, and the musician the power of arranging sounds in an harmonious order that is possibly a copy of an ideal harmony on high.''

'' There is his everlasting system of medicine, arbitrary, monarchical, and pious,'' muttered Brisset.

'' Gentlemen,'' Maugredie broke in hastily, to distract attention from Brisset's comment, '' don't let us lose sight of the patient.''

'' What is the good of science?'' Raphael moaned. '' Here is my recovery halting between a string of beads and a rosary of leeches, between Dupuytren's bistoury and Prince Hohenlohe's prayer. There is Maugredie suspending his judgment on the line that divides facts from words, mind from matter. Man's ' it is,' ' and it is not,' is always on my track; it is the *Carymary Carymara* of Rabelais for evermore : my disorder is spiritual, *Carymary*, or material, *Carymara*. Shall I live? They have no idea. Planchette was more straightforward with me, at any rate, when he said, ' I do not know.'

Just then Valentin heard Maugredie's voice.

'' The patient suffers from monomania; very good, I am quite of that opinion,'' he said, '' but he has two hundred thousand a year; monomaniacs of that kind are very uncommon. As for knowing whether his epigastric region has affected his brain, or his brain his epigastric region, we shall find that out, perhaps, whenever he dies. But to resume. There is no disputing the fact that he is ill; some sort of treatment he must have. Let us leave theories alone, and put leeches on him, to counteract the nervous and intestinal irritation, as to the existence of which we all agree; and let us send him to drink the waters, in that way we shall act on both systems at once. If there really is tubercular disease, we can hardly expect to save his life; so that——''

Raphael abruptly left the passage, and went back to his armchair. The four doctors very soon came out of the study; Horace was the spokesman.

"These gentlemen," he told him, "have unanimously agreed that leeches must be applied to the stomach at once, and that both physical and moral treatment are imperatively needed. In the first place, a carefully prescribed rule of diet, so as to soothe the internal irritation"—here Brisset signified his approval; "and in the second, a hygienic regimen, to set your general condition right. We all, therefore, recommend you to go to take the waters at Aix in Savoy; or, if you like it better, at Mont Dore in Auvergne; the air and the situation are both pleasanter in Savoy than in the Cantal, but you will consult your own taste."

Here it was Caméristus who nodded assent.

"These gentlemen," Bianchon continued, "having recognized a slight affection of the respiratory organs, are agreed as to the utility of the previous course of treatment that I have prescribed. They think that there will be no difficulty about restoring you to health, and that everything depends upon a wise and alternate employment of these various means. And——"

"And that is the cause of the milk in the cocoanut," said Raphael, with a smile, as he led Horace into his study to pay the fees for this useless consultation.

"Their conclusions are logical," the young doctor replied. "Caméristus feels, Brisset examines, Maugredie doubts. Has not a man a soul, a body, and an intelligence? One of these three elemental constituents always influences us more or less strongly; there will always be the personal element in human science. Believe me, Raphael, we effect no cures; we only assist them. Another system—the use of mild remedies while nature exerts her powers—lies between the extremes of theory of Brisset and Caméristus, but one ought to have known the patient for some ten years or so to obtain a good result on these lines. Negation lies at the back of all medicine, as in every other science. So endeavor to live wholesomely; try a trip to Savoy; the best course is, and always will be, to trust to nature."

It was a month later, on a fine summer-like evening, that several people, who were taking the waters at Aix, returned from the promenade and met together in the salons of the Club. Raphael remained alone by a window for a long time. His back was turned upon the gathering, and he himself was deep in those involuntary musings in which thoughts arise in succession and fade away, shaping themselves indistinctly, passing over us like thin, almost colorless clouds. Melancholy is sweet to us then, and delight is shadowy, for the soul is half-asleep. Valentin gave himself up to this life of sensations; he was steeping himself in the warm, soft twilight, enjoying the pure air with the scent of the hills in it, happy in that he felt no pain, and had tranquillized his threatening Wild Ass' Skin at last. It grew cooler as the red glow of the sunset faded on the mountain-peaks; he shut the window and left his place.

"Will you be so kind as not to close the windows, sir?" said an old lady; "we are being stifled——"

The peculiar sharp and jarring tones in which the phrase was uttered grated on Raphael's ears; it fell on them like an indiscreet remark let slip by some man in whose friendship we would fain believe, a word which reveals unsuspected depths of selfishness and destroys some pleasing sentimental illusion of ours. The Marquis glanced, with the cool inscrutable expression of a diplomatist, at the old lady, called a servant, and, when he came, curtly bade him

"Open that window."

Great surprise was clearly expressed on all faces at the words. The whole roomful began to whisper to each other, and turned their eyes upon the invalid, as though he had given some serious offence. Raphael, who had never quite managed to rid himself of the bashfulness of his early youth, felt a momentary confusion; then he shook off his torpor, exerted his faculties, and asked himself the meaning of this strange scene.

A sudden and rapid impulse quickened his brain; the past weeks appeared before him in a clear and definite vision; the reasons for the feelings he inspired in others stood out for him in relief, like the veins of some corpse which a naturalist, by some cunningly contrived injection, has colored so as to show their least ramifications.

He discerned himself in this fleeting picture; he followed out his own life in it, thought by thought, day after day. He saw himself, not without astonishment, an absent gloomy figure in the midst of these lively folk, always musing over his own fate, always absorbed by his own sufferings, seemingly impatient of the most harmless chat. He saw how he had shunned the ephemeral intimacies that travelers are so ready to establish—no doubt because they feel sure of never meeting each other again—and how he had taken little heed of those about him. He saw himself like the rocks without, unmoved by the caresses or the stormy surgings of the waves.

Then, by a gift of insight seldom accorded, he read the thoughts of those about him. The light of a candle revealed the sardonic profile and yellow cranium of an old man; he remembered now that he had won from him, and had never proposed that the other should have his revenge; a little further on he saw a pretty woman, whose lively advances he had met with frigid coolness; there was not a face there that did not reproach him with some wrong done, inexplicably to all appearance, but the real offence in every case lay in some mortification, some invisible hurt dealt to self-love. He had unintentionally jarred on all the small susceptibilities of the circle round about him.

His guests on various occasions, and those to whom he had loaned his horses, had taken offence at his luxurious ways;

their ungraciousness had been a surprise to him; he had spared them further humiliation of that kind, and they had considered that he looked down upon them, and had accused him of haughtiness ever since. He could read their inmost thoughts as he fathomed their natures in this way. Society with its polish and varnish grew loathsome to him. He was envied and hated for his wealth and superior ability; his reserve baffled the inquisitive; his humility seemed like haughtiness to these petty superficial natures. He guessed the secret unpardonable crime which he had committed against them; he had overstepped the limits of the jurisdiction of their mediocrity. He had resisted their inquisitorial tyranny; he could dispense with their society; and all of them, therefore, had instinctively combined to make him feel their power, and to take revenge upon this incipient royalty by submitting him to a kind of ostracism, and so teaching him that they in their turn could do without him.

Pity came over him, first of all, at this aspect of mankind, but very soon he shuddered at the thought of the power that came thus, at will, and flung aside for him the veil of flesh under which the moral nature is hidden away. He closed his eyes, so as to see no more. A black curtain was drawn all at once over this unlucky phantom show of truth; but still he found himself in the terrible loneliness that surrounds every power and dominion. Just then a violent fit of coughing seized him. Far from receiving one single word—indifferent and meaningless, it is true, but still containing, among well-bred people brought together by chance, at least, some pretence of civil commiseration—he now heard hostile ejaculations and muttered complaints. Society there assembled disdained any pantomime on his account, perhaps because he had gauged its real nature too well.

"His complaint is contagious."

"The president of the club ought to forbid him to enter the salon."

"It is contrary to all rules and regulations to cough in that way!"

"When a man is as ill as that, he ought not to come to take the waters——"

"He will drive me away from the place."

Raphael rose and walked about the room to screen himself from their unanimous execrations. He thought to find a shelter, and went up to a young lady who sat doing nothing, minded to address some pretty speeches to her; but as he came towards her, she turned her back upon him, and pretended to be watching the dancers. Raphael feared lest he might have made use of the talisman already that evening; and feeling that he had neither the wish nor the courage to break into the conversation, he left the salon and took refuge in the billiard-room. No one there greeted him, nobody spoke to him, no one sent so much as a friendly glance in his direction. His turn of mind, naturally meditative, had discovered instinctively the general grounds and reasons for the aversions he inspired. This little world was obeying, unconsciously perhaps, the sovereign law which rules over polite society; its inexorable nature was becoming apparent in its entirety to Raphael's eyes. A glance into the past showed it to him, as a type completely realized in Fœdora.

He would no more meet with sympathy here for his bodily ills than he had received it at her hands for the distress in his heart. The fashionable world expels every suffering creature from its midst, just as the body of a man in robust health rejects any germ of disease. The world holds suffering and misfortune in abhorrence; it dreads them like the plague; it never hesitates between vice and trouble, for vice is a luxury. Ill-fortune may possess a majesty of its own, but society can belittle it and make it ridiculous by an epigram. Society draws caricatures, and in this way flings in the teeth of fallen kings the affronts which it fancies it has received from them; society, like the Roman youth at the circus, never shows mercy to the fallen gladiator; mockery and money are its vital necessities. "Death to the weak!" That is the oath taken by this kind of equestrian order, instituted in their midst by all the nations of the world; everywhere it makes for the elevation of the rich, and its motto is deeply graven in hearts that wealth has turned to stone, or that have been reared in aristocratic prejudices.

Assemble a collection of school-boys together. That will give you a society in miniature, a miniature which represents life more truly, because it is so frank and artless; and in it you will always find poor isolated beings, relegated to some place in the general estimation between pity and contempt, on account of their weakness and suffering. To these the Evangel promises heaven hereafter. Go lower yet in the scale of organized creation. If some bird among its fellows in the court-yard sickens, the others fall upon it with their beaks, pluck out its feathers, and kill it. The whole world, in accordance with its charter of egotism, brings all its severity to bear upon wretchedness that has the hardihood to spoil its festivities, and to trouble its joys.

Any sufferer in mind or body, any helpless or poor man, is a pariah. He had better remain in his solitude; if he crosses the boundary-line, he will find winter everywhere; he will find freezing cold in other men's looks, manners, words, and hearts; and lucky indeed is he if he does not receive an insult where he expected that sympathy would be expended upon him. Let the dying keep to their bed of neglect, and age sit lonely by its fireside. Portionless maids, freeze and burn in your solitary attics. If the world tolerates misery of any kind, it is to turn it to account for its own purposes, to make some use of it, saddle and bridle it, put a bit in its mouth, ride it about, and get some fun out of it.

Crotchety spinsters, ladies' companions, put a cheerful face upon it, endure the humors of your so-called benefactress, carry her lapdogs for her; you have an English poodle for your rival, and you must seek to understand the moods of your patroness, and amuse her, and—keep silence about yourselves. As for you, unblushing parasite, uncrowned king of unliveried servants, leave your real character at home, let your digestion keep pace with your host's, laugh when he laughs, mingle your tears with his, and find his epigrams amusing; if you want to relieve your mind about him, wait till he is ruined. That is the way the world shows its respect for the unfortunate; it persecutes them, or slays them; it deprives them of their manhood, or humbles them in the dust.

Such thoughts as these welled up in Raphael's heart with the suddenness of poetic inspiration. He looked around him, and felt the influence of the forbidding gloom that society breathes out in order to rid itself of the unfortunate; it nipped his soul more effectually than the east wind grips the body in December. He locked his arms over his chest, set his back against the wall, and fell into a deep melancholy. He mused upon the meagre happiness that this depressing way of living can give. What did it amount to? Amusement with no pleasure in it, gaiety without gladness, joyless festivity, fevered dreams empty of all delight, firewood or ashes on the hearth without a spark of flame in them. When he raised his head he found himself alone, all the billiard players had gone.

"I have only to let them know my power to make them worship my coughing fits," he said to himself, and wrapped himself against the world in the cloak of his contempt.

Next day the resident doctor came to call upon him, and took an anxious interest in his health. Raphael felt a thrill of joy at the friendly words addressed to him. The doctor's face, to his thinking, wore an expression that was kind and pleasant; the pale curls of his wig seemed redolent of philanthropy; the square cut of his coat, the loose folds of his trousers, his big Quaker-like shoes, everything about him down to the powder shaken from his queue and dusted in a circle upon his slightly stooping shoulders, revealed an apostolic nature, and spoke of Christian charity and of the self-sacrifice of a man, who, out of sheer devotion to his patients, had compelled himself to learn to play whist and tric-trac so well that he never lost money to any of them.

"My Lord Marquis," said he, after a long talk with Raphael, "I can dispel your uneasiness beyond all doubt. I know your constitution well enough by this time to assure you that the doctors in Paris, whose great abilities I know, are mistaken as to the nature of your complaint. You can live as long as Methuselah, my Lord Marquis, accidents only excepted. Your lungs are as sound as a blacksmith's bellows, your stomach would put an ostrich to the blush; but if you persist in living at a high altitude, you are running the risk of prompt interment in consecrated soil. A few words, my Lord Marquis, will make my meaning clear to you.

"Chemistry," he began, "has shown us that man's breathing is a real process of combustion, and the intensity of its action varies according to the abundance or scarcity of the phlogistic element stored up by the organism of each individual. In your case, the phlogistic or inflammatory element is abundant; if you will permit me to put it so, you generate superfluous oxygen, possessing as you do the inflammatory temperament of a man destined to experience strong emotions. While you breathe the keen, pure air that stimulates life in men of lymphatic constitution, you are accelerating an expenditure of vitality already too rapid. One of the conditions of existence for you is the heavier atmosphere of the plains and valleys. Yes, the vital air for a man consumed by his genius lies in the fertile pasture-lands of Germany, at Toplitz or Baden-Baden. If England is not obnoxious to you, its misty climate would reduce your fever; but the situation of our baths, a thousand feet above the level of the Mediterranean, is dangerous for you. That is my opinion at least," he said, with a deprecatory gesture, " and I give it in opposition to our interests, for, if you act upon it, we shall unfortunately lose you."

But for these closing words of his, the affable doctor's seeming good-nature would have completely won Raphael over; but he was too profoundly observant not to understand the meaning of the tone, the look and gesture that accompanied that mild sarcasm, not to see that the little man had been sent on this errand, no doubt, by a flock of his rejoicing patients. The florid-looking idlers, tedious old women, nomad English people, and fine ladies who had given their husbands the slip, and were escorted hither by their lovers—one and all were in a plot to drive away a wretched, feeble creature about to die, who seemed unable to hold out against a daily renewed persecution! Raphael accepted the challenge; he foresaw some amusement to be derived from their manœuvres.

" As you would be so grieved at losing me," said he to the doctor, " I will endeavor to avail myself of your good advice without leaving the place. I will set about having a house built to-morrow, and the atmosphere within it shall be regulated by your instruction."

The doctor understood the sarcastic smile that lurked about Raphael's mouth, and took his leave without finding another word to say.

The Lake of Bourget lies seven hundred feet above the Mediterranean, in a great hollow among the jagged peaks of the hills; it sparkles there, the bluest drop of water in the world. From the summit of the Cat's Tooth the lake below looks like a stray turquoise. This lovely sheet of water is about twenty-seven miles round, and in some places is nearly five hundred feet deep.

Under the cloudless sky, in your boat in the midst of the great expanse of water, with only the sound of the oars in your ears, only the vague outline of the hills on the horizon before you; you admire the glittering snows of the French Maurienne; you pass now by masses of granite clad in the velvet of green turf or in low-growing shrubs, now by pleasant sloping meadows; there is always a wilderness on the one hand and fertile lands on the other, and both harmonies and dissonances compose a scene for you where everything is at once small and vast, and you feel yourself to be a poor onlooker at a grand banquet. The configuration of the mountains brings about misleading optical conditions and illusions of perspective; a pine-tree a hundred feet in height looks to be a mere reed; wide valleys look as narrow as meadow paths. The lake is the only one where the confidences of heart and heart can be exchanged. There one can love; there one can meditate. Nowhere on earth will you find a closer understanding between the water, the sky, the mountains, and the fields. There is a balm there for all the agitations of life. The place keeps the secrets of sorrow to itself, the sorrow that grows less beneath its soothing influence; and to love, it gives a grave and meditative cast, deepening passion and purifying it. A kiss there becomes something great. But beyond all things it is a lake for memories; it aids them by lending to them the hues of its own waves; it is a mirror in which everything is reflected. Only here, with this lovely landscape all round him, could Raphael endure the burden laid upon him; here he could remain as a languid dreamer, without a wish of his own.

He went out upon the lake after the doctor's visit, and was landed at a lonely point on the pleasant slope where the village of Saint-Innocent is situated. The view from this promontory, as one may call it, comprises the heights of Bugey with the Rhone flowing at their foot, and at the end of the lake; but Raphael liked to look at the opposite shore from thence, at the melancholy looking Abbey of Haute-Combe, the burying-place of the Sardinian kings, who lie prostrate there before the hills, like pilgrims come at last to their journey's end.

The silence of the landscape was broken by the even rhythm of the strokes of the oar; it seemed to find a voice for the place, in monotonous cadences like the chanting of monks. The Marquis was surprised to find visitors to this usually lonely part of the lake; and as he mused, he watched the people seated in the boat, and recognized in the stern the elderly lady who had spoken so harshly to him the evening before.

No one took any notice of Raphael as the boat passed, except the elderly lady's companion, a poor old maid of noble family, who bowed to him, and whom it seemed to him that he saw for the first time. A few seconds later he had already forgotten the visitors, who had rapidly disappeared behind the promontory, when he heard the fluttering of a dress, and the sound of light footsteps not far from him. He turned about and saw the companion; and, guessing from her embarrassed manner that she wished to speak with him, he walked towards her.

She was somewhere about thirty-six years of age, thin and tall, reserved and prim, and, like all old maids, seemed puzzled to know which way to look, an expression no longer in keeping with her measured, springless, and hesitating steps. She was both young and old at the same time, and, by a certain dignity in her carriage, showed the high value which she set upon her charms and perfections. In addition, her movements were all demure and discreet, like those of women who are accustomed to take great care of themselves, no doubt because they desire not to be cheated of love, their destined end.

"Your life is in danger, sir; do not come to the Club again!" she said, stepping back a pace or two from Raphael, as if her reputation had been already compromised.

"But, mademoiselle," said Raphael, smiling, "please explain yourself more clearly, since you have condescended so far——"

"Ah," she answered, "unless I had had a very strong motive, I should never have run the risk of offending the

Countess, for if she ever came to know that I had warned you——"

"And who would tell her, mademoiselle?" cried Raphael.

"True," the old maid answered. She looked at him, quaking like an owl out in the sunlight. "But think of yourself," she went on; "several young men, who want to drive you away from the baths, have agreed to pick a quarrel with you, and to force you into a duel."

The elderly lady's voice sounded in the distance.

"Mademoiselle," began the Marquis, "my gratitude——" But his protectress had fled already; she had heard the voice of her mistress squeaking afresh among the rocks.

"Poor girl! unhappiness always understands and helps the unhappy," Raphael thought, and sat himself down at the foot of a tree.

The key of every science is, beyond cavil, the mark of interrogation; we owe most of our greatest discoveries to a *Why?* and all the wisdom in the world, perhaps, consists in asking *Wherefore?* in every connection. But, on the other hand, this acquired prescience is the ruin of our illusions.

So Valentin, having taken the old maid's kindly action for the text of his wandering thoughts, without the deliberate promptings of philosophy, must find it full of gall and wormwood.

"It is not at all extraordinary that a gentlewoman's gentlewoman should take a fancy to me," said he to himself. "I am twenty-seven years old, and I have a title and an income of two hundred thousand a year. But that her mistress, who hates water like a rabid cat—for it would be hard to give the palm to either in that matter—that her mistress should have brought her here in a boat! Is not that very strange and wonderful? Those two women came into Savoy to sleep like marmots; they ask if day has dawned at noon; and to think that they could get up this morning before eight o'clock to take their chance in running after me!"

Very soon the old maid and her elderly innocence became, in his eyes, a fresh manifestation of that artificial, malicious little world. It was a paltry device, a clumsy artifice, a piece of priest's or woman's craft. Was the duel a myth, or did they merely want to frighten him? But these petty creatures, impudent and teasing as flies, had succeeded in wounding his vanity, in rousing his pride, and exciting his curiosity. Unwilling to become their dupe, or to be taken for a coward, and even diverted perhaps by the little drama, he went to the Club that very evening.

He stood leaning against the marble chimney-piece, and stayed there quietly in the middle of the principal salon, doing his best to give no one any advantage over him; but he scrutinized the faces about him, and gave a certain vague offence to those assembled, by his inspection. Like a dog aware of his strength, he awaited the contest on his own ground, without unnecessary barking. Towards the end of the evening he strolled into the card-room, walking between the door and another that opened into the billiard-room, throwing a glance from time to time over a group of young men that had gathered there. He heard his name mentioned after a turn or two. Although they lowered their voices, Raphael easily guessed that he had become the topic of their debate, and he ended by catching a phrase or two spoken aloud.

" You ? "

" Yes, I."

" I dare you to do it ! "

" Let us make a bet on it ! "

" Oh, he will do it."

Just as Valentin, curious to learn the matter of the wager, came up to pay closer attention to what they were saying, a tall, strong, good-looking young fellow, who, however, possessed the impertinent stare peculiar to people who have material force at their back, came out of the billiard-room.

"I am deputed, sir," he said coolly, addressing the Marquis, "to make you aware of something which you do not seem to know ; your face and person generally are a source of annoyance to every one here, and to me in particular. You have too much politeness not to sacrifice yourself to the public good, and I beg that you will not show yourself in the Club again."

"This sort of joke has been perpetrated before, sir, in garrison towns at the time of the Empire ; but nowadays it is exceedingly bad form," said Raphael drily.

"I am not joking," the young man answered ; "and I repeat it : your health will be considerably the worse for a stay here ; the heat and light, the air of the salon, and the company are all bad for your complaint."

"Where did you study medicine?" Raphael inquired.

"I took my bachelor's degree on Lepage's shooting-ground in Paris, and was made a doctor at Cerizier's, the king of foils."

"There is one last degree left for you to take," said Valentin ; "study the ordinary rules of politeness, and you will be a perfect gentleman."

The young men all came out of the billiard-room just then, some disposed to laugh, some silent. The attention of other players was drawn to the matter ; they left their cards to watch a quarrel that rejoiced their instincts. Raphael, alone among this hostile crowd, did his best to keep cool, and not to put himself in any way in the wrong ; but his adversary having ventured a sarcasm containing an insult couched in unusually keen language, he replied gravely—

"We cannot box men's ears, sir, in these days, but I am at a loss for any word by which to stigmatize such cowardly behavior as yours."

"That's enough, that's enough. You can come to an explanation to-morrow," several young men exclaimed, interposing between the two champions.

Raphael left the room in the character of aggressor, after he had accepted a proposal to meet near the Château de Bordeau, in a little sloping meadow, not very far from the newly made road, by which the man who came off victorious could reach Lyons.   Raphael must now either take to his bed or leave the baths.   The visitors had gained their point.   At eight o'clock next morning his antagonist, followed by two seconds and a surgeon, arrived first on the ground.

" We shall do very nicely here ; glorious weather for a duel," he cried gaily, looking at the blue vault of sky above, at the waters of the lake, and the rocks, without a single melancholy presentiment or doubt of the issue.   " If I wing him," he went on, " I shall send him to bed for a month ; eh, doctor ? "

" At the very least," the surgeon replied ; " but let that willow twig alone, or you will weary your wrist, and then you will not fire steadily.   You might kill your man then instead of wounding him."

The noise of a carriage was heard approaching.

" Here he is," said the seconds, who soon descried a calèche coming along the road ; it was drawn by four horses, and there were two postilions.

" What a queer proceeding ! " said Valentin's antagonist ; " here he comes post-haste to be shot."

The slightest incident about a duel, as about a stake at cards, makes an impression on the minds of those deeply concerned in the results of the affair ; so the young man awaited the arrival of the carriage with a kind of uneasiness. It stopped in the road ; old Jonathan laboriously descended from it, in the first place, to assist Raphael to alight ; he supported him with his feeble arms, and showed him all the minute attentions that a lover lavishes upon his mistress. Both became lost to sight in the footpath that lay between the high-road and the field where the duel was to take place ; they were walking slowly, and did not appear again for some time after. The four onlookers at this strange spectacle felt deeply moved by the sight of Valentin as he leaned on his servant's arm ; he was wasted and pale ; he limped as if he had the gout, went with his head bowed down, and said not a word. You might have taken them for a couple of old men, one broken with years, the other worn out with thought ; the elder bore his age visibly written in his white hair, the younger was of no age.

"I have not slept all night, sir ; " so Raphael greeted his antagonist.

The icy tone and terrible glance that went with the words made the real aggressor shudder ; he knew that he was in the wrong, and felt in secret ashamed of his behavior. There was something strange in Raphael's bearing, tone and gesture ; the Marquis stopped, and every one else was likewise silent. The uneasy and constrained feeling grew to a height.

"There is yet time," he went on, " to offer me some slight apology ; and offer it you must, or you will die, sir ! You rely even now on your dexterity, and do not shrink from an encounter in which you believe all the advantage to be upon your side. Very good, sir ; I am generous, I am letting you know my superiority beforehand. I possess a terrible power. I have only to wish to do so, and I can neutralize your skill, dim your eyesight, make your hand and pulse unsteady, and even kill you outright. I have no wish to be compelled to exercise my power ; the use of it costs me too dear. You would not be the only one to die. So if you refuse to apologize to me, no matter what your experience in murder, your ball will go into the waterfall there, and mine will speed straight to your heart though I do not aim it at you."

Confused voices interrupted Raphael at this point. All the time that he was speaking, the Marquis had kept his intolerably keen gaze fixed upon his antagonist ; now he drew himself up and showed an impassive face, like that of a dangerous madman.

"Make him hold his tongue," the young man had said to one of his seconds; "that voice of his is tearing the heart out of me."

"Say no more, sir; it is quite useless," cried the seconds and the surgeon, addressing Raphael.

"Gentlemen, I am fulfilling a duty. Has this young gentleman any final arrangements to make?"

"That is enough; that will do."

The Marquis remained standing steadily, never for a moment losing sight of his antagonist; and the latter seemed, like a bird before a snake, to be overwhelmed by a well-nigh magical power. He was compelled to endure that homicidal gaze; he met and shunned it incessantly.

"I am thirsty; give me some water——" he said again to the second.

"Are you nervous?"

"Yes," he answered. "There is a fascination about that man's glowing eyes."

"Will you apologize?"

"It is too late now."

The two antagonists were placed at fifteen paces distant from each other. One of them had a brace of pistols at hand, and, according to the programme prescribed for them, each was to fire twice when and how he pleased, but after the signal had been given by the seconds.

"What are you doing, Charles?" exclaimed the young man who acted as second to Raphael's antagonist; "you are putting in the ball before the powder!"

"I am a dead man," he muttered, by way of answer; "you have put me facing the sun——"

"The sun lies behind you," said Valentin sternly and solemnly, while he coolly loaded his pistol without heeding the fact that the signal had been given, or that his antagonist was carefully taking aim.

There was something so appalling in this supernatural uncon-

VALENTIN HURRIEDLY SOUGHT THE WILD ASS' SKIN TO
SEE WHAT ANOTHER MAN'S LIFE HAD COST HIM.

VALENTIN HURRIEDLY SOUGHT THE WILD ASS' SKIN TO
SEE WHAT ANOTHER MAN'S LIFE HAD COST HIM.

cern, that it affected the two postilions, brought thither by a cruel curiosity. Raphael was either trying his power or playing with it, for he talked to Jonathan, and looked towards him as he received his adversary's fire. Charles' bullet broke a branch of willow, and ricocheted over the surface of the water; Raphael fired at random, and shot his antagonist through the heart. He did not heed the young man as he dropped; he hurriedly sought the Wild Ass' Skin to see what another man's life had cost him. The talisman was no larger than a small oak-leaf.

"What are you gaping at, you postilions over there? Let us be off," said the Marquis.

That same evening he crossed the French border, immediately set out for Auvergne, and reached the springs of Mont Dore. As he traveled, there surged up in his heart, all at once, one of those thoughts that come to us as a ray of sunlight pierces through the thick mists in some dark valley—a sad enlightenment, a pitiless sagacity that lights up the accomplished fact for us, that lays our errors bare, and leaves us without excuse in our own eyes. It suddenly struck him that the possession of power, no matter how enormous, did not bring with it the knowledge how to use it. The sceptre is a plaything for a child, an axe for a Richelieu, and for a Napoleon a lever by which to move the world. Power leaves us just as it finds us; only great natures grow greater by its means. Raphael had had everything in his power, and he had done nothing.

At the springs of Mont Dore he came again in contact with a little world of people, who invariably shunned him with the eager haste that animals display when they scent afar off one of their own species lying dead, and flee away. The dislike was mutual. His late adventure had given him a deep distaste for society; his first care, consequently, was to find a lodging at some distance from the neighborhood of the springs. Instinctively he felt within him the need of close contact with nature, of natural emotions, and of the vegetative life into which we sink so gladly among the fields.

The day after he arrived he climbed the Pic de Sancy, not without difficulty, and visited the higher valleys, the skyey nooks, undiscovered lakes, and peasants' huts about Mont Dore, a country whose stern and wild features are now beginning to tempt the brushes of our artists, for sometimes wonderfully fresh and charming views are to be found there, affording a strong contrast to the frowning brows of those lonely hills.

Barely a league from the village Raphael discovered a nook where nature seemed to have taken a pleasure in hiding away all her treasures like some glad and mischievous child. At the first sight of this unspoiled and picturesque retreat, he determined to take up his abode in it. There, life must needs be peaceful, natural, and fruitful, like the life of a plant.

Imagine for yourself an inverted cone of granite hollowed out on a large scale, a sort of basin with its sides divided up by queer winding paths. On one side lay level stretches with no growth upon them, a bluish uniform surface, over which the rays of the sun fell as upon a mirror; on the other lay cliffs split open by fissures and frowning ravines; great blocks of lava hung suspended from them, while the action of rain slowly prepared their impending fall; a few stunted trees, tormented by the wind, often crowned their summits; and here and there in some sheltered angle of their ramparts a clump of chestnut-trees grew tall as cedars, or some cavern in the yellowish rock showed the dark entrance into its depths, set about by flowers and brambles, decked by a little strip of green turf.

"At the bottom of this cup, which perhaps had been the crater of an old-world volcano, lay a pool of water as pure and bright as a diamond. Granite boulders lay around the deep basin, and willows, mountain-ash trees, yellow-flag lilies, and numberless aromatic plants bloomed about it, in a realm of meadow as fresh as an English bowling-green. The fine soft grass was watered by the streams that trickled through the fissures in the cliffs; the soil was continually enriched by the deposits of loam which storms washed down from the heights above. The pool might be some three acres in extent; its shape was irregular, and the edges were scalloped like the hem of a dress; the meadow might be an acre or two acres in extent. The cliffs and the water approached and receded from each other; here and there, there was scarcely width enough for the cows to pass between them.

After a certain height the plant life ceased. Aloft in air the granite took upon itself the most fantastic shapes, and assumed those misty tints that give to high mountains a dim resemblance to clouds in the sky. The bare, bleak cliffs, with the fearful rents in their sides, pictures of wild and barren desolation, contrasted strongly with the pretty view of the valley; and so strange were the shapes they assumed, that one of the cliffs had been called "The Capuchin," because it was so like a monk. Sometimes these sharp-pointed peaks, these mighty masses of rock, and airy caverns were lighted up one by one, according to the direction of the sun or the caprices of the atmosphere; they caught gleams of gold, dyed themselves in purple, took a tint of glowing rose-color, or turned dull and gray. Upon the heights a drama of color was always to be seen, a play of ever-shifting iridescent hues like those on a pigeon's breast.

Oftentimes at sunrise or at sunset a ray of bright sunlight would penetrate between two sheer surfaces of lava, that might have been split apart by a hatchet, to the very depths of that pleasant little garden, where it would play in the waters of the pool, like a beam of golden light which gleams through the chinks of a shutter into a room in Spain, that has been carefully darkened for a siesta. When the sun arose above the old crater that some antediluvian revolution had filled with water, its rocky sides took warmer tones, the extinct volcano glowed again, and its sudden heat quickened the sprouting seeds and vegetation, gave color to the flowers, and ripened the fruits of this forgotten corner of the earth.

As Raphael reached it, he noticed several cows grazing in the pasture-land; and when he had taken a few steps towards the water, he saw a little house built of granite and roofed with shingle in the spot where the meadow-land was at its widest. The roof of this little cottage harmonized with everything about it; for it had long been overgrown with ivy, moss, and flowers of no recent date. A thin smoke, that did not scare the birds away, went up from the dilapidated chimney. There was a great bench at the door between huge honeysuckle bushes, that were pink with blossom and full of scent. The walls could scarcely be seen for branches of vine and sprays of rose and jessamine that interlaced and grew entirely as chance and their own will bade them; for the inmates of the cottage seemed to pay no attention to the growth which adorned their house, and to take no care of it, leaving to it the fresh capricious charm of nature.

Some clothes spread out on the gooseberry bushes were drying in the sun. A cat was sitting on a machine for stripping hemp; beneath it lay a newly scoured brass caldron, among a quantity of potato-parings. On the other side of the house Raphael saw a sort of barricade of dead thorn-bushes, meant no doubt to keep the poultry from scratching up the vegetables and pot-herbs. It seemed like the end of the earth. The dwelling was like some bird's-nest ingeniously set in a cranny of the rocks, a clever and at the same time a careless bit of workmanship. A simple and kindly nature lay round about it; its rusticity was genuine, but there was a charm like that of poetry in it; for it grew and throve at a thousand miles' distance from our elaborate and conventional poetry. It was like none of our conceptions; it was a spontaneous growth, a masterpiece due to chance.

As Raphael reached the place, the sunlight fell across it from right to left, bringing out all the colors of its plants and trees ; the yellowish or gray bases of the crags, the different shades of the green leaves, the masses of flowers, pink, blue, or white, the climbing plants with their bell-like blossoms, and the shot velvet of the mosses, the purple-tinted blooms of the heather,—everything was either brought into relief or made fairer yet by the enchantment of the light or by the contrasting shadows ; and this was the case most of all with the sheet of water, wherein the house, the trees, the granite peaks, and the sky were all faithfully reflected. Everything had a radiance of its own in this delightful picture, from the sparkling mica stone to the bleached tuft of grass hidden away in the soft shadows ; the spotted cow with its glossy hide, the delicate water-plants that hung down over the pool like fringes in a nook where blue or emerald colored insects were buzzing about, the roots of trees like a sand-besprinkled shock of hair above grotesque faces in the flinty rock surface, —all these things made a harmony for the eye.

The odor of the tepid water, the scent of the flowers, and the breath of the caverns which filled the lonely place, gave Raphael a sensation that was almost enjoyment. Silence reigned in majesty over these woods, which possibly are unknown to the tax-collector ; but the barking of a couple of dogs broke the stillness all at once ; the cows turned their heads towards the entrance of the valley, showing their moist noses to Raphael, stared stupidly at him, and then fell to browsing again. A goat and her kid, that seemed to hang on the side of the crags in some magical fashion, capered and leaped to a slab of granite near to Raphael, and stayed there a moment, as if to seek to know who he was. The yapping of the dogs brought out a plump child, who stood agape, and next came a white-haired old man of middle height. Both of these two beings were in keeping with the surroundings, the air, the flowers, and the dwelling. Health appeared to overflow in this fertile region ; old age and childhood thrived there. There seemed to be, about all these types of existence, the freedom and carelessness of the life of primitive times, a happiness of use and wont that gave the lie to our philosophical platitudes, and wrought a cure of all its swelling passions in the heart.

The old man belonged to the type of model dear to the masculine brush of Schnetz. The countless wrinkles upon his brown face looked as if they would be hard to the touch ; the straight nose, the prominent cheek-bones, streaked with red veins like a vine-leaf in autumn, the angular features, all were characteristics of strength, even where strength existed no longer. The hard hands, now that they toiled no longer, had preserved their scanty white hair ; his bearing was that of an absolutely free man ; it suggested the thought that, had he been an Italian, he would have perhaps turned brigand, for the love of the liberty so dear to him. The child was a regular mountaineer, with the black eyes that can face the sun without flinching, a deeply-tanned complexion, and rough brown hair. His movements were like a bird's—swift, decided, and unconstrained ; his clothing was ragged ; the white, fair skin showed through the rents in his garments. There they both stood in silence, side by side, both obeying the same impulse ; in both faces were clear tokens of an absolutely identical and idle life. The old man had adopted the child's amusements, and the child had fallen in with the old man's humor ; there was a sort of tacit agreement between two kinds of feebleness, between failing powers well-nigh spent and powers just about to unfold themselves.

Very soon a woman who seemed to be about thirty years old appeared on the threshold of the door, spinning as she came. She was an Auvergnate, a high-colored, comfortable-looking, straightforward sort of person, with white teeth ; her cap and dress, the face, full figure, and general appearance were of the Auvergne peasant stamp. So was her dialect ; she was a thorough embodiment of her district ; its hard-working ways, its thrift, ignorance, and heartiness all met in her.

She greeted Raphael, and they began to talk. The dogs quieted down ; the old man went and sat on a bench in the sun ; the child followed his mother about wherever she went, listening without saying a word, and staring at the stranger.

"You are not afraid to live here, good woman?"

"What should we be afraid of, sir? When we bolt the door, whoever could get inside? Oh, no, we aren't afraid at all. And besides," she said, as she brought the Marquis into the principal room in the house, "what should thieves come to take from us here?"

She designated the room as she spoke ; the smoke-blackened walls, with some brilliant pictures in blue, red and green, an "End of Credit," a Crucifixion, and the "Grenadiers of the Imperial Guard," for their sole ornament ; the furniture here and there, the old wooden four-post bedstead, the table with crooked legs, a few stools, the chest that held the bread, the flitch that hung from the ceiling, a jar of salt, a stove, and on the mantel-shelf a few discolored yellow plaster figures. As he went out again Raphael noticed a man half-way up the crags, leaning on a hoe, and watching the house with interest.

"That's my man, sir," said the Auvergnate, unconsciously smiling in peasant fashion ; "he is at work up there."

"And that old man is your father?"

"Asking your pardon, sir, he is my man's grandfather. Such as you see him, he is a hundred and two, and yet quite lately he walked over to Clermont with our little chap! Oh, he has been a strong man in his time ; but he does nothing now but sleep and eat and drink. He amuses himself with the little fellow. Sometimes the child trails him up the hillsides, and he will just go up there along with him.

Valentin made up his mind immediately. He would live between this child and old man, breathe the same air, eat their bread, drink the same water, sleep with them, make the blood in his veins like theirs. It was a dying man's fancy. For him the prime model, after which the customary

18

existence of the individual should be shaped, the real formula
for the life of a human being, the only true and possible life,
the life-ideal, was to become one of the oysters adhering to
this rock, to save his shell a day or two longer by paralyzing
the power of death. One profoundly selfish thought took
possession of him, and the whole universe was swallowed up
and lost in it. For him the universe existed no longer ; the
whole world had come to be within himself. For the sick,
the world begins at their pillow and ends at the foot of the
bed ; and this country-side was Raphael's sick bed.

Who has not, at some time or other in his life, watched the
comings and goings of an ant, slipped straws into a yellow
slug's one breathing-hole, studied the vagaries of a slender
dragon-fly, pondered admiringly over the countless veins in
an oak-leaf, that bring the colors of a rose window in some
Gothic cathedral into contrast with the reddish background ?
Who has not looked long in delight at the effects of sun and
rain on a roof of brown tiles, at the dewdrops, or at the
variously shaped petals of the flower-cups ? Who has not
sunk into these idle, absorbing meditations on things without,
that have no conscious end, yet lead to some definite thought
at last ? Who, in short, has not led a lazy life, the life of
childhood, the life of the savage without his labor ? This life
without a care or a wish, Raphael led for some days' space.
He felt a distinct improvement in his condition, a wonderful
sense of ease, that quieted his apprehensions and soothed his
sufferings.

He would climb the crags, and then find a seat high up on
some peak whence he could see a vast expanse of distant
country at a glance, and he would spend whole days in this
way, like a plant in the sun, or a hare in its form. And at
last, growing familiar with the appearance of the plant-life
about him, and of the changes in the sky, he minutely noted
the progress of everything working around him in the water,
or in the air. He tried to share the secret impulses of nature,

sought by passive obedience to become a part of it, and to lie within the conservative and despotic jurisdiction that regulates instinctive existence. He no longer wished to steer his own course.

Just as criminals in olden times were safe from the pursuit of justice, if they took refuge under the shadow of the altar, so Raphael made an effort to slip into the sancturary of life. He succeeded in becoming an integral part of the great and mighty fruit-producing organization ; he had adapted himself to the inclemency of the air, and dwelt in every cave among the rocks. He had learned the ways and habits of growth of every plant, had studied the laws of the watercourses and their beds, and had come to know the animals ; he was at last so perfectly at one with this teeming earth, that he had in some way discerned its mysteries and caught the spirit of it.

The infinitely varied forms of every natural kingdom were, to his thinking, only developments of one and the same substance, different combinations brought about by the same impulse, endless emanations from a measureless Being which was aching, thinking, moving, and growing, and in harmony with which he longed to grow, to move, to think, and act. He had fancifully blended his life with the life of the crags ; he had deliberately planted himself there. During the earliest days of his sojourn in these pleasant surroundings, Valentin tasted all the pleasures of childhood again, thanks to the strange hallucination of apparent convalescence, which is not unlike the pauses of delirium that nature mercifully provides for those in pain. He went about making trifling discoveries, setting to work on endless things, and finishing none of them; the evening's plans were quite forgotten in the morning ; he had no cares, he was happy ; he thought himself saved.

One morning he had lain in bed till noon, deep in the dreams between sleep and waking, which give to realities a fantastic appearance, and make the wildest fancies seem solid facts ; while he was still uncertain that he was not dreaming yet, he suddenly heard his hostess giving a report of his health to Jonathan, for the first time. Jonathan came to inquire after him daily; and the Auvergnate, thinking no doubt that Valentin was still asleep, had not lowered the tones of a voice developed in mountain air.

"No better and no worse," she said. "He coughed all last night again fit to kill himself. Poor gentleman, he coughs and spits till it is piteous. My husband and I often wonder to each other where he gets the strength from to cough like that. It goes to your heart. What a cursed complaint it is! He has no strength at all. I am always afraid I shall find him dead in his bed some morning. He is every bit as pale as a waxen Christ. *Dame!* I watch him as he dresses; his poor body is as thin as a nail. And he does not feel well now; but no matter. It's all the same; he wears himself out with running about as if he had health and to spare. All the same, he is very brave, for he never complains at all. But really he would be better under the earth than on it, for he is enduring the agonies of Christ. I don't wish that myself, sir; it is quite against our interests; but even if he didn't pay us what he does, I should be just as fond of him; it is not our own interest that is our motive."

"Ah, mon Dieu!" she continued, "Parisians are the people for these dogs' diseases. Where did he catch it, now? Poor young man! And he is so sure that he is going to get well! That fever just gnaws him, you know; it eats him away; it will be the death of him. He has no notion whatever of that; he does not know it, sir; he sees nothing—— You mustn't cry about him, M. Jonathan; you must remember that he will be happy, and will not suffer any more. You ought to make a novena for him; I have seen wonderful cures come of a nine days' prayer, and I would gladly pay for a wax taper to save such a gentle creature, so good he is, a paschal lamb——"

As Raphael's voice had grown too weak to allow him to

make himself heard, he was compelled to listen to this horrible statement. His irritation, however, drove him out of bed at length, and he appeared upon the threshold.

"Old scoundrel!" he shouted to Jonathan; "do you mean to put me to death?"

The peasant woman took him for a ghost, and fled.

"I forbid you to have any anxiety whatever about my health," Raphael went on.

"Yes, my Lord Marquis," said the old servant, wiping away his tears.

"And for the future you had very much better not come here without my orders."

Jonathan meant to be obedient, but in the look full of pity and devotion that he gave the Marquis before he went, Raphael read his own death-warrant. Utterly disheartened, brought all at once to a sense of his real position, Valentin sat down on the threshold, locked his arms across his chest, and bowed his head. Jonathan turned to his master in alarm, with "My Lord ——"

"Go away, go away," cried the invalid.

In the hours of the next morning, Raphael climbed the crags, and sat down in a mossy cleft in the rocks, whence he could see the narrow path along which the water for the dwelling was carried. At the base of the hill he saw Jonathan in conversation with the Auvergnate. Some malicious power interpreted for him all the woman's head-shakings, melancholy gestures, and garrulous forebodings, and filled the breeze and the silence with her ominous words. Thrilled with horror, he took refuge among the highest summits of the mountains, and stayed there till the evening; but yet he could not drive away the gloomy presentiments awakened within him in such an unfortunate manner by a cruel solicitude on his account.

The Auvergne peasant herself suddenly appeared before him like a shadow in the dusk; a perverse freak of the poet within him found a vague resemblance between her black and white striped petticoat and the bony frame of a spectre.

"The damp is falling now, sir," said she. "If you stop out there, you will go off just like rotten fruit. You must come in. It isn't healthy to breathe the damp, and you have taken nothing since the morning, besides."

"God's thunder! old witch," he cried; "let me live after my own fashion, I tell you, or I shall be off altogether. It is quite bad enough to dig my grave every morning; you might let it alone in the evenings at least ——"

"Your grave, sir! I dig your grave!—and where may your grave be? I want to see you as old as father there, and not in your grave by any manner of means. The grave! that comes soon enough for us all; in the grave——"

"That is enough," said Raphael.

"Take my arm, sir."

"No."

The feeling of pity in others is very difficult for a man to bear, and it is hardest of all when the pity is deserved. Hatred is a tonic—it quickens life and stimulates revenge; but pity is death to us—it makes our weakness weaker still. It is as if distress simpered ingratiatingly at us; contempt lurks in the tenderness, or tenderness in an affront. In the centenarian Raphael saw triumphant pity, a wondering pity in the child's eyes, an officious pity in the woman, and in her husband a pity that had an interested motive; but no matter how the sentiment declared itself, death was always its import.

A poet makes a poem of everything; it is tragical or joyful, as things happen to strike his imagination; his lofty soul rejects all half-tones; he always prefers vivid and decided colors. In Raphael's soul this compassion produced a terrible poem of mourning and melancholy. When he had wished to live in close contact with nature, he had of course forgotten how freely natural emotions are expressed. He would think himself quite alone under a tree, whilst he struggled with an obstinate coughing fit, a terrible combat from which he never issued victorious without utter exhaustion afterwards; and then he would meet the clear, bright eyes of the little boy, who occupied the post of sentinel, like a savage in a bent of grass; the eyes scrutinized him with a childish wonder, in which there was as much amusement as pleasure, and an indescribable mixture of indifference and interest. The awful *Brother, you must die,* of the Trappists seemed constantly legible in the eyes of the peasants with whom Raphael was living; he scarcely knew which he dreaded most, their unfet-tered talk or their silence; their presence became torture.

One morning he saw two men in black prowling about in his neighborhood, who furtively studied him and took obser-vations. They acted as though they had come there for a stroll, and asked him a few indifferent questions, to which he returned short answers. He recognized them both. One was the curé and the other the doctor at the springs; Jona-than had no doubt sent them, or the people in the house had called them in, or the scent of an approaching death had drawn them thither. He beheld his own funeral, heard the chanting of the priests, and counted the tall wax candles; and all that lovely fertile nature around him, in whose lap he had thought to find life once more, he saw no longer, save through a veil of crape. Everything that but lately had spoken of length of days to him, now prophesied a speedy end. He set out the next day for Paris, not before he had been inundated with cordial wishes, which the people of the house uttered in melancholy and wistful tones for his benefit.

He traveled through the night, and awoke as they passed through one of the pleasant valleys of the Bourbonnais. View after view swam before his gaze, and passed rapidly away like the vague pictures of a dream. Cruel nature spread herself out before his eyes with tantalizing grace. Sometimes the Allier, a liquid shining riband, meandered through the distant fertile landscape; then followed the steeples of hamlets, hiding modestly in the depths of a ravine with its yellow cliffs ; sometimes, after the monotony of vineyards, the water-mills of a little valley would be suddenly seen ; and everywhere there were pleasant châteaux, hillside villages, roads with their fringes of queenly poplars ; and the Loire itself, at last, with its wide sheets of water sparkling like diamonds amid its golden sands. Attractions everywhere, without end ! This nature, all astir with a life and gladness like that of childhood, scarcely able to contain the impulses and sap of June, possessed a fatal attraction for the darkened gaze of the invalid. He drew the blinds of his carriage windows, and betook himself again to slumber.

Towards evening, after they had passed Cesne, he was awakened by lively music, and found himself confronted with a village fair. The horses were changed near the market-place. Whilst the postilions were engaged in making the transfer, he saw the people dancing merrily, pretty and attractive girls with flowers about them, excited youths, and finally the jolly wine-flushed countenances of the old peasants. Children prattled, old women laughed and chatted ; everything spoke in one voice, and there was a holiday gaiety about everything, down to their clothing and the tables that were set out. A cheerful expression pervaded the square and the church, the roofs and windows ; even the very doorways of the village seemed likewise to be in holiday trim.

Raphael could not repress an angry exclamation, nor yet a wish to silence the fiddles, annihilate the stir and bustle, stop the clamor, and disperse the ill-timed festival ; like a dying man, he felt unable to endure the slightest sound, and he entered his carriage much annoyed. When he looked out upon the square from the window, he saw that all the happiness was scared away ; the peasant women were in flight, and the benches were deserted. Only a blind musician, on the scaffolding of the orchestra, went on playing a shrill tune on his clarionette. That piping of his, without dancers to it, and the solitary old man himself, in the shadow of the lime-tree, with his curmudgeon's face, scanty hair, and ragged clothing, was like a fantastic picture of Raphael's wish. The heavy rain was pouring in torrents; it was one of those thunder-storms that June brings about so rapidly, to cease as suddenly. The thing was so natural that, when Raphael had looked out and seen some pale clouds driven by a gust of wind, he did not think of looking at the piece of skin. He lay back again in the corner of his carriage, which was very soon rolling upon its way.

The next day found him back in his home again, in his own room, beside his own fireside. He had had a large fire lighted; he felt cold. Jonathan brought him some letters; they were all from Pauline. He opened the first one without any eagerness, and unfolded it as if it had been the gray-paper form of application for taxes made by the revenue collector. He read the first sentence :—

"Gone! This really is a flight, my Raphael. How is it? No one can tell me where you are. And who should know if not I."

He did not wish to learn any more.. He calmly took up the letters and threw them in the fire, watching with dull and lifeless eyes the perfumed paper as it was twisted, shriveled, bent, and devoured by the capricious flames. Fragments that fell among the ashes allowed him to see the beginning of a sentence, or a half-burnt thought or word; he took a pleasure in deciphering them—a sort of mechanical amusement.

"Sitting at your door—expected—Caprice—I obey—Rivals —I, never!—thy Pauline—love—no more of Pauline?—If you had wished to leave me forever, you would not have deserted me—Love eternal—To die——"

The words caused him a sort of remorse; he seized the tongs, and rescued a last fragment of the letter from the flames.

"I have murmured," so Pauline wrote, "but I have never

complained, my Raphael! If you have left me so far behind
you, it was doubtless because you wished to hide some heavy
grief from me. Perhaps you will kill me one of these days,
but you are too good to torture me. So do not go away from
me like this. There! I can bear the worst of torment, if
only I am at your side. Any grief that you could cause me
would not be grief. There is far more love in my heart for
you than I have ever yet shown you. I can endure any-
thing, except this weeping far away from you, this ignorance
of your——"

Raphael laid the scorched scrap on the mantel-piece, then
all at once he flung it in the fire. This bit of paper was too
clearly a symbol of his own love and luckless existence.

"Go and find M. Bianchon," he told Jonathan.

Horace came and found Raphael in bed.

"Can you prescribe a draught for me—some mild opiate
which will always keep me in a somnolent condition, a draught
that will not be injurious although taken constantly."

"Nothing is easier," the young doctor replied; "but you
will have to keep on your feet for a few hours daily, at any
rate, so as to take your food."

"A few hours!" Raphael broke in; "no, no! I only
wish to be out of bed for an hour at most."

"What is your object?" inquired Bianchon.

"To sleep; for so one keeps alive, at any rate," the
patient answered. "Let no one come in, not even Mlle.
Pauline de Vitschnau!" he added to Jonathan, as the doctor
was writing out his prescription.

"Well, M. Horace, is there any hope?" the old servant
asked, going as far as the flight of steps before the door, with
the young doctor.

"He may live for some time yet, or he may die to-night.
The chances of life and death are evenly balanced in his case.
I can't understand it at all," said the doctor, with a doubtful
gesture. "His mind ought to be diverted."

"Diverted! Ah, sir, you don't know him! He killed a man the other day without a word!—Nothing can divert him!"

For some days Raphael lay plunged in the torpor of this artificial sleep. Thanks to the material power that opium exerts over the immaterial part of us, this man with the powerful and active imagination reduced himself to the level of those sluggish forms of animal life that lurk in the depths of forests, and take the form of vegetable refuse, never stirring from their place to catch their easy prey. He had darkened the very sun in heaven; the daylight never entered his room. About eight o'clock in the evening he would leave his bed, with no very clear consciousness of his own existence; he would satisfy the claims of hunger and return to bed immediately. One dull blighted hour after another only brought confused pictures and appearances before him, and lights and shadows against a background of darkness. He lay buried in deep silence; movement and intelligence were completely annihilated for him. He woke later than usual one evening, and found that his dinner was not ready. He rang for Jonathan.

"You can go," he said. "I have made you rich; you shall be happy in your old age; but I will not let you muddle away my life any longer. Miserable wretch! I am hungry —where is my dinner? How is it?—Answer me!"

A satisfied smile stole over Jonathan's face. He took a candle that lit up the great dark rooms of the mansion with its flickering light; brought his master, who had again become an automaton, into a great gallery, and flung a door suddenly open. Raphael was all at once dazzled by a flood of light and amazed by an unheard-of scene.

His chandeliers had been filled with wax-lights; the rarest flowers from his conservatory were carefully arranged about the room; the table sparkled with silver, gold, crystal, and porcelain; a royal banquet was spread—the odors of the tempting dishes tickled the nervous fibres of the palate. There sat his friends; he saw them among beautiful women in full evening dress, with bare necks and shoulders, with flowers in their hair; fair women of every type, with sparkling eyes, attractively and fancifully arrayed. One had adopted an Irish jacket, which displayed the alluring outlines of her form; one wore the "basquina" of Andalusia, with its wanton grace; here was a half-clad Dian the huntress, there the costume of Mlle. de la Vallière, amorous and coy; and all of them alike were given up to the intoxication of the moment.

As Raphael's death-pale face showed itself in the doorway, a sudden outcry broke out, as vehement as the blaze of this improvised banquet. The voices, perfumes, and lights, the exquisite beauty of the women, produced their effect upon his senses, and awakened his desires. Delightful music, from unseen players in the next room, drowned the excited tumult in a torrent of harmony—the whole strange vision was complete.

Raphael felt a caressing pressure of his own hand, a woman's white, youthful arms were stretched out to grasp him, and the hand was Aquilina's. He knew now that this scene was not a fantastic illusion like the fleeting pictures of his disordered dreams; he uttered a dreadful cry, slammed the door, and dealt his heartbroken old servant a blow in the face.

"Monster!" he cried, "so you have sworn to kill me!" and trembling at the risks he had just now run, he summoned all his energies, reached his room, took a powerful sleeping draught, and went to bed.

"The devil!" cried Jonathan, recovering himself. "And M. Bianchon most certainly told me to divert his mind."

It was close upon midnight. By that time, owing to one of those physical caprices that are the marvel and the despair of science, Raphael, in his slumber, became radiant with beauty. A bright color glowed on his pale cheeks. There was an almost girlish grace about the forehead in which his genius was revealed. Life seemed to bloom on the quiet face that lay there at rest. His sleep was sound; a light, even breath was drawn in between the red lips; he was smiling—he had passed no doubt through the gate of dreams, into a noble life. Was he a centenarian now? Did his grandchildren come to wish him length of days? Or, on a rustic bench set in the sun and under the trees, was he scanning, like the prophet on the mountain-heights, a promised land, a far-off time of blessing.

"Here you are!"

The words, uttered in silver tones, dispelled the shadowy faces of his dreams. He saw Pauline, in the lamplight, sitting upon the bed; Pauline grown fairer yet through sorrow and separation. Raphael remained bewildered by the sight of her face, white as the petals of some water flower, and the shadow of her long, dark hair about it seemed to make it whiter still. Her tears had left a gleaming trace upon her cheeks, and hung there yet, ready to fall at the least movement. She looked like an angel fallen from the skies, or a spirit that a breath might waft away, as she sat there all in white, with her head bowed, scarcely creasing the quilt beneath her weight.

"Ah, I have forgotten everything!" she cried, as Raphael opened his eyes. "I have no voice left except to tell you, 'I am yours.' There is nothing in my heart but love. Angel of my life, you have never been so beautiful before! Your eyes are blazing—— But come, I can guess it all. You have been in search of health without me; you were afraid of me ——well——"

"Go! go! leave me," Raphael uttered at last. "Why do you not go? If you stay, I shall die. Do you want to see me die?"

"Die?" she echoed. "Can you die without me? Die? But you are young; and I love you! Die?" she asked, in a deep, hollow voice. She seized his hands with a frenzied movement. "Cold!" she wailed. "Is it all an illusion?"

Raphael drew the little bit of skin from under his pillow ; it was as tiny and as fragile as a periwinkle-petal.   He showed it to her.

" Pauline ! " he said, " fair image of my fair life, let us say good-bye."

" Good-bye ? " she echoed, looking surprised.

" Yes.   This is a talisman that grants all my wishes, and that represents my span of life.   See here, this is all that remains of it.   If you look at me any longer, I shall die——"

The young girl thought that Valentin had grown light-headed ; she took the talisman and went to fetch the lamp. By its tremulous light which she shed over Raphael and the talisman, she scanned her lover's face and the last morsel of the magic skin.   As Pauline stood there, in all the beauty of love and terror, Raphael was no longer able to control his thoughts ; memories of tender scenes, and of passionate and fevered joys, overwhelmed the soul that had so long lain dormant within him, and kindled a fire not quite extinct.

" Pauline ! Pauline !   Come to me——"

A dreadful cry came from the girl's throat, her eyes dilated with horror, her eyebrows were distorted and drawn apart by an unspeakable anguish ; she read in Raphael's eyes the vehement desire in which she had once exulted, but as it grew she felt a light movement in her hand, and the skin contracted. She did not stop to think ; she fled into the next room, and locked the door.

" Pauline ! Pauline ! " cried the dying man, as he rushed after her ; " I love you, I adore you, I want you, Pauline !   I must curse you if you will not open the door for me.   I wish to die in your arms ! "

With unnatural strength, the last effort of ebbing life, he broke down the door, and saw his mistress writhing upon a sofa.   Pauline had vainly tried to pierce her heart, and now thought to find a rapid death by strangling herself with her shawl.

"If I die, he will live," she said, trying to tighten the knot that she had made.

In her struggle with death her hair hung loose, her shoulders were bare, her clothing was disordered, her eyes were bathed in tears, her face was flushed and drawn with the horror of despair; yet as her exceeding beauty met Raphael's intoxicated eyes, his delirium grew. He sprang towards her like a bird of prey, tore away the shawl, and tried to take her in his arms.

The dying man sought for words to express the wish that was consuming his strength; but no sounds would come except the choking death-rattle in his chest. Each breath he drew sounded hollower than the last, and seemed to come from his very entrails. At the last moment, no longer able to utter a sound, he set his teeth in Pauline's breast. Jonathan appeared, terrified by the cries he had heard, and tried to tear away the dead body from the grasp of the girl who was crouching with it in a corner.

" What do you want?" she asked. " He is mine; I have killed him. Did I not foresee how it would be?"

EPILOGUE.

" And what became of Pauline?"

" Pauline? Ah! Do you sometimes spend a pleasant winter evening by your own fireside, and give yourself up luxuriously to memories of love or youth, while you watch the glow of the fire where the logs of oak are burning? Here, the fire outlines a sort of chessboard in red squares, there it has a sheen like velvet; little blue flames start up and flicker and play about in the glowing depths of the brasier. A mysterious artist comes and adapts that flame to his own ends; by a secret of his own he draws a visionary face in the midst of those flaming violet and crimson hues, a face with unimaginable delicate outlines, a fleeting apparition which no chance will ever bring back again. It is a woman's face, her hair is blown back by the wind, her features speak of a rapture of delight; she breathes fire in the midst of the fire. She smiles, she dies, you will never see her any more. Farewell, flower of the flame! Farewell, essence incomplete and unforeseen, come too early or too late to make the spark of some glorious diamond.''

"But, Pauline.''

"You do not see, then? I will begin again. Make way! make way! She comes, she is here, the queen of illusions, a woman fleeting as a kiss, a woman bright as lightning, issuing in a blaze like lightning from the sky, a being uncreated, of spirit and love alone. She has wrapped her shadowy form in flame, or perhaps the flame betokens that she exists but for a moment. The pure outlines of her shape tell you that she comes from heaven. Is she not radiant as an angel? Can you not hear the beating of her wings in space? She sinks down beside you more lightly than a bird, and you are entranced by her awful eyes; there is a magical power in her light breathing that draws your lips to hers; she flies and you follow; you feel the earth beneath you no longer. If you could but once touch that form of snow with your eager, deluded hands, once twine the golden hair around your fingers, place one kiss on those shining eyes! There is an intoxicating vapor around, and the spell of a siren music is upon you. Every nerve in you is quivering; you are filled with pain and longing. O joy for which there is no name! You have touched the woman's lips, and you are wakened at once by a horrible pang. Oh! ah! yes, you have struck your head against the corner of the bedpost, you have been clasping its brown mahogany sides, and chilly gilt ornaments; embracing a piece of metal, a brazen cupid.''

"But how about Pauline, sir?''

"What, again? Listen. One lovely morning at Tours a young man, who held the hand of a pretty woman in his, went on board the " Ville d' Angers." Thus united they both looked and wondered long at a white form that rose elusively out of the mists above the broad waters of the Loire, like some child of the sun and the river, or some freak of air and cloud. This translucent form was a sylph or a naiad by turns; she hovered in the air like a word that haunts the memory, which seeks in vain to grasp it ; she glided among the islands, she nodded her head here and there among the tall poplar trees ; then she grew to a giant's height; she shook out the countless folds of her drapery to the light ; she shot light from the aureole that the sun had lit about her face; she hovered above the slopes of the hills and their little hamlets, and seemed to bar the passage of the Château d'Ussé. You might have thought that *La dame des belles cousines* * sought to protect her country from modern intrusion.

" Well, well, I understand. So it went with Pauline. But how about Fœdora?"

" Oh ! Fœdora, you are sure to meet with her ! She was at the Bouffons last night, and she will go to the opera this evening, and if you like to take it so, she is society."

19   * The lady with pretty cousins.

THE ELIXIR OF LIFE.

(L'Elixir de longue Vie.)

To the Reader.

At the very outset of the writer's literary career, a friend, long since dead, gave him the subject of this study. Later on he found the same story in a collection published about the beginning of the present century. To the best of his belief, it is some stray fancy of the brain of Hoffmann, of Berlin ; probably it appeared in some German almanac, and was omitted in the published editions of his collected works. The "Comédie Humaine" is sufficiently rich in original creations for the author to own to this innocent piece of plagiarism ; when, like the worthy La Fontaine, he has told unwittingly, and after his own fashion, a tale already related by another. This is not one of the hoaxes in vogue in the year 1830, when every author wrote his "tale of horror" for the amusement of young ladies. When you have read the account of Don Juan's decorous parricide, try to picture to yourself the part which would be played under very similar circumstances by honest folk who, in this nineteenth century, will take a man's money and undertake to pay him a life annuity on the faith of a chill, or let a house to an ancient lady for the term of her natural life? Would they be for resuscitating their clients? I should dearly like a connoisseur in consciences to consider how far there is a resemblance between a Don Juan and fathers who marry their children to great expectations. Does humanity, which, according to certain philosophers, is making progress, look on the art of waiting for dead men's shoes as a step in the right direction? To this art we owe sev-

(286)

eral honorable professions, which open up ways of living on death. There are people who rely entirely on an expected demise; who brood over it, crouching each morning upon a corpse, that serves again for their pillow at night. To this class belong bishops' coadjutors, cardinals' supernumeraries, *tontiniers*,* and the like. Add to the list many delicately scrupulous persons eager to buy landed property beyond their means, who calculate with dry logic and in cold blood the probable duration of the life of a father or of a stepmother, some old man or woman of eighty or ninety, saying to themselves, "I shall be sure to come in for it in three years' time, and then——" A murderer is less loathsome to us than a spy. The murderer may have acted on a sudden mad impulse; he may be penitent and amend; but a spy is always a spy, night and day, in bed, at table, as he walks abroad; his vileness pervades every moment of his life. Then what must it be to live when every moment of your life is tainted with murder? And have we not just admitted that a host of human creatures in our midst are led by our laws, customs, and usages to dwell without ceasing on a fellow-creature's death. There are men who put the weight of a coffin into their deliberations as they bargain for Cashmere shawls for their wives, as they go up the staircase of a theatre, or think of going to the Bouffons, or of setting up a carriage; who are murderers in thought when dear ones, with the irresistible charm of innocence, hold up childish foreheads to be kissed with a "Good-night, father!" Hourly they meet the gaze of eyes that they would fain close for ever, eyes that still open each morning to the light, like Belvidero's in this study. God alone knows the number of those who are parricides in thought. Picture to yourself the state of mind of a man who must pay a life annuity to some old woman whom he scarcely knows; both live in the country with a brook between them, both sides are free to hate cordially, without offending

* Possessors of Tontine Annuities on Survivorships.

against the social conventions that require two brothers to wear a mask if the older will succeed to the entail, and the other to the fortune of a younger son. The whole civilization of Europe turns upon the principle of hereditary succession as upon a pivot; it would be madness to subvert the principle; but could we not, in an age that prides itself upon its mechanical inventions, perfect this essential portion of the social machinery?

If the author has preserved the old-fashioned style of address "To the Reader" before a work wherein he endeavors to represent all literary forms, it is for the purpose. of making a remark that applies to several of the studies, and very specially to this. Every one of his compositions has been based upon ideas more or less novel, which, as it seemed to him, needed literary expression; he can claim priority for certain forms and for certain ideas which have since passed into the domain of literature, and have there, in some instances, become common property; so that the date of the first publication of each study cannot be a matter of indifference to those of his readers who would fain do him justice.

Reading brings us unknown friends, and what friend is like a reader! We have friends in our own circle who read nothing of ours. The author hopes to pay his debt, by dedicating this work *Diis ignotis*.

ONE winter evening, in a princely palace at Ferrara, Don Juan Belvidero was giving a banquet to a prince of the house of Este. A banquet in those times was a marvelous spectacle which only royal wealth or the power of a mighty lord could furnish forth. Seated about a table lit up with perfumed tapers, seven laughter-loving women were interchanging sweet talk. The white marble of the noble works of art about them stood out against the red stucco walls, and made strong contrasts with the rich Turkey carpets. Clad in satin, glittering with gold, and covered with gems less brilliant than their eyes, each told a tale of energetic passions as diverse as their styles of beauty. They differed neither in their ideas nor in their language; but the expression of their eyes, their glances, occasional gestures, or the tones of their voices supplied a commentary, dissolute, wanton, melancholy, or satirical, to their words.

One seemed to be saying—"The frozen heart of age might kindle at my beauty."

Another—"I love to lounge upon cushions, and think with rapture of my adorers."

A third, a neophyte at these banquets, was inclined to blush. "I feel remorse in the depths of my heart! I am a Catholic, and afraid of hell. But I love you, I love you so that I can sacrifice my hereafter to you."

The fourth drained a cup of Chian wine. "Give me a joyous life!" she cried; "I begin life afresh each day with the dawn. Forgetful of the past, with the intoxication of yesterday's rapture still upon me, I drink deep of life—a whole lifetime of pleasure and of love!"

The woman who sat next to Juan Belvidero looked at him with a feverish glitter in her eyes. She was silent. Then—"I should need no hired bravo to kill my lover if he forsook me!" she cried at last, and laughed, but the marvelously wrought comfit box in her fingers was crushed by her convulsive clutch.

"When are you to be Grand Duke?" asked the sixth. There was the frenzy of a Bacchante in her eyes, and her teeth gleamed between the lips parted with a smile of cruel glee.

"Yes, when is that father of yours going to die?" asked the seventh, throwing her bouquet at Don Juan with bewitching playfulness. It was a childish girl who spoke, and the speaker was wont to make sport of sacred things.

"Oh! don't talk about it," cried Don Juan, the young

and handsome giver of the banquet. "There is but one eternal father, and, as ill luck will have it, he is mine."

The seven Ferrarese, Don Juan's friends, the prince himself, gave a cry of horror. Two hundred years later, in the days of Louis XV., people of taste would have laughed at this witticism. Or was it, perhaps, that at the outset of an orgy there is a certain unwonted lucidity of mind? Despite the taper light, the clamor of the senses, the gleam of gold and silver, the fumes of wine, and the exquisite beauty of the women, there may perhaps have been in the depths of the revelers' hearts some struggling glimmer of reverence for things divine and human, until it was drowned in glowing floods of wine? Yet even then the flowers had been crushed, eyes were growing dull, and drunkenness, in Rabelais' phrase, had "taken possession of them down to their sandals."

During that brief pause a door opened; and as once the Divine presence was revealed at Belshazzar's feast, so now it seemed to be manifest in the apparition of an old white-haired servant, who tottered in, and looked sadly from under knitted brows at the revelers. He gave a withering glance at the garlands, the golden cups, the pyramids of fruit, the dazzling lights of the banquet, the flushed scared faces, the hues of the cushions pressed by the white arms of the women.

"My Lord, your father is dying!" he said; and at those solemn words, uttered in hollow tones, a veil of crape seemed to be drawn over the wild mirth.

Don Juan rose to his feet with a gesture to his guests that might be rendered by, "Excuse me; this kind of thing does not happen every day."

Does it so seldom happen that a father's death surprises youth in the full-blown splendor of life, in the midst of the mad riot of an orgy? Death is as unexpected in his caprice as a courtesan in her disdain; but death is truer—death has never forsaken any man.

Don Juan closed the door of the banqueting-hall; and as

he went down the long gallery, through the cold and darkness, he strove to assume an expression in keeping with the part he had to play; he had thrown off his mirthful mood, as he had thrown down his table-napkin, at the first thought of this *rôle*. The night was dark. The mute servitor, his guide to the chamber where the dying man lay, lighted the way so dimly that death, aided by cold, silence, and darkness, and it may be by a reaction of drunkenness, could send some sober thoughts through the spendthrift's soul. He examined his life, became thoughtful, like a man involved in a lawsuit on his way to the court.

Bartolommeo Belvidero, Don Juan's father, was an old man of ninety, who had devoted the greatest part of his life to business pursuits. He had acquired vast wealth in many a journey in magical Eastern lands, and knowledge, so it was said, more valuable than the gold and diamonds, which had almost ceased to have any value for him.

" I would give more to have a tooth in my head than for a ruby," he would say at times with a smile. The indulgent father loved to hear Don Juan's story of this and that wild freak of youth. "So long as these follies amuse you, dear boy "—he would say laughingly, as he lavished money on his son. Age never took such pleasure in the sight of youth; the fond father did not remember his own decaying powers while he looked on that brilliant young life.

Bartolommeo Belvidero, at the age of sixty, had fallen in love with an angel of peace and beauty. Don Juan had been the sole fruit of this late and short-lived love. For fifteen years the widower had mourned the loss of his beloved Juana; and to this sorrow of age, his son and his numerous household had attributed the strange habits that he had contracted. He had shut himself up in the least comfortable wing of his palace, and very seldom left his apartments; even Don Juan himself must first ask permission before seeing his father. If this hermit, unbound by vows, came or went in his palace or in the streets of Ferrara, he walked as if he were in a dream, wholly engrossed, like a man at strife with a memory, or a wrestler with some thought.

The young Don Juan might give princely banquets, the palace might echo with clamorous mirth, horses pawed the ground in the courtyards, pages quarrelled and flung dice upon the stairs, but Bartolommeo ate his seven ounces of bread daily and drank water. A fowl was occasionally dressed for him, simply that the black poodle, his faithful companion, might have the bones. Bartolommeo never complained of the noise. If huntsmen's horns and baying dogs disturbed his sleep during his illness, he only said, "Ah! Don Juan has come back again." Never on earth has there been a father so little exacting and so indulgent ; and, in consequence, young Belvidero, accustomed to treat his father unceremoniously, had all the faults of a spoiled child. He treated old Bartolommeo as a wilful courtesan treats an elderly adorer ; buying indemnity for insolence with a smile, selling good-humor, submitting to be loved.

Don Juan, beholding scene after scene of his younger years, saw that it would be a difficult task to find his father's indulgence at fault. Some newborn remorse stirred the depths of his heart ; he felt almost ready to forgive this father now about to die for having lived so long. He had an accession of filial piety, like a thief's return in thought to honesty at the prospect of a million adroitly stolen.

Before long Don Juan had crossed the lofty, chilly suite of rooms in which his father lived ; the penetrating influences of the damp, close air, the mustiness diffused by old tapestries and presses thickly covered with dust had passed into him, and now he stood in the old man's antiquated room, in the repulsive presence of the death-bed, beside a dying fire. A flickering lamp on a Gothic table sent broad uncertain shafts of light, fainter or brighter, across the bed, so that the dying man's face seemed to wear a different look at every moment.

The bitter wind whistled through the crannies of the ill-fitting casements; there was a smothered sound of snow lashing the windows. The harsh contrast of these sights and sounds with the scenes which Don Juan had just quitted was so sudden that he could not help shuddering. He turned cold as he came towards the bed; the lamp flared in a sudden vehement gust of wind and lighted up his father's face; the features were wasted and distorted; the skin that cleaved to their bony outlines had taken wan, livid hues, all the more ghastly by force of contrast with the white pillows on which he lay. The muscles about the toothless mouth had contracted with pain and drawn apart the lips; the moans that issued between them with appalling energy found an accompaniment in the howling of the storm without.

In spite of every sign of coming dissolution, the most striking thing about the dying face was its incredible power. It was no ordinary spirit that wrestled there with death. The eyes glared with strange fixity of gaze from the cavernous sockets hollowed by disease. It seemed as if Bartolommeo sought to kill some enemy sitting at the foot of his bed by the intent gaze of dying eyes. That steady remorseless look was the more appalling because the head that lay upon the pillow was passive and motionless as a skull upon a doctor's table. The outlines of the body, revealed by the coverlet, were no less rigid and stiff; he lay there as one dead, save for those eyes. There was something automatic about the moaning sounds that came from the mouth. Don Juan felt something like shame that he must be brought thus to his father's bedside, wearing a courtesan's bouquet, redolent of the fragrance of the banqueting-chamber and the fumes of wine.

"You were enjoying yourself!" the old man cried as he saw his son.

Even as he spoke the pure high notes of a woman's voice, sustained by the sound of the viol on which she accompanied her song, rose above the rattle of the storm against the casements, and floated up to the chamber of death. Don Juan stopped his ears against the barbarous answer to his father's speech.

"I bear you no grudge, my child," Bartolommeo went on.

The words were full of kindness, but they hurt Don Juan; he could not pardon this heart-searching goodness on his father's part.

"What a remorseful memory for me!" he cried, hypocritically.

"Poor Juanino," the dying man went on in a smothered voice, "I have always been so kind to you, that you could not surely desire my death?"

"Oh, if it were only possible to keep you here by giving up a part of my own life!" cried Don Juan.

("We can always *say* this sort of thing," the spendthrift thought; "it is as if I laid the whole world at my mistress' feet.")

The thought had scarcely crossed his mind when the old poodle barked. Don Juan shivered; the response was so intelligent that he fancied the dog must have understood him.

"I was sure that I could count on you, my son!" cried the dying man. "I shall live. So be it; you shall be satisfied. I shall live, but without depriving you of a single day of your life."

"He is raving," thought Don Juan. Aloud he added, "Yes, dearest father, yes; you shall live, of course, as long as I live, for your image will be forever in my heart."

"It is not that kind of life that I mean," said the old noble, summoning all his strength to sit up in bed; for a thrill of doubt ran through him, one of those suspicions that come into being under a dying man's pillow. "Listen, my son," he went on, in a voice grown weak with that last effort," I have no more wish to give up life than you to give up wine and mistresses, horses and hounds, and hawks and gold——"

"I can well believe it," thought the son; and he knelt

down by the bed and kissed Bartolommeo's cold hands. "But, father, my dear father," he added aloud, " we must submit to the will of God."

" I am God ! " muttered the dying man.

" Do not blaspheme ! " cried the other, as he saw the menacing expression on his father's face. " Beware what you say ; you have received extreme unction, and I should be inconsolable if you were to die before my eyes in mortal sin."

" Will you listen to me?" cried Bartolommeo, and his mouth twitched.

Don Juan held his peace ; an ugly silence prevailed. Yet above the muffled sound of the beating of the snow against the windows rose the sounds of the beautiful voice and the viol in unison, far off and faint as the dawn. The dying man smiled.

" Thank you," he said, " for bringing those singing voices and the music, a banquet, young and lovely women with fair faces and dark tresses, all the pleasures of life ! Bid them wait for me ; for I am about to begin life anew."

" The delirium is at its height," said Don Juan to himself.

" I have found out a way of coming to life again," the speaker went on. " There, just look in that table drawer, press the spring hidden by the griffin, and it will fly open."

" I have found it, father."

" Well, then, now take out a little phial of rock crystal."

" I have it."

" I have spent twenty years in——" but even as he spoke the old man felt how very near the end had come, and summoned all his dying strength to say, " As soon as the breath is out of me, rub me all over with that liquid, and I shall come to life again."

" There is very little of it," his son remarked.

Though Bartolommeo could no longer speak, he could still hear and see. When those words dropped from Don Juan, his head turned with appalling quickness, his neck was twisted like the throat of some marble statue which the sculptor has condemned to remain stretched out forever, the wide eyes had come to have a ghastly fixity.

He was dead, and in death he lost his last and sole illusion.

He had sought a shelter in his son's heart, and it had proved to be a sepulchre, a pit deeper than men dig for their dead. The hair on his head had risen and stiffened with horror, his agonized glance still spoke. He was a father rising in just anger from his tomb, to demand vengeance at the throne of God.

"There! it is all over with the old man!" cried Don Juan.

He had been so interested in holding the mysterious phial to the lamp, as a drinker holds up the wine-bottle at the end of a meal, that he had not seen his father's eyes fade. The cowering poodle looked from his master to the elixir, just as Don Juan himself glanced again and again from his father to the flask. The lamplight flickered. There was a deep silence; the viol was mute. Juan Belvidero thought that he saw his father stir, and trembled. The changeless gaze of those accusing eyes frightened him; he closed them hastily, as he would have closed a loose shutter swayed by the wind of an autumn night. He stood there motionless, lost in a world of thought.

Suddenly the silence was broken by a shrill sound like the creaking of a rusty spring. It startled Don Juan; he all but dropped the phial. A sweat, colder than the blade of a dagger, issued through every pore. It was only a piece of clockwork, a wooden cock that sprang out and crowed three times, an ingenious contrivance by which the learned of that epoch were wont to be awakened at the appointed hour to begin the labors of the day. Through the windows there came already a flush of dawn. The thing, composed of wood, and cords, and wheels, and pulleys, was more faithful in its service than he in his duty to Bartolommeo—he, a man with that pecular piece of human mechanism within him, that we call a heart.

Don Juan the sceptic shut the flask again in the secret drawer in the gothic table—he meant to run no more risks of losing the mysterious liquid.

Even in that solemn moment he heard the murmur of a crowd in the gallery, a confused sound of voices, of stifled laughter and light footfalls, and the rustling of silks—the sounds of a band of revelers struggling for gravity. The door opened, and in came the Prince and Don Juan's friends, the seven courtesans, and the singers, disheveled and wild like dancers surprised by the dawn, when the tapers that have burned through the night struggle with the sunlight.

They had come to offer the customary condolence to the young heir.

"Oho! is poor Don Juan really taking this seriously?" said the Prince in Brambilla's ear.

"Well, his father was very good," she returned.

But Don Juan's night-thoughts had left such unmistakable traces on his features, that the crew was awed into silence. The men stood motionless. The women, with wine-parched lips and cheeks marbled with kisses, knelt down and began a prayer. Don Juan could scarce help trembling when he saw splendor and mirth and laughter and song and youth and beauty and power bowed in reverence before death. But in those times, in that adorable Italy of the sixteenth century, religion and revelry went hand in hand; and religious excess became a sort of debauch, and a debauch a religious rite!

The Prince grasped Don Juan's hand affectionately, then when all faces had simultaneously put on the same grimace—half-gloomy, half-indifferent—the whole masque disappeared, and left the chamber of death empty. It was like an allegory of life.

As they went down the staircase, the Prince spoke to Rivabarella : " Now, who would have taken Don Juan's impiety for a boast ? He loves his father."

" Did you see that black dog ? " asked La Brambilla.

" He is enormously rich now," sighed Bianca Cavatolino.

" What is that to me ? " cried the proud Veronese (she who had crushed the comfit-box).

" What does it matter to you, forsooth ? " cried the Duke. " With his money he is as much a prince as I am."

At first Don Juan was swayed hither and thither by countless thoughts, and wavered between two decisions. He took counsel with the gold heaped up by his father, and returned in the evening to the chamber of death, his whole soul brimming over with hideous selfishness. He found all his household busy there. " His lordship " was to lie in state to-morrow ; all Ferrara would flock to behold the wonderful spectacle ; and the servants were busy decking the room and the couch on which the dead man lay. At a sign from Don Juan all his people stopped, dumbfounded and trembling.

"Leave me alone here," he said, and his voice was changed," " and do not return till I leave the room."

When the footsteps of the old servitor, who was the last to go, echoed but faintly along the paved gallery, Don Juan hastily locked the door, and, sure that he was quite alone, " Let us try," he said to himself.

Bartolommeo's body was stretched on a long table. The embalmers had laid a sheet over it, to hide from all eyes the dreadful spectacle of a corpse so wasted and shrunken that it seemed like a skeleton, and only the face was uncovered. This mummy-like form lay in the middle of the room. The limp clinging linen conformed itself to the outlines it shrouded —so sharp, bony, and thin. Large violet patches had already begun to spread over the face ; the embalmer's work had not been finished too soon.

Don Juan, strong as he was in his scepticism, felt a tremor as he opened the magic crystal flask. When he stood over that face, he was trembling so violently that he was actually obliged to wait for a moment. But Don Juan had acquired an early familiarity with evil; his morals had been corrupted by a licentious court, a reflection worthy of the Duke of Urbino crossed his mind, and it was a keen sense of curiosity that goaded him into boldness. The devil himself might have whispered the words that were echoing through his brain, *Moisten one of the eyes with the liquid!* He took up a linen cloth, moistened it sparingly with the precious fluid, and passed it lightly over the right eyelid of the corpse. The eye unclosed.

"Aha!" said Don Juan. He gripped the flask tightly, as we clutch in dreams the branch from which we hang suspended over a precipice.

For the eye was full of life. It was a young child's eye set in a death's head; the light quivered in the depths of its youthful liquid brightness. Shaded by the long dark lashes, it sparkled like the strange lights that travelers see in lonely places in winter nights. That eye seemed as if it would fain dart fire at Don Juan; he saw it thinking, upbraiding, condemning, uttering accusations, threatening doom; it cried aloud, and gnashed upon him. All anguish that shakes human souls was gathered there; supplications the most tender, the wrath of kings, the love in a girl's heart pleading with the headsman; then, and after all these, the deeply searching glance a man turns on his fellows as he mounts the last step of the scaffold. Life so dilated in this fragment of life that Don Juan shrank back; he walked up and down the room, he dared not meet that gaze, but he saw nothing else. The ceiling and the hangings, the whole room was sown with living points of fire and intelligence. Everywhere those gleaming eyes haunted him.

" He might very likely have lived another hundred years," he cried involuntarily. Some diabolical influence had drawn him to his father, and again he gazed at that luminous spark.

The eyelid closed and opened again abruptly; it was like a woman's sign of assent. It was an intelligent movement. If a voice had cried, "Yes!" Don Juan could not have been more startled.

"What is to be done?" he thought.

He nerved himself to try to close the white eyelid. In vain.

"Kill it? That would perhaps be parricide," he debated with himself.

"Yes," the eye said, with a strange sardonic quiver of the lid.

"Aha!" said Don Juan to himself, "here is witchcraft at work!" And he went closer to crush the thing. A great tear trickled over the hollow cheeks, and fell on Don Juan's hand.

"It is scalding!" he cried. He sat down. This struggle exhausted him; it was as if, like Jacob of old, he was wrestling with an angel.

At last he rose. "So long as there is no blood——" he muttered.

Then, summoning all the courage needed for a coward's crime, he extinguished the eye, pressing it with the linen cloth, turning his head away. A terrible groan startled him. It was the poor poodle, who died with a long-drawn howl.

"Could the brute have been in the secret?" thought Don Juan, looking down at the faithful creature.

Don Juan Belvidero was looked upon as a dutiful son. He reared a white marble monument on his father's tomb, and employed the greatest sculptors of the time upon it. He did not recover perfect ease of mind till the day when his father knelt in marble before religion, and the heavy weight of the stone had sealed the mouth of the grave in which he had laid the one feeling of remorse that sometimes flitted through his soul in moments of physical weariness.

He had drawn up a list of the wealth heaped up by the old merchant in the East, and he became a miser; had he not to provide for a second lifetime? His views of life were the more profound and penetrating; he grasped its significance, as a whole, the better, because he saw it across a grave. All men, all things, he analyzed once and for all; he summoned up the past, represented by its records; the present in the law, its crystallized form; the future, revealed by religion. He took spirit and matter, and flung them into his crucible, and found—nothing. Thenceforward he became Don Juan.

At the outset of his life, in the prime of youth and the beauty of youth, he knew the illusions of life for what they were; he despised the world, and made the utmost of the world. His felicity could not have been of the bourgeois kind, rejoicing in periodically recurrent boiled meat, in the comforts of a warming-pan, a lamp of a night, and a new pair of slippers once a quarter. Nay, rather he seized upon existence as a monkey snatches a nut, and after no long toying with it, proceeds deftly to strip off the mere husks to reach the savory kernel within.

Poetry and the sublime transports of passion scarcely reached ankle-depth with him now. He in nowise fell into the error of strong natures who flatter themselves now and again that little souls will believe in a great soul, and are willing to barter their own lofty thoughts of the future for the small change of our life-annuity ideas. He, even as they, had he chosen, might well have walked with his feet on the earth and his head in the skies; but he liked better to sit on earth, to wither the soft, fresh, fragrant lips of a woman with kisses, for, like death, he devoured everything without scruple as he passed; he would have full fruition; he was an Oriental lover, seeking prolonged pleasures easily obtained. He sought nothing but a woman in women, and cultivated cynicism, until it became with him a habit of mind. When his mistress, from the couch on which she lay, soared

20

and was lost in regions of ecstatic bliss, Don Juan followed suit, earnest, expansive, serious as any German student. But he said "I," while she, in the transports of intoxication, said "We." He understood to admiration the art of abandoning himself to the influence of a woman; he was always clever enough to make her believe that he trembled like some boy fresh from college before his first partner at a dance, when he asks her, "Do you like dancing?" But, no less, he could be terrible at need, could unsheath a formidable sword and make short work of commandants. Banter lurked beneath his simplicity, mocking laughter behind his tears—for he had tears at need, like any woman nowadays who says to her husband, "Give me a carriage, or I shall go into a consumption."

For a merchant the world is a bale of goods or a mass of circulating bills; for most young men it is a woman, and for a woman here and there it is a man; for a certain order of mind it is a salon, a coterie, a quarter of the town, or some single city; but Don Juan found his world in himself.

This model of grace and dignity, this captivating wit, moored his bark by every shore; but wherever he was led he was never carried away, and was only steered in a course of his own choosing. The more he saw, the more he doubted. He watched men narrowly, and saw how, beneath the surface, courage was often rashness; and prudence, cowardice; generosity, a clever piece of calculation; justice, a wrong; delicacy, pusillanimity; honesty, a *modus vivendi;* and by some strange dispensation of fate, he must see that those who at heart were really honest, scrupulous, just, generous, prudent, or brave were held cheaply by their fellow-men.

"What a cold-blooded jest!" said he to himself. "It was not devised by a God."

From that time forth he renounced a better world, and never uncovered himself when a name was pronounced, and for him the carven saints in the churches became works of art. He understood the mechanism of society too well to clash wantonly with its prejudices; for, after all, he was not as powerful as the executioner, but he evaded social laws with the wit and grace so well rendered in the scene with M. Dimanche. He was, in fact, Moliére's Don Juan, Goethe's Faust, Byron's Manfred, Mathurin's Melmoth—great allegorical figures drawn by the greatest men of genius in Europe, to which Mozart's harmonies, perhaps, do no more justice than Rossini's lyre. Terrible allegorical figures that shall endure as long as the principle of evil existing in the heart of man shall produce a few copies from century to century. Sometimes the type becomes half-human when incarnate as a Mirabeau, sometimes it is an inarticulate force in a Bonaparte, sometimes it overwhelms the universe with irony as a Rabelais; or, yet again, it appears when a Maréchal de Richelieu elects to laugh at human beings instead of scoffing at things, or when one of the most famous of our ambassadors goes a step further and scoffs at both men and things. But the profound genius of Juan Belvidero anticipated and resumed all these. All things were a jest to him. He was the life of a mocking spirit. All men, all institutions, all realities, all ideas were within its scope. As for eternity, after half an hour of familiar conversation with Pope Julius II. he had said, laughing—

"If it is absolutely necessary to make a choice, I would rather believe in God than in the devil; power combined with goodness always offers more resources than the spirit of evil can boast."

"Yes; still God requires repentance in this present world ——"

"So you always think of your indulgences," returned Don Juan Belvidero. "Well, well, I have another life in reserve in which to repent of the sins of my previous existence."

"Oh, if you regard old age in that light," cried the Pope, "you are in danger of canonization."

" After your elevation to the Papacy nothing is incredible." And they went to watch the workmen who were building the huge basilica dedicated to Saint Peter.

" Saint Peter, as the man of genius who laid the foundation of our double power," the Pope said to Don Juan, "deserves this monument. Sometimes, though, at night, I think that a deluge will wipe all this out as with a sponge, and it will be all to begin over again."

Don Juan and the Pope began to laugh; they understood each other. A fool would have gone on the morrow to amuse himself with Julius II. in Raphael's studio or at the delicious Villa Madama; not so Belvidero. He went to see the Pope as pontiff, to be convinced of any doubts that he (Don Juan) entertained. Over his cups the Rovere would have been capable of denying his own infallibility and of commenting on the Apocalypse.

Nevertheless, this legend has not been undertaken to furnish materials for future biographies of Don Juan; it is intended to prove to honest folk that Belvidero did not die in a duel with stone, as some lithographers would have us believe.

When Don Juan Belvidero reached the age of sixty he settled in Spain, and there in his old age he married a young and charming Andalusian wife. But of set purpose he was neither a good husband nor a good father. He had observed that we are never so tenderly loved as by women to whom we scarcely give a thought. Doña Elvira had been devoutly brought up by an old aunt in a castle a few leagues from San-Lucar in a remote part of Andalusia. She was a model of devotion and grace. Don Juan foresaw that this would be a woman who would struggle long against a passion before yielding, and therefore hoped to keep her virtuous until his death. It was a jest undertaken in earnest, a game of chess which he meant to reserve till his old age. Don Juan had learned wisdom from the mistakes made by his father, Barto-lommeo; he determined that the least details of his life in old age should be subordinated to one object—the success of the drama which was to be played out upon his deathbed.

For the same reason the largest part of his wealth was buried in the cellars of his palace at Ferrara, whither he seldom went. As for the rest of his fortune, it was invested in a life annuity, with a view to give his wife and children an interest in keeping him alive; but this Machiavellian piece of foresight was scarcely necessary. His son, young Felipe Belvidero, grew up as a Spaniard as religiously conscientious as his father was irreligious, in virtue, perhaps, of the old rule, "A miser has a spendthrift son." The Abbot of San-Lucar was chosen by Don Juan to be director of the consciences of the Duchess of Belvidero and her son Felipe. The ecclesiastic was a holy man, well shaped and admirably well proportioned. He had fine dark eyes, a head like that of Tiberius, worn with fasting, bleached by an ascetic life, and, like all dwellers in the wilderness, was daily tempted. The noble lord had hopes, it may be, of despatching yet another monk before his term of life was out.

But whether because the Abbot was every whit as clever as Don Juan himself, or Doña Elvira possessed more discretion or more virtue than Spanish wives are usually credited with, Don Juan was compelled to spend his declining years beneath his own roof, with no more scandal under it than if he had been an ancient country parson. Occasionally he would take wife and son to task for negligence in the duties of religion, peremptorily insisting that they should carry out to the letter the obligations imposed upon the flock by the Court of Rome. Indeed, he was never so well pleased as when he had set the courtly Abbot discussing some case of conscience with Doña Elvira and Felipe.

At length, however, despite the prodigious care that the great magnifico, Don Juan Belvidero, took of himself, the days of decrepitude came upon him, and with those days the constant importunity of physical feebleness, an importunity all the more distressing by contrast with the wealth of memories of his impetuous youth and the sensual pleasures of middle age. The unbeliever who in the height of his cynical humor had been wont to persuade others to believe in laws and principles at which he scoffed, must repose nightly upon a *perhaps.* The great Duke, the pattern of good breeding, the champion of many a carouse, the proud ornament of courts, the man of genius, the graceful winner of hearts that he had wrung as carelessly as a peasant twists an osier withe, was now the victim of a cough, of a ruthless sciatica, of an unmannerly gout. His teeth gradually deserted him, as at the end of an evening the fairest and best-dressed women take their leave one by one till the room is left empty and desolate. The active hands became palsy-stricken, the shapely legs tottered as he walked. At last, one night, a stroke of apoplexy caught him by the throat in its icy clutch. After that fatal day he grew morose and stern.

He would reproach his wife and son with their devotion, casting it in their teeth that the affecting and thoughtful care that they lavished so tenderly upon him was bestowed because they knew that his money was invested in a life annuity. Then Elvira and Felipe would shed bitter tears and redouble their caresses, and the wicked old man's insinuating voice would take an affectionate tone—" Ah, you will forgive me, will you not, dear friends, dear wife? I am rather a nuisance. Alas, Lord in heaven, how canst Thou use me as the instrument by which Thou provest these two angelic creatures? I who should be the joy of their lives am become their scourge——"

In this manner he kept them tethered to his pillow, blotting out the memory of whole months of fretfulness and unkindness in one short hour when he chose to display for them the ever-new treasures of his pinchbeck tenderness and charm of manner—a system of paternity that yielded him an infinitely better return than his own father's indulgence had formerly gained. At length his bodily infirmities reached a point when the task of laying him in bed became as difficult as the navigation of a felucca in the perils of an intricate channel. Then came the day of his death; and this brilliant sceptic, whose mental faculties alone had survived the most dreadful of all destructions, found himself between his two special antipathies—the doctor and the confessor. But he was jovial with them. Did he not see a light gleaming in the future beyond the veil? The pall that is like lead for other men was thin and translucent for him; the light-footed, irresistible delights of youth danced beyond it like shadows.

It was on a beautiful summer evening that Don Juan felt the near approach of death. The sky of Spain was serene and cloudless; the air was full of the scent of orange-blossom; the stars shed clear, pure gleams of light; nature without seemed to give the dying man assurance of 'resurrection; a dutiful and obedient son sat there watching him with loving and respectful eyes. Towards eleven o'clock he desired to be left alone with this single-hearted being.

"Felipe," said the father, in tones so soft and affectionate that the young man trembled, and tears of gladness came to his eyes; never had that stern father spoken his name in such a tone. "Listen, my son," the dying man went on. "I am a great sinner. All my life long, however, I have thought of my death. I was once the friend of the great Pope Julius II.; and that illustrious Pontiff, fearing lest the excessive excitability of my senses should entangle me in mortal sin between the moment of my death and the time of my anointing with the holy oil, gave me a flask that contains a little of the holy water that once issued from the rock in the wilderness. I have kept the secret of this squandering of a treasure belonging to Holy Church, but

I am permitted to reveal the mystery *in articulo mortis* to my son. You will find the flask in a drawer in that Gothic table that always stands by the head of the bed. The precious little crystal flask may be of use yet again for you, dearest Felipe. Will you swear to me, by your salvation, to carry out my instructions faithfully?"

Felipe looked at his father, and Don Juan was too deeply learned in the lore of the human countenance not to die in peace with that look as his warrant, as his own father had died in despair at meeting the expression in his son's eyes.

"You deserved to have a better father," Don Juan went on. "I dare to confess, my child, that while the reverend Abbot of San-Lucar was administering the Viaticum I was thinking of the incompatibility of the coexistence of two powers so infinite as God and the devil——"

"Oh, father!"

"And I said to myself, when Satan makes his peace he ought surely to stipulate for the pardon of his followers, or he will be the veriest scoundrel. The thought haunted me; so I shall go to hell, my son, unless you carry out my wishes."

"Oh, quick; tell me quickly, father."

"As soon as I have closed my eyes," Don Juan went on, "and that may be in a few minutes, you must take my body before it grows cold and lay it on a table in this room. Then put out the lamp; the light of the stars should be sufficient. Take off my clothes, reciting *Aves* and *Paters* the while, raising your soul to God in prayer, and carefully anoint my lips and eyes with this holy water; begin with the face, and proceed successively to my limbs and the rest of my body; my dear son, the power of God is so great that you must be astonished at nothing."

Don Juan felt death so near, that he added in a terrible voice, "Be careful not to drop the flask."

Then he breathed his last gently in the arms of his son, and his son's tears fell fast over his sardonic, haggard features.

It was almost midnight when Don Felipe Belvidero laid his father's body upon the table. He kissed the sinister brow and the gray hair; then he put out the lamp.

By the soft moonlight that lit strange gleams across the country without, Felipe could dimly see his father's body, a vague white thing among the shadows. The dutiful son moistened a linen cloth with the liquid, and, absorbed in prayer, he anointed the revered face. A deep silence reigned. Felipe heard faint, indescribable rustlings; it was the breeze in the tree-tops, he thought. But when he had moistented the right arm, he felt himself caught by the throat, a young, strong hand held him in a tight grip—it was his father's hand! He shrieked aloud; the flask dropped from his hand and broke in pieces. The liquid evaporated; the whole household hurried into the room, holding torches aloft. That shriek had startled them, and filled them with as much terror as if the trumpet of the angel sounding on the last day had rung through earth and sky. The room was full of people, and a horror-stricken crowd beheld the fainting Felipe upheld by the strong arm of his father, who clutched him by the throat. They saw another thing, an unearthly spectacle— Don Juan's face grown young and beautiful as Antinoüs, with its dark hair and brilliant eyes and red lips, a head that made horrible efforts, but could not move the dead, wasted body.

An old servitor cried, "A miracle! a miracle!" and all the Spaniards echoed, "A miracle! a miracle!"

Doña Elvira, too pious to attribute this to magic, sent for the Abbot of San-Lucar; and the Prior beholding the miracle with his own eyes, being a clever man, and withal an Abbot desirous of augmenting his revenues, determined to turn the occasion to profit. He immediately gave out that Don Juan would certainly be canonized; he appointed a day for the celebration of the apotheosis in his convent, which thenceforward, he said, should be called the convent of San Juan of

Lucar.   At these words a sufficiently facetious grimace passed over the features of the late Duke.

The taste of the Spanish people for ecclesiastical solemnities is so well known that it should not be difficult to imagine the religious pantomime by which the Convent of San-Lucar celebrated the translation of the blessed Don Juan Belvidero to the abbey-church.   The tale of the partial resurrection had spread so quickly from village to village, that a day or two after the death of the illustrious nobleman the report had reached every place within fifty miles of San-Lucar, and it was as good as a play to see the roads covered already with crowds flocking in on all sides, their curiosity whetted still further by the prospect of a *Te Deum* sung by torchlight. The old abbey-church of San-Lucar, a marvelous building erected by the Moors, a mosque of Allah, which for three centuries had heard the name of Christ, could not hold the throng that poured in to see the ceremony.   Hidalgos in their velvet mantles, with their good swords at their sides, swarmed like ants, and were so tightly packed in among the pillars that they had not room to bend the knees, which never bent save to God.   Charming peasant girls, in the basquina that defines the luxuriant outlines of their figures, lent an arm to white-haired old men.   Young men, with eyes of fire, walked beside aged crones in holiday array.   Then came couples tremulous with joy, young lovers led thither by curiosity, newly-wedded folk ; children timidly clasping each other by the hand.   This throng, so rich in coloring, in vivid contrasts, laden with flowers, enameled like a meadow, sent up a soft murmur through the quiet night.   Then the great door of the church opened.

Late comers who remained without saw afar, through the three great open doorways, a scene of which the theatrical illusions of modern opera can give but a faint idea.   The vast church was lighted up by thousands of candles, offered by saints and sinners alike eager to win the favor of this new can-

didate for canonization, and these self-commending illumina-
tions turned the great building into an enchanted fairyland.
The black archways, the shafts and capitals, the recessed
chapels with gold and silver gleaming in their depths, the gal-
leries, the Arab traceries, all the most delicate outlines of that
delicate sculpture, burned in the excess of light like the fan-
tastic figures in the red heart of a brazier. At the further end
of the church, above that blazing sea, rose the high altar like
a splendid dawn. All the glories of the golden lamps and
silver candlesticks, of banners and tassels, of the shrines of
the saints and votive offerings, paled before the gorgeous
brightness of the reliquary in which Don Juan lay. The
blasphemer's body sparkled with gems, and flowers, and
crystal, with diamonds and gold, and plumes white as the
wings of seraphim; they had set it up on the altar, where the
picture of Christ had stood. All about him blazed a host of
tall candles; the air quivered in the radiant light. The
worthy Abbot of San-Lucar, in pontifical robes, with his
mitre set with precious stones, his rochet and golden crosier,
sat enthroned in imperial state among his clergy in the
choir. Rows of impassive aged faces, silver-haired old men
clad in fine linen albs, were grouped about him, as the
saints who confessed Christ on earth are set by painters,
each in his place, about the throne of God in heaven. The
precentor and the dignitaries of the chapter, adorned with
the gorgeous insignia of ecclesiastical vanity, came and went
through the clouds of incense, like stars upon their courses
in the firmament.

When the hour of triumph arrived, the bells awoke the
echoes far and wide, and the whole vast crowd raised to
God the first cry of praise that begins the *Te Deum.* A
sublime cry! High, pure notes, the voices of women in
ecstasy, mingled in it with the sterner and deeper voices
of men; thousands of voices sent up a volume of sound so
mighty, that the straining, groaning organ-pipes could not

dominate that harmony. But the shrill sound of children's singing among the choristers, the reverberation of deep bass notes, awakened gracious associations, visions of childhood, and of man in his strength, and rose above that entrancing harmony of human voices blended in one sentiment of love.

Te Deum laudamus !

The chant went up from the black masses of men and women kneeling in the cathedral, like a sudden breaking out of light in darkness, and the silence was shattered as by a peal of thunder. The voices floated up with the clouds of incense that had begun to cast thin bluish veils over the fanciful marvels of the architecture, and the aisles were filled with splendor and perfume and light and melody. Even at the moment when that music of love and thanksgiving soared up to the altar, Don Juan, too well bred not to express his acknowledgments, too witty not to understand how to take a jest, bridled up in his reliquary, and responded with an appalling burst of laughter. Then the devil having put him in mind of the risk he was running of being taken for an ordinary man, a saint, a Boniface, a Pantaleone, he interrupted the melody of love by a yell ; the thousand voices of hell joined in it. Earth blessed, Heaven banned. The church was shaken to its ancient foundations.

Te Deum laudamus ! cried the many voices.

" Go to the devil, brute beasts that you are ! *Dios ! Dios ! Carajos demonios !* Idiots ! What fools you are with your dotard-God ! " and a torrent of imprecations poured forth like a stream of red-hot lava from the mouth of Vesuvius.

" *Deus Sabaoth ! Sabaoth !* " cried the believers.

" You are insulting the majesty of hell," shouted Don Juan, gnashing his teeth. In another moment the living arm struggled out of the reliquary, and was brandished over the assembly in mockery and despair.

" The saint is blessing us," cried the old women, children, lovers, and the credulous among the crowd.

And note how often we are deceived in the homage we pay ; the great man scoffs at those who praise him, and pays compliments now and again to those whom he laughs at in the depths of his heart.

Just as the Abbot, prostrate before the altar, was chanting *" Sancte Johannes ora pro nobis ! "* he heard a voice exclaim sufficiently distinct : *" O coglione ! "*

" What can be going on up there ? " cried the sub-prior, as he saw the reliquary move.

" The saint is playing the devil," replied the Abbot.

Even as he spoke, the living head tore itself away from the lifeless body, and dropped upon the sallow cranium of the officiating priest.

" Remember Doña Elvira ! " cried the thing, with its teeth set fast in the Abbot's head.

The Abbot's horror-stricken shriek disturbed the ceremony ; all the ecclesiastics hurried up and crowded about their chief.

" Idiot, tell us now if there is a God ! " the voice cried, as the Abbot, bitten through the brain, drew his last breath.

PARIS, *October*, 1830.

A STUDY OF WOMAN

(Étude de Femme)

Dedicated to the Marquis Jean-Charles di Negro.

THE Marquise de Listomère is a young woman brought up in the spirit of the Restoration. She has principles, she fasts in season, she takes the sacrament, she goes very much dressed to balls, to the Bouffons, to the opera; her spiritual director allows her to combine the sacred and the profane. Always on good terms with the church and the world, she is an incarnation of the present time, and seems to have taken the word "Legality" for her motto. The Marquise's conduct is marked by exactly enough devotion to enable her, under another Maintenon, to achieve the gloomy piety of the last days of Louis XIV., and enough worldliness to adopt the manners and gallantry of the earlier years of his reign, if they ever could return.

Just now she is virtuous from interest, or, perhaps, by taste. Married some seven years since to the Marquis de Listomère, a deputy who expects a peerage, she perhaps thinks that her conduct may promote the ambitions of the family. Some women wait to pass judgment on her till Monsieur de Listomère is made Pair de France, and till she is six-and-thirty—a time of life when most women discover that they are the dupes of social laws.

The Marquis is an insignificant personage; he is in favor at court; his good qualities, like his faults, are negative; the former can no more give him a reputation for virtue than the latter can give him the sort of brilliancy bestowed by vice. As a deputy he never speaks, but he votes "straight;" and at

(314)

home, he behaves as he does in the Chamber. He is considered the best husband in France. Though he is incapable of enthusiasms, he never scolds, unless he is kept waiting. His friends nickname him " Cloudy weather ;" and, in fact, there is in him no excessively bright light, and no utter darkness. He is exactly like all the ministers that have succeeded each other in France since the charter.

A woman with principles could hardly have fallen into better hands. Is it not a great thing for a virtuous woman to have married a man incapable of folly? Dandies have been known to venture on the impertinence of slightly pressing the Marquise's hand when dancing with her ; they met only looks of scorn, and all have experienced that insulting indifference which, like spring frosts, chills the germs of the fairest hopes. Handsome men, witty men, coxcombs, sentimental men who derive nourishment from sucking the knob of their walking-sticks, men of name and men of fame, men of high birth and of low, all have blanched before her. She has won the right of talking as long and as often as she pleases with men whom she thinks intelligent, without being entered in the calendar of scandal. Some coquettes are capable of pursuing this plan for seven years on end, to gratify their fancy at last ; but to ascribe such a covert motive to Madame de Listomère would be to calumniate her. I had been so fortunate as to meet this phœnix of a marquise ; she talks well, I am a good listener. I pleased her, and I go to her evening parties. This was the object of my ambition.

Neither plain nor pretty, Madame de Listomère has white teeth, a brilliant complexion, and very red lips; she is tall and well made, has a small, slender foot, which she does not display; her eyes, far from being dulled, as most eyes are in Paris, have a soft gleam which becomes magical when by chance she is animated. You feel there is a soul under this ill-defined personality. When she is interested in the conversation, she reveals the grace that lies buried under the prudery of cold demeanor, and then she is charming. She does not crave for success, and she gets it. We always find the thing we do not seek. This statement is too often true not to become a proverb one day. It will be the moral of this tale, which I should not allow myself to relate if it were not at this moment the talk of every drawing-room in Paris.

One evening, about a month since, the Marquise de Listomère danced with a young man as modest as he is heedless, full of good qualities, but showing only his bad ones; he is impassioned, and laughs at passion; he has talent, and hides it; he assumes the savant with aristocrats, and affects to be aristocratic with savants.

Eugène de Rastignac is one of those very sensible young men who try everything, and seem to sound other men to discover what the future will bring forth. Pending the age when he will be ambitious, he laughs at everything; he has grace and originality—two qualities which are rare, because they exclude each other. Without aiming at success, he talked to Madame de Listomère for about half an hour. While following the deviations of a conversation which, beginning with William Tell, went on to the duties of woman, he looked at the Marquise more than once in a way to embarrass her; then he left her, and spoke to her no more all the evening. He danced, sat down to *écarté*, lost a little money, and went home to bed. I have the honor of assuring you that this is exactly what happened. I have added, I have omitted nothing.

The next morning Rastignac woke late, remained in bed, where he gave himself up, no doubt, to some of those morning day-dreams in which a young man glides, like a sylph, behind more than one curtain of silk, wool, or cotton. At such moments, the heavier the body is with sleep, the more nimble is the fancy. Finally Rastignac got up without yawning too much, as so many ill-bred people do, rang for his man-servant, ordered some tea, and drank of it immoderately —which will not seem strange to those who like tea; but, to account for this to those persons who only regard tea as a panacea for indigestion, I will add that Eugène was writing; he sat at his ease, and his feet were more often on the fire-dogs than in his foot-muff.

Oh! to sit with your feet on the polished bar that rests on the two brackets of a fender, and dream of your love affairs while wrapped in your dressing-gown, is so delightful a thing that I deeply regret having no mistress, no fire-dogs, and no dressing-gown. When I shall have all these good things, I shall not write my experiences, I shall take the benefit of them.

The first letter Eugène had to write was finished in a quarter of an hour. He folded it, sealed it, and left it lying in front of him without any address. The second letter, begun at eleven o'clock, was not finished till noon. The four pages were written all over.

"That woman runs in my head," said he to himself as he folded the second missive, leaving it there, and intending to address it after ending his involuntary reverie. He crossed the fronts of his flowered dressing-gown, put his feet on a stool, stuffed his hands into the pockets of his red cashmere trousers, and threw himself back in a delicious armchair with deep ears, of which the seat and back were set at the comfortable angle of a hundred and twenty degrees. He drank no more tea, but remained passive, his eyes fixed on the little gilt fist which formed the knob of his fire-shovel, without seeing the shovel, or the hand, or the gilding. He did not even make up the fire. This was a great mistake! Is it not an intense pleasure to fidget with the fire when dreaming of women? Our fancy lends speech to the little blue tongues which suddenly burst up and babble on the hearth. We can find a meaning in the sudden and noisy language of a *bourguignon.*

At this word I must pause and insert, for the benefit of the ignorant, an explanation vouchsafed by a very distinguished

etymologist, who wishes to remain anonymous. *Bourguignon*
is the popular and symbolical name given, ever since the reign
of Charles VI., to the loud explosions which result in the
ejection on to a rug or a dress of a fragment of charcoal, the
germ of a conflagration. The heat, it is said, explodes a
bubble of air remaining in the heart of the wood, in the trail
of some gnawing grub. *Inde amor, inde Burgundus.* We
quake as we see the charred pieces coming down like an
avalanche when we had balanced them so industriously be-
tween two blazing logs. Oh ! making up a wood-fire when
you are in love is the material expression of your sentiments.

It was at this moment that I entered Eugène's room; he
started violently, and said—

"So there you are, my dear Horace. How long have you
been here?"

"I have this moment come."

"Ah !"

He took the two letters, addressed them, and rang for his
servant.

"Take these two notes."

And Joseph went without a remark. Excellent servant!

And we proceeded to discuss the expedition to the Morea,
in which I wanted to be employed as surgeon. Eugène
pointed out that I should lose much by leaving Paris, and we
then talked of different things. I do not think I shall be
blamed for omitting our conversation.

When Madame de Listomère rose at about two in the after-
noon, her maid Caroline handed her a letter, which she read
while Caroline was dressing her hair. (An imprudence com-
mitted by a great many young wives.)

"Ah, dear angel of love, my treasure of life and happi-
ness!"—on reading these words, the Marquise was going to
throw the letter into the fire; but a fancy flashed through her
head, which any virtuous woman will understand to a marvel,
namely, to see how a man might end who began in this strain,

She read on. When she turned her fourth page, she dropped her arms like a person who is tired.

"Caroline," said she, "go and find out who left this letter for me."

"Madame, I took it from M. le Baron de Rastignac's man-servant."

There was a long silence.

"Will Madame dress now?"

"No."

"He must be excessively impertinent!" thought the Marquise. I may ask any woman to make her own commentary.

Madame de Listomère closed hers with a formal resolution to shut her door on Monsieur Eugène, and, if she should meet him in company, to treat him with more than contempt; for his audacity was not to be compared with any of the other instances which the Marquise had at last forgiven. At first she thought she would keep the letter, but, on due reflection, she burned it.

"Madame has just received such a flaming love-letter, and she read it!" said Caroline to the housemaid.

"I never should have thought it of Madame," said the old woman, quite astonished.

That evening the Marquise was at the house of the Marquise de Beauséant, where she would probably meet Rastignac. It was a Saturday. The Marquise de Beauséant was distantly related to Monsieur de Rastignac, so the young man could not fail to appear in the course of the evening. At two in the morning, Madame de Listomère, who had stayed so late solely to crush Eugène by her coldness, had waited in vain. A witty writer, Stendahl, has given the whimsical name of crystallization to the process worked out by the Marquise's mind before, during, and after this evening.

"Four days later Eugène was scolding his man-servant.

"Look here, Joseph; I shall be obliged to get rid of you, my good fellow."

"I beg your pardon, sir ?"

"You do nothing but blunder. Where did you take the two letters I gave you on Friday ?"

Joseph was bewildered. Like a statue in a cathedral porch he stood motionless, wholly absorbed in the travail of his ideas. Suddenly he smiled foolishly, and said——

"Monsieur, one was for Madame la Marquise de Listomère, Rue Saint-Dominique, and the other was for Monsieur's lawyer——"

"Are you sure of what you say ?"

Joseph stood dumbfounded. I must evidently interfere—happening to be present at the moment.

"Joseph is right," said I. Eugène turned round to me. "I read the addresses quite involuntarily, and——"

"And," said Eugène, interrupting me, "was not one of them for Madame de Nucingen ?"

"No, by all the devils ! And so I supposed, my dear boy, that your heart had pirouetted from the Rue Saint-Lazare to the Rue Saint-Dominique."

Eugène struck his forehead with the palm of his hand, and began to smile. Joseph saw plainly that the fault was none of his.

Now, there are certain moral reflections on which all young men should meditate. Mistake the first : Eugene thought it amusing to have made Madame de Listomère laugh at the blunder that had put her in possession of a love-letter which was not intended for her. Mistake the second : He did not go to see Madame de Listomère till four days after the misadventure, thus giving the thoughts of a virtuous young woman time to crystallize. And there were a dozen more mistakes which must be passed over in silence to give ladies *ex professo* the pleasure of deducing them for the benefit of those who cannot guess them.

Eugène arrived at the Marquise's door ; but as he was going in, the porter stopped him, and told him that Madame de Listomère was out. As he was getting into his carriage again, the Marquis came in.

"Come up, Eugène," said he; "my wife is at home."

Oh! forgive the Marquis. A husband, however admirable, scarcely ever attains to perfection.

Rastignac as he went upstairs discerned the ten fallacies in worldly logic which stood on this page of the fair book of his life.

When Madame de Listomère saw her husband come in with Eugène, she could not help coloring. The young Baron observed the sudden flush. If the most modest of men never quite loses some little dregs of conceit, which he can no more get rid of than a woman can throw off her inevitable vanities, who can blame Eugène for saying to himself, "What! this stronghold, too?"—and he settled his head in his cravat. Though young men are not very avaricious, they all love to add a head to their collection of medals.

Monsieur de Listomère seized on the *Gazette de France*, which he saw in a corner by the fire-place, and went to the window to form, by the help of the newspaper, an opinion of his own as to the state of France. No woman, not even a prude, is long in embarrassment even in the most difficult situations in which she can find herself; she seems always to carry in her hand the fig-leaf given to her by our mother Eve. And so, when Eugène, having interpreted the orders given to the porter in a sense flattering to his vanity, made his bow to Madame de Listomère with a tolerably deliberate air, she was able to conceal all her thoughts behind one of those feminine smiles, which are more impenetrable than a king's speech.

"Are you unwell, Madame? You had closed your door."

"No, Monsieur."

"You were going out perhaps?"

"Not at all."

"You are expecting somebody?"

"Nobody."

"If my visit is ill-timed, you have only the Marquis to blame. I was obeying your mysterious orders when he himself invited me into the sanctuary."

"Monsieur de Listomère was not in my confidence. There are certain secrets which it is not always prudent to share with one's husband."

The firm, mild tone in which the Marquise spoke these words, and the imposing dignity of her glance, were enough to make Rastignac feel that he had been in too much haste to plume himself.

"I understand, Madame," said he, laughing; "I must therefore congratulate myself all the more on having met Monsieur le Marquis; he has procured me an opportunity for offering you an explanation, which would be fraught with danger, but that you are kindness itself."

The Marquise looked at the young Baron with considerable astonishment, but she replied with dignity.

"On your part, Monsieur, silence will be the best excuse. On my side I promise you to forget entirely—a forgiveness you scarcely merit.

"Forgiveness is needless, Madame, where there has been no offence. The letter you received," he added in an undertone, "and which you must have thought so unseemly, was not intended for you."

The Marquise smiled in spite of herself; she wished to appear offended.

"Why tell a falsehood?" she replied with an air of disdainful amusement, but in a very friendly tone. "Now that I have scolded you enough, I am quite ready to laugh at a stratagem not devoid of skill. I know some poor women who would be caught by it. "Good heavens, how he loves me !" they would say. She forced a laugh, and added with an indulgent air, "If we are to remain friends, let me hear nothing more of mistakes of which I cannot be the dupe."

"On my honor, Madame, you are far more so than you fancy," Eugène eagerly replied.

"What are you talking about?" asked Monsieur de Listomère, who for a minute had been listening to the conversation, without being able to pierce the darkness of its meaning.

"Oh, nothing that will interest you," said Madame de Listomère.

The Marquis quietly returned to his paper, saying, "I see Madame de Mortsauf is dead; your poor brother is at Clochegourde no doubt."

"Do you know, Monsieur," said the Marquise, addressing Eugène, "that you have just made a very impertinent speech?"

"If I did not know the strictness of your principles," he replied simply, "I should fancy you either meant to put ideas into my head which I dare not allow myself, or to wring my secret from me; or perhaps, indeed, you wish to make fun of me."

The Marquise smiled. This smile put Eugène out of patience.

"May you always believe, Madame, in the offence I did not commit!" said he. "And I fervently hope that chance may not lead you to discover in society the person who was intended to read that letter——"

"What! Still Madame de Nucingen?" cried Madame de Listomère, more anxious to master the secret than to be revenged on the young man for his retort.

Eugène reddened. A man must be more than five-and-twenty not to redden when he is blamed for the stupid fidelity which women laugh at only to avoid betraying how much they envy its object. However, he said, calmly enough, "Why not, Madame?"

These are the blunders we commit at five-and-twenty. This confession agitated Madame de Listomère violently;

but Eugène was not yet able to analyze a woman's face as seen in a glimpse, or from one side. Only her lips turned white. She rang to have some wood put on the fire, and so obliged Eugène to rise to take leave. "If that is the case," said the Marquise, stopping Eugène by her cold, precise manner, "you will find it difficult, Monsieur, to explain by what chance my name happened to come to your pen. An address written on a letter is not like the first-come crush hat which a man may heedlessly take for his own on leaving a ball."

Eugène, put quite out of countenance, looked at the Marquise with a mingled expression of stupidity and fatuousness; he felt that he was ridiculous, stammered out some schoolboy speech, and left. A few days later Madame de Listomère had indisputable proof of Eugène's veracity.

For more than a fortnight she has not gone into society.

The Marquis tells every one who asks him the reason of this change—

"My wife has a gastric attack."

I, who attend her, and who know her secret, know that she is only suffering from a little nervous crisis, and takes advantage of it to stay quietly at home.

PARIS, *February*, 1839.

www.ingramcontent.com/pod-product-compliance
Lightning Source LLC
Chambersburg PA
CBHW051526100726
47898CB00005B/1593